The Full Extent

An Inquiry into Reality and Destiny

Richard Botelho

Copyright © 2022 by Richard Botelho

ISBN: 978-0-9643926-3-2 (softcover)
ISBN: 978-0-9643926-0-1 (ebook)

Library of Congress Control Number: 2021917327

Published by Windstream Publishing Company
303 Windstream Place
Danville, CA 94526

Manufactured in the United States of America
First Edition 2022

Publisher's Cataloging-In-Publication Data
Names: Botelho, Richard, author.
Title: The full extent : an inquiry into reality and destiny / Richard Botelho.
Description: First edition. | Danville, CA : Windstream Publishing Company, 2022. | Includes bibliographical references.
Identifiers: ISBN 9780964392632 (softcover) | ISBN 9780964392601 (ebook)
Subjects: LCSH: Reality. | Fate and fatalism. | Philosophy. | Spirituality.
Classification: LCC BD331 .B68 2022 (print) | LCC BD331 (ebook) | DDC 110—dc23

For anyone who ever contemplated a nighttime sky

All matter originates and exists only by virtue of a force.... We must assume behind this force the existence of a conscious and intelligent Mind. This Mind is the matrix of all matter.

—Max Planck, the Father of Quantum Mechanics

CONTENTS

INTRODUCTION

I remember being in my early thirties when I first discovered Quantum Mechanics, the study of matter and energy at the atomic and subatomic levels. The article in my old encyclopedia started with the words (paraphrasing) "you will not believe what follows, but it is proven without exception." It had me there. Naturally a skeptic, I always require proof. The only thing I take on faith is God. So I began my inquiry with dubious curiosity.

What was written was incomprehensible—matter and energy as a product of Consciousness; particles behaving as waves, and waves behaving as particles; nothing real until observed; the past, present, and future occurring at once; things connected regardless of the distance; everything behaving counterintuitively and illogically. Fascination? Sure, but a larger realization soon followed. Since everything is made of atoms, the quantum is a *gateway to truth*. Little did I realize I had stumbled upon the greatest question of our age—how does quantum bizarreness form the physical world we witness with a foundation that is literally unreal?

So I read on.

What I learned is that reality is layered and often at odds with itself, an enigma beyond comparison eluding definitive description and confident comprehension. Moreover, we are only beginning to understand the relationship between the micro (Quantum Mechanical) and the macro (Classical Physical) worlds. The former forms the latter, the small composing the large, but the quantum follows radically different laws, possessing nonsensical and even baffling properties, its nature incompatible with common sense experience. We see reality as independently actual when experiment after experiment proves that reality is a product of Mind.

Thus, Consciousness is the ground of all being. Mind preceded the universe, a force responsible for individual minds. The same applies to concepts such as Body, Soul, and Spirit, with individual bodies, souls, and spirits derivative of these larger essences. Everything we experience results from something grander. Consciousness existed prior to the Big Bang—before history even began and before anything else existed, including time and us. That is the truth. Believing otherwise is like believing the world is flat or the Sun revolves around the Earth. False beliefs are an impediment to our advance, with adherence to inaccurate foundations deleterious to society and causative of our current stagnation.

That last statement is controversial considering historical advances in science and more specifically, in information technology. After all, we have smartphones, computers, artificial intelligence, the Internet, and advanced spacecraft. Nevertheless, the low-hanging fruit has been plucked from the tree, and true scientific breakthroughs are sorely lacking. For those who doubt this, consider these examples of our lack of progress: educational spending produces ever-diminishing returns; few cures for diseases exist; ground and air transportation are antiquated; we have no colonies on the Moon; time travel and teleportation are still fantasies; academic disciplines show little improvement; wealth inequality is rampant; no protection exists against nuclear or biological weapons. In short, unresolved, age-old problems abound as science and technology fail to provide solutions.

As a result, this work contains much criticism by science and its consequent philosophy—scientific materialism. Criticism is not condemnation. Science has forwarded humanity in astounding ways, improving the lives of billions. Yet as we will see, science has become ideological and obdurate, resistant to unconventional facts and obfuscatory of truth. Hence, our criticism is necessary and valid.

To extend ourselves, we must decipher the true nature of existence. Prioritization of the physical realm has its limitations, whereas the immaterial realm is filled with endless opportunity. Intimations of truth surround us; many challenge the status quo, while others are so unbelievable they make us question our own cognitive processes. Yet understand we must. For as we will discover in this investigation, if Mind—and, by extension, Spirit—is truly the basis of reality, then we must embrace both regardless of conventional interpretations or dogmatic objections. An understanding of reality is to be wonderstruck, certain to rearrange individual priorities and hopefully societal ones as the truth enlightens us into an era of unparalleled opportunity.

The structure of this book is to introduce one incredibly compelling experiment, investigate the primacy of Consciousness, consider the course of Spirit, review the management of destiny, position the human future, and demonstrate the progression of the universe to its teleological end. During our exploration, we will consider the opinions of various experts and integrate their findings into a synthetic whole; where appropriate, we will also apply some basic logic and mathematical formulations for further consideration of our concepts. Note that some of the references are intentionally exterior to traditional science since its dogma represents a single, exclusionary worldview. This study cites and appreciates many unconventional thinkers since their courage forwards our wisdom and advances our future.

Therefore, we can think of this work as an architecture for subsequent explorations since it relies on many contradistinct opinions while incorporating established scientific truths. We must expand our perspectives in order to break through societal stagnation. That is the great directive of our time. From our investigations, we will develop a megatheory of reality, no doubt highly speculative in nature but nevertheless grounded in empirical observations and confirmable facts. We also will see a new paradigm emerging, one that challenges the past and forwards our species into a spiritualistic reality full of purpose and creativity.

So let us begin.

PART I:

THE QUESTION
OF REALITY

CHAPTER 1

The Experiment

The grandest experiment in history comes from Quantum Mechanics, and its results—the *Double Slit Experiment*—are not only astonishing but revolutionary. Everything humans believed about the nature of reality was obliterated with this one, simple experimental result.

First, let us get a little context. Atoms and their constituent parts are the basic building blocks of everything in the universe. Electrons, as well as protons and neutrons that together form the nucleus of the atom, exist in all atoms, and electrons orbit the nucleus in an imprecise cloud of possible locations. It was known since 1801 that light had wave and particle properties. In 1927, Davisson and Germer demonstrated that electrons show the same behavior as light, and that was subsequently extended to atoms and molecules.[1] That meant electrons also had wave and particle properties. Particles are *localized*; that is, they exist as a specific point at a specific time. Waves, on the other hand, are *nonlocalized* and are therefore spread out. It also is significant to note that electrons are the glue that binds atoms together in chemical bonds. These chemical bonds form the physical environment around us—the constitution of matter itself—that we simply term the *material world* (although as we shall see shortly, the underpinning of atoms is invisible energy, so atoms are therefore actually immaterial). In no small way, then, electrons are the basis of the universe and of reality itself.

Astonishment

In the *Double Slit Experiment*, electrons were shot at a partition with two open slits (there was a screen behind the partition to record the paths of the electrons). What emerged was a wave-like arrangement on the screen when the expectation was two distinct columns of dots representing individual particles. The results showed that the electrons were behaving like waves, transversing through both slits when they should have traveled through one slit or the other. Remember, a wave could pass through both slits, whereas particles would have to choose one or the other slit. Physicists initially thought the electrons were bouncing off each other, forming the wave arrangement. So they reduced the electron stream to one electron at a time. When the electrons were fired singularly and slowly (supposedly ensuring their particle-like nature), each electron also passed through the two slits. What was thought to be a single particle was behaving like a wave by passing through both slits at the same time. This is the famous *wave-particle duality* of Quantum Mechanics since an electron is both a wave and a particle existing as one. To this day, there is no satisfactory explanation for this phenomenon.

Obviously, this baffled early physicists. In fact, these findings were so bizarre that physicists tried to peek at the electrons to catch them in their curious behavior. They used measuring devices to actually see the electrons pass through the slits. Much to their astonishment, when they observed the electron, it behaved like a particle and passed through only one slit. The mere act of observing the electron (called the *Observer Effect*) caused it to assume particle characteristics and abandon its wave-like nature.

So let us get directly to the point:

> **Our observation of the electron creates its nature. When we are observing, the electron behaves as a particle; when we are not observing, the electron behaves as a wave. Our observation (Consciousness) determines the electron's properties and actualizes it.**

Then some extremely high-level mathematics was applied, and the calculations demonstrated that an electron in its natural state can go through both slits, neither slit, one slit, or the other slit. All the potentials of the electron exist before observation in what is known as a *superposition*. At once, the electron is everywhere! It does not have a definite state or position. That is also known as the *wave function* of the atom where the electron exists in many orbital positions above the nucleus (behaving like a wave). Yet if we want to observe the electron at a specific point, the electron appears as a particle (as opposed to a wave) in that exact location and ceases its other potential positions. That is known as *collapse of the wave function*. This bizarre collapse is caused by the observation made by an observer where literally Consciousness collapses the wave function and forces the electron into one position with nothing more than the intention of a human observer.[2]

Thus, the *Double Slit Experiment* is the definitive glance into reality. Mind compels electrons to become real things, controlling their characteristics and behavior. Without Consciousness observing them, electrons exist only as clouds of potential and would never become actual things. Again, the same dynamic extends to atoms and simple molecules that form the building blocks of the entire universe, so reality is inexorably linked to observation and Mind. Fundamentally, it is Consciousness that brings things into existence by materializing potential into matter.

Implications

So how can this be? How can a supposedly objective and independent universe exist only through an association with Consciousness? How is it that Consciousness brings the universe to life? How can matter and energy behave in ways that appear so counterintuitive and absurd to our everyday senses? What does the *Double Slit Experiment* say about the nature of reality?

Consider the following:

> **The universe is not a real thing in the materialist sense of the term. As Nobel Prize–winning physicist Neils Bohr once famously remarked, "Everything we call real is made of things that cannot be regarded as real." Physicists have discovered that atoms and subatomic particles are vortices of invisible energy, perpetually spinning and vibrating, existing in a type of physical void with no actual material structure. Things become real only by connection to Mind. Thus, Consciousness creates the universe.**

This puts Consciousness at the forefront as the organizer of existence, arranging innumerable potentials into the one actuality we know as reality. But the question remains—"of whose Consciousness?" Where does this Mind come from? Is this Mind evenly dispersed throughout the universe or located in just one place? We obviously have some of this Universal Mind in us, but we are not its source. Moreover, since the ingredients forming the universe are immaterial and unreal, that fact alone attests to a source that is incorporeal, transcendental, or even spiritual.

Therefore, Consciousness is likely related to Spirit, comprised of the same incorporeal essence. In addition, the Observer Effect noted earlier connotes a *first observer* where an initial observation (or something similar) brought an entire universe into existence. This original observer would possess both mental and spiritual properties, offering considerable challenge to scientific orthodoxy that cannot account for Mind and believes Spirit is ridiculous. After all, science is based on things being physically real, our common sense notion of reality premised on matter as actually existing in material form. The quantum, however, clearly demonstrates that this is false. Consider the following from *Collective Evolution*:

> **According to the quantum mechanic laws that govern subatomic affairs, a particle like an electron exists in a murky**

state of possibility—to be anywhere, everywhere or nowhere at all—until clicked into substantiality by a laboratory detector or an eyeball.[3]

Think about that. Nothing exists without Mind. That is not the reality we were all taught to believe in. The scientific materialist preference for an objective and independent reality apart from Consciousness literally doesn't exist. Their doctrine that everything is matter and its movements, including all mental processes leading to Consciousness, is eviscerated by the *Double Slit Experiment* and the primacy of Mind. Matter is merely a product of Consciousness.

Scientific materialists hate this fact (partly because it was derived scientifically) and for additional reasons to be explored in subsequent chapters, but consider the words of physicist David Deutsch:

> **Despite the unrivalled empirical success of quantum theory, the very suggestion that it may be *literally true as a description of nature* is still greeted with cynicism, incomprehension, and even anger.**[4]

Put another way, some of our greatest minds are struggling to accept reality. That cannot be good for the human future.

Ultimately, what does that mean? Let us consider some indisputable and glaring implications of a reality created by Consciousness as learned from the *Double Slit Experiment* to assist in our embrace of the truth.

> **Reality is a structure that appears real but is made of unreal things, coming into its "realness" only through the observational power of Mind. Consider reality as a great painting. Mind creates the art, filling a blank canvas with a visible masterwork. Yet if you remove Consciousness from the equation, the art literally disappears. Consciousness doesn't so much witness the image as actually create it; the prodigious painter of the art we term reality is simply the Mind being the Mind. Without Consciousness, there is no art.**

That causes some troubling questions. Is reality an illusion? Can the universe and, by extension, reality ever truly be understood? As with the *Double Slit Experiment*, perhaps other revelations within Quantum Mechanics might provide answers to questions about the true nature of things. Be warned, however, that every further exploration into the inner workings of the atom reveals more unbelievable truths. Virtually nothing is as we thought. Let us turn to that exploration next.

CHAPTER 2

The Incredible World
of Quantum Mechanics

The *Double Slit Experiment* is only the beginning of the astonishing truths inside an atom. Nevertheless, much division occurs within science concerning the experimental results of Quantum Mechanics, largely because the findings are so impossibly bizarre. The debate is often heated, and each new, experimental result causes yet more divisive opinions. Seldom is there widespread agreement on what the experiments actually mean. So for our purposes, we will focus on the generally accepted conclusions and develop logical linkages to larger truths.

To further understand the subject, we start with a definition that extends beyond our earlier description. Quantum Mechanics is "the branch of mechanics, based on the quantum theory used for interpreting the behaviour of elementary particles and atoms, which do not obey Newtonian mechanics."[5] This definition is significant because it identifies the central problem within any examination of reality—the incompatibility of the macro classical physics of Newton and the micro quantum mechanical physics that govern the atom. **Classical physics and quantum physics are radically different, displaying different behaviors and obeying different rules. Classical physics cannot adequately describe the quantum world.** Classical physics is logical and easily deducible, whereas quantum physics is counterintuitive and esoteric. Moreover, there is no grand unification theory that incorporates both into a comprehensive whole.

Thus, physics is stagnant, caught between two apparently incompatible worlds. The classical world exists in a state of astonishment at the inherent outlandishness of the quantum, while a goodly bunch of quantum physicists consider classical physics anachronistically limiting. Simply, the results of the *Double Slit Experiment* are so invalidating that classical physics has never recovered. Its worldview of mechanistic determinism (belief that the universe is reducible to its constituent parts and their interrelations) is destroyed when the constituent parts are immaterial and random.

As a result, Quantum Mechanics rather points to *spiritualistic indeterminism* (i.e., the immaterial and probabilistic nature of things) as the only valid explanation of reality. This perfectly positions the philosophical debate between *idealism* (reality is fundamentally mental and spiritual) and *realism* (reality is independent of Mind); classical physics is naturally *realistic*, whereas quantum physics is naturally *idealistic*. Newtonians, although providing much utility in their understanding and manipulation of the macro environment, are simply unsuited to explore the enigmas of the quantum. It is like asking a whale to climb a tree.

Atomic Truth

An atom is 99.9999999% empty space. You read that correctly. Even the particles that comprise the "matter" within the atom (protons, neutrons, and electrons) are actually just waves of probability. So the universe—and by extension our reality—is comprised of empty space and matter that is invisible. When the ancient sages claimed that reality was an illusion, they meant it.

As mentioned in Chapter 1, electrons are spread out into an electron cloud or superposition known as a wave function. In some respects, this cloud fills the empty space, although since the electron is merely a probability wave, the space in the atom is actually empty (debates on this empty space versus electron cloud rage on, but it is merely a technicality). Fundamental forces of nature bond particles within the atom, and when electrons in atoms come into contact with other atoms, attractive and repulsive forces provide the appearance and feel of solidity. In this way, a reality made of immaterial and unreal things can appear solid and feel real.

Therefore, things look actual, but underneath there is nothing there. Reality begins to appear as a type of hologram or simulation. As discussed in Chapter 1, measurement (observation) collapses the wave function so all of an electron's potentials manifest at one particular point known as a particle. Without doubt, that ascribes huge significance to the powers of Mind since Consciousness not only collapses the wave function but directly influences or even creates the properties of matter and energy. Mind literally compels electrons to become actual things out of a wavy cloud of potential. To Neils Bohr and Werner Heisenberg, the experimental results were obvious. Their explanation for the results of the *Double Slit Experiment* is known as the *Copenhagen Interpretation* (since Bohr was from Copenhagen) and is the preponderant interpretation of Quantum Mechanics.

Naturally, the Copenhagen Interpretation was challenged by classical physicists who invented twenty-two other interpretations of Quantum Mechanics that supported their belief systems. None of these twenty-two interpretations (Many Worlds Interpretation, Pilot Wave Theory, and Decoherence, to name a few) have ever been proven, but the theoretical landscape is littered with unsubstantiated nonsense so scientific materialism can maintain its belief in a solid, physical reality that doesn't exist. Further on, we will discredit many of these other interpretations, some of which are truly preposterous. Consider the following quote from Nobel Prize winner Max Planck:

> **There is no matter as such! All matter originates and exists only by virtue of a force. . . . We must assume behind this force the existence of a conscious and intelligent Mind. This Mind is the matrix of all matter.**[6]

Nobel prize–winning physicist Erwin Schrödinger said in an interview in 1931 that Consciousness is how the world "first becomes manifest." It is made up of components of Consciousness.[7]

And again from Schrödinger:

> **Consciousness cannot be accounted for in physical terms.**
> **For consciousness is absolutely fundamental. It cannot be**
> **accounted for in terms of anything else.**[8]

Since the primacy of Consciousness is experimentally validated, it should be widely accepted; unfortunately, it is disputed without cause. That implies willful intent by the scientific community to deny the primacy of Consciousness in order to fulfill some deeper agenda. So what is this hidden objective? What is so concerning about the centrality of Mind? We may be able to learn the answer by examining a rather famous question by Albert Einstein concerning Consciousness and the state of the moon.

First, let us look at a little context. As previously mentioned, Consciousness, through the act of observation or measurement, collapses the wave function of an atom; obviously, that was an unexpected result, especially for Einstein. It appeared completely illogical for Mind to have a "power" or directing influence over what should be neutral or indifferent material. To Einstein, the experimental results of the *Double Slit Experiment* appeared non-deterministic, without cause and effect, so something undiscovered must describe the impossible behavior of electrons. He termed these "hidden variables." Unfortunately for Einstein, they have never been found. Nevertheless, Einstein challenged the *Copenhagen Interpretation* of Quantum Mechanics by posing this question: "Are you saying the moon is not there if we are not looking at it?"

Remarkably, we can use Einstein's question to make the absurd appear logical. Einstein was a realist, while quantum truths are idealist. The question remains—"of whose Mind?" Does the moon exist because our individual minds observe it? Or do our individual minds share a universal Consciousness? Consider a theoretical Realist and Idealist debate using the initial question Einstein posed:

> **Realist: You know, Galileo observed the moon hundreds of**
> **years before us with one of the first telescopes. So the moon**
> **was there.**

Idealist: Of course. Galileo had Consciousness.

Realist: What about the fossil record revealing that 250 million years ago dinosaurs were being affected by the tides of the Earth's oceans? Tides are caused by the gravitational effects of the moon. So the moon was there.

Idealist: Sure. Dinosaurs had Consciousness.

Realist: So how far in history does Consciousness go?

Idealist: To the beginning. The *Observer Effect* demonstrates that Consciousness brings matter and energy into existence. The universe is matter and energy. That mandates a first observer manifesting an entire universe.

Realist: That would be a powerful first observer. Who might that be?

Idealist: Apparently, a Great Consciousness or God.

Perhaps the reluctance of scientific materialists to embrace the *Copenhagen Interpretation* and the primacy of Consciousness is because it leads inexorably to God. Scientific materialists tend to be atheists. A First Mind sounds an awful lot like a Creator. Would an atheistic, scientific materialist welcome quantum experimental results that inevitably point to a Divine Being? Of course not. Hence, there are twenty-two interpretations of Quantum Mechanics. The *Double Slit Experiment* provides a direct linkage through time of the observational antecedence of Mind to a Great Consciousness, one who created the entire universe with nothing more than focused intention or observation.

Since experiments demonstrate that observation creates reality, the Copenhagen Interpretation was correct—the moon doesn't exist without the presence of Mind. If one believes in the scientific method, one must accept even those experimental results that conflict with common sense. **Essentially, that is the materialist dilemma—how to accept scientific facts that undermine scientific beliefs.**

Entanglement

Another bizarre, inner working of the atom leading to a radically new perspective of reality is known as Quantum Entanglement. It occurs when subatomic pairs of particles interact physically. When measurements are made on their spin, momentum, position, and polarization, they are correlated. An effect on one particle immediately affects the other, determining its behavior regardless of distance. That, of course, is also nonsensical, but it has been proven experimentally, the latest being a Chinese experiment of entangled particles separated by almost 750 miles.[9] The math has been worked out, and particles can be entangled even through distances of billions of light years.

Entanglement suggests that the particle "knows" what manipulation has been performed on its equivalent, and because of Einstein's Theory of Relativity, no "message" that exceeds the speed of light can be sent between the particles. Yet Quantum Entanglement is irrespective of this limitation. Such experimental results are nondeterministic, counterintuitive to all that is logical. Two separate objects behaving as one, regardless of distance? That certainly doesn't sound like traditional interpretations of reality.

So what does Quantum Entanglement say about the relationship between particles? How can electrons be so incredibly connected as to defy common sense?

Experiments have told the story. Since the speed of light limitation is verified and so are physical distances, the net result is that no message is actually being sent as a form of communication between the two distinct particles; rather, entanglement is simply a fundamental property of nature with two separate objects behaving as one, regardless of the distances involved. The classical speed of light limitation is maintained because there is no movement in the intervening space between the entangled particles and no signal sent between them, nor is one necessary. Although they are two separate entities, entangled particles behave as one system.

The experiments also demonstrate another incredible truth: Quantum Entanglement is a direct assault on the foundations of classical physics because it violates a stalwart of Newtonian orthodoxy known as *locality* where objects are influenced only by their immediate surroundings.[10] *Locality* dictates that in the case of entangled particles, a communication would have to travel between them in order to bring the message from one particle to the other; essentially, there has to be a physical, real force to cause the influence. Yet no such force exists.

Therefore, Quantum Entanglement also violates the concept of *realism* in physics, the assumption that quantum states have defined properties independent of measurement.[11] *Superposition* has shown that no such defined properties exist. Moreover, a materialist interpretation of reality necessitates a belief in *local realism*, an Einsteinian principle combining *locality* and *realism*. Things are supposed to exist on their own, have defined properties, and only be influenced by nearby objects. Quantum Entanglement, however, violates *local realism* because experiments have shown that matter is naturally *nonlocal* (spread out) and that nothing exists before measurement (observation). Contrary to things being influenced only by their immediate surroundings and thus definitively "real," quantum realities demonstrate instead that nature is universally connected and physically unreal.

The further we look into the quantum world, the more bizarre it becomes. The next phenomenon is virtually incomprehensible.

Consider when Quantum Entanglement is combined with the classic *Double Slit Experiment* in what is known as *Delayed Choice* and *Quantum Eraser* experiments. Originally, the concept of *Delayed Choice* was formulated as a thought experiment by John Archibald Wheeler portending the actual Quantum Eraser experiments. Be advised, however, that these experiments will challenge the limits of rationality and credulity. First, we shall examine *Delayed Choice* as a thought experiment.

Imagine a distant star emits light. Between that star and the Earth is a galaxy, but instead of blocking the light, it bends light towards the Earth. It bends light in of [sic] two different ways. A single photon, going from the star, can take one of two paths, to the left of the galaxy or the right of the galaxy. Suddenly, we have a Double-Slit experiment

in space. The photons make their way to Earth, and we can observe them. We can observe either exactly where they come from, or we can neglect to see which side of the galaxy they came around. Again, we have a Double-Slit experiment in space . . . and we would get the same results – interference pattern if we do not check the exact origin of the photons, and no interference pattern if we do check the exact origin of the photons.

The interesting thing is, these photons would have made "the choice" between going through one path, the other, or both, millions or billions of years ago. There is no way we could have messed up and measured them as they were coming around the galaxy. And yet, depending on whether we measure them, we will have determined whether they passed through one path, the other, or possibly both. Can we determine, now, events that happened millions of years ago?[12]

Fortunately, this is no longer conjecture. In 2015, an experiment was conducted at the Australian National University that demonstrated that measurements in the present can determine a particle's past. Consider their following press release:

The bizarre nature of reality as laid out by quantum theory has survived another test, with scientists performing a famous experiment and proving that reality does not exist until it is measured. Physicists at The Australian National University (ANU) have conducted John Wheeler's delayed-choice thought experiment, which involves a moving object that is given the choice to act like a particle or a wave. Wheeler's experiment then asks – at which point does the object decide? Common sense says the object is either wave-like or particle-like, independent of how we measure it. But quantum physics predicts that whether you observe wave like behavior (interference) or particle behavior (no interference) depends only on how it is actually measured at the end of its journey. This is exactly what the ANU team found. "It proves that measurement is everything. At the quantum level, reality does not exist if you are not looking at it," said Associate Professor Andrew Truscott from the ANU Research School of Physics and Engineering. . . . The ANU team not only succeeded in building the experiment, which seemed nearly impossible when it was proposed in 1978, but reversed Wheeler's original concept of light beams being bounced by mirrors, and instead used atoms scattered by laser light. . . . Professor Truscott's team first trapped a collection of helium atoms in a suspended state known as a Bose-Einstein condensate, and then ejected them until there was only a single atom left. The single atom was then dropped through a pair of counter-propagating laser beams, which formed a grating that acted as crossroads in the same way a solid grating would scatter light. A second light grating to recombine the paths was randomly added, which led to constructive or destructive interference as if the atom had travelled both paths. When the second light grating was not added, no interference was observed as if the atom chose only one path. However, the random number determining whether the grating was added was only generated after the atom had passed through the crossroads. If one chooses to believe that the atom really did take a particular path or paths then one has to accept that a future measurement is affecting the atom's past, said Truscott. "The atoms did not travel from A to B. It was only when they were measured at the end of the journey that their wave-like or particle-like behavior was brought into existence," he said.[13]

We should think seriously about the implications of this experiment. These findings are antithetical to our common-sense notions of reality, specifically the passage of time. So here is the new reality. **Measurements made in the present can determine the past. The ironclad forward motion of time is not so ironclad after all. Time can proceed into the past, the present, and the future. That contradicts everything we have been taught.**

Next, we can consider *Quantum Eraser* experiments, further extensions of the *Double Slit Experiment* that attempt to find "which path" information for how particles travel through the slits. The foundation of these experiments was the dubiety, even intransigence, of scientific materialists to accept that Consciousness collapses the wave function—that Mind creates reality. They were convinced that some property of the measuring devices or other physical equipment was causing the collapse. They named this physical phenomenon *decoherence*, which has never been proved and is actually disproven by *Quantum Eraser* experiments.

In *Quantum Eraser* experiments, the major difference to the famous *Double Slit Experiment* is that the measuring devices observing the paths of electrons are placed behind the slits. In short, the electrons are viewed after rather than before they pass through the slits. Observation before the slits collapses their *superposition* (wave) and changes electrons to particles; if unobserved, experiments always show that electrons pass through as waves. But in *Quantum Eraser* experiments, observation is made after electrons pass through the slits as waves and are then observed—as particles! Observation changes their nature from wave to particle, even past the point of no return (the two, open slits). **Moreover, a new history is loaded so the particles actually went through the two open slits as particles, even though they first passed through as a wave. History is rewritten. Observation in the present literally changes the past.**

As a result, it becomes obvious that *Quantum Entanglement* not only links particles spatially but also links them temporally (in time). A technique developed in 2007 termed *entanglement swapping* demonstrated quantum correlations across time, but an experiment in 2013 further demonstrated that particles can be entangled, never having concurrently existed.[14]

Although too complicated to discuss at length here, in 1999 a famous experiment known as *Delayed Choice Quantum Eraser* extended even further the exploration of "which path" information. An excellent video on YouTube goes into great detail yet offers simple explanations of the results.[15] Briefly, it is knowledge of "which path" in the present can change the past history of a particle. Choices observers make in the present can change the past, so it proves that time is not set. Time can travel in different directions, and the mere knowledge of "which path" information an observer has can literally change the properties and histories of the particles.

We have been taught to believe that the past determines the present and the present determines the future. In reality, that is true, but so can **the present determine the past, the future determine the present, and the future determine the past**. That is retrocausality, and it is a staple of the quantum world. Hence systems, including the universe and reality, should be viewed as wholes, not just a collection of parts. Moreover, the materialist explanation for the nature of things, what is known as *determinism* where everything has a rational cause and effect, is obviously false. The quantum world makes little sense, at least according to our physicalist sensibilities, yet its outlandish peculiarities form the basis of reality. Thus, scientific materialism is both inaccurate and anachronistic.

So what are the implications of Quantum Entanglement? Consider the following possibilities:

- Everything is connected.

- Since particles are brought into physical existence by Consciousness and everything is associated, the universe is entangled with Mind.

- Since Quantum Entanglement is fundamental in nature, potentially any activity affects everything else.

- Spacetime may result from Quantum Entanglement. The "grid" of the universe may result from the interconnectedness of everything.

- Quantum Entanglement suggests a "one state" nature to reality. If superposition is the natural, unobserved state (all potentialities existing concurrently), then Consciousness brings single state reality into existence by observation. That does not preclude different levels of reality, only that we share a common one.

- Consciousness allows parts to become separate from the whole so they can be experienced. Without Consciousness, all possibilities exist, but they are not known. Consciousness allows separateness without separation.

- *Determinism,* the concept that everything is determined by previously existing causes and is therefore exceedingly rational, is obliterated. Quantum Entanglement points more toward *indeterminism,* the belief that everything is probabilistic, fundamentally random, and likely unknowable.

Basic applications of Quantum Entanglement exist (the preponderance in early formulation and experimental stages), but the future of this phenomenon is incredibly promising. Possibilities include advanced encryption technologies, teleported information, precision clocks, superior microscopes, vastly more powerful computers, and unfortunately more lethal weapons systems. All will utilize entanglement as the means of transmission, although only information can be transmitted, not actual matter (or what we call matter). The effects on reality as we know it can only be imagined.

The Inevitability of Consciousness

It must be mentioned that some believe the aforementioned bizarre behavior of electrons and other particles is best described by particles having their own Consciousness. This is known as *panpsychism*—that everything, no matter how small, has its own mind. Experiments have shown that when measuring devices are left in place in the *Double Slit Experiment* and turned off (no longer observing), the interference nature of a wave returns (instead of the particle characteristic typical of observation).[16] Somehow, electrons appear to "know" when the detector is off and they are no longer being observed.

Two possible explanations exist for an electron's apparently conscious behavior: (1) the Great Consciousness watches everything and gives electrons the direction required to conform to human observation, or (2) electrons have their own mind. The first is self-explanatory. The second, although it sounds absurd, mandates a new understanding of Mind since electrons have no physical brain yet demonstrate intelligence and choice. Could it be that Mind does not result from physical processes in the brain such as neural networks and synaptic firings? Could it be that brain chemistry is not required in order for Mind to exist?

What are required in order to lend credibility to the notion of electrons having their own mind are other examples from nature of things that demonstrate Consciousness without a physical brain. We digress some here, but since nature consists of atomic structure, including, of course, electrons, establishing this linkage proves the potential of *panpsychism*. We can consider these examples next.

Amoebas, planarian flatworms, starfish, and mold are just some of the many organisms on Earth that demonstrate self-awareness and intelligence without a physical brain. Recently, a plant whose natural enemy, a caterpillar, makes a scrunching sound when it eats the leaves of the plant was placed in a room by itself. In nature, when the caterpillar eats the leaves, the plant emits a chemical that is its defense mechanism against the caterpillar. This time, with no caterpillar on its leaves or anywhere in the room, the sound of the caterpillar munching the leaves was broadcast, and the plant immediately emitted the chemical.[17] Somehow, the plant "heard" the threat with ears it doesn't have and processed the threat with a brain it doesn't have. The plant clearly demonstrated intelligence and intention with no physical brain. How did the plant perform this incredible feat? How does a plant with no physical brain demonstrate awareness and the presence of Mind? Consider another example.

It is common knowledge that mold demonstrates Consciousness. ResearchGate searches identified numerous experimental results, but perhaps we can summarize their collective findings using a representative example. Mold was placed in a dish with four paths ahead of it: white, gold, beige, and grey. As good mold should do, it went exploring all paths for food. Only the gold path provided food. Immediately, the mold travelled only to the gold path. More impressively, some of the mold in the rear of the dish (that did not explore) was separated and kept in a separate dish for thirty days. Placed into another dish with the same four color paths ahead of it, the mold instantly proceeded toward the gold because it "knew" that meant food. Mold demonstrates high levels of intelligence and awareness and has at least a thirty-day memory. Not a scientist in the world will tell you that mold has a physical brain.

Next, consider another experiment conducted by biologist Monica Gagliano that demonstrates how a mimosa plant can learn from experience. Michael Pollan stated in an interview that because Gagliano used the term "learn," ten scientific journals rejected her paper before it was published (scientific materialism dies slowly). Below is an excerpt from the article.

> **Mimosa is a plant, which looks something like a fern, that collapses its leaves temporarily when it is disturbed. So Gagliano set up a contraption that would drop the mimosa plant, without hurting it. When the plant dropped, as expected, its leaves collapsed. She kept dropping the plants every five to six seconds. "After five or six drops, the plants would stop responding, as if they'd learned to tune out the stimulus as irrelevent," Pollan says. "This is a very important part of learning – to learn what you can safely ignore in your environment." Maybe the plant was just getting worn out from all the dropping? To test that, Gagliano took the plants that had stopped responding to the drops and shook them instead. "They would continue to collapse," Pollan says. "They had made the distinction that [dropping] was a signal they could safely ignore. And what was more incredible is that [Gagliano] would retest them every week for four weeks and, for a month, they continued to remember their lesson.**[18]

We must remember that plants do not have brains, yet they clearly demonstrate Mind. Finally, consider this example from John Kehoe:

**Seeing this reminded me of being on safari several years ear-
lier where a game ranger pointed out a species of tree that not
only reacted to animals eating its leaves, but also transmitted
signals to other trees of the same species as well. It seems that
these particular leaves were very delicate and tasty favourites
of the giraffe. So whenever a family of giraffes would begin
eating them, within 15 minutes the taste of the leaves would
turn sour. What was so interesting, however, was that it was
not only the leaves on that particular tree that turned sour,
but the leaves on all the identical trees within a half-mile
radius! The tree whose leaves were being eaten was able to
somehow communicate with the other trees in the area and
warn of impending danger.**[19]

The aforementioned sounds like a tree version of Quantum Entanglement, the
strange behavior of electrons extending into macro objects (such as trees) with
a level of connectivity that cannot be described through scientific materialism.
Mind is firmly entrenched into every living organism on Earth and possibly
even into the inanimate. The above examples conclusively point to Mind, not
brain, as the source of awareness and intelligence since no other satisfactory
explanation exists.

The primary ramification of the experimental evidence reviewed so far
is that Consciousness is paramount to existence. Nothing is more essential or
causative of being than Mind. Max Planck, the Nobel Prize–winning physicist
and father of quantum theory, stated:

**I regard consciousness as fundamental. I regard matter as
derivative from consciousness. We cannot get behind consciousness. Everything that we talk about, everything that
we regard as existing, postulates consciousness.**[20]

The supremacy of Consciousness necessitates a restructuring of our conceptual
foundations. Our worldview is flawed. First, consider the following organization
of reality according to physicalism:

- **Big Bang creates the universe.**

- **Matter appears, governed by fundamental laws.**

- **Galaxies form, filled with billions of stars and planets.**

- **Time passes.**

- **On some of these planets, life happens. Evolution begins.**

- **On Earth, after billions of years of evolution, humans emerge.**

- **Humans, having a highly advanced brain, develop Consciousness.**

- **Consciousness is thus born of materialism.**

This framework reigned until the arrival of Quantum Mechanics. What replaces physicalism is a revolution. Consider the correct framework:

- **Matter doesn't exist without Mind observing it.**

- **The history of antecedental observation mandates a First Mind.**

- **First Mind brings the universe into existence.**

- **Mind therefore precedes the Big Bang and all physical processes.**

- **Humans have Consciousness as a derivative of First Mind, not because of a physical brain.**

- **Thus, Materialism doesn't cause Consciousness, rather Consciousness causes Materialism.**

To fully grasp the far-reaching implications of a reality based on the essentiality of Mind, we must first understand the historical attempts of leading thinkers to interpret their world. These sophists provided the classical descriptions of reality that contrast with the emerging truths of our time. After all, a structure must exist in order for a revolution to topple it. Let us consider this traditional framework next in our study.

CHAPTER 3

Reality Defined

As we have noted, we require an interpretation of reality that is far deeper, far more comprehensive, and far more accurate than scientific materialism. First, however, we must examine and even appreciate earlier attempts to describe reality since traditional interpretations largely prevail and are instructional for their contrast to the primacy of Consciousness.

Definitions

We can start with a classic definition of reality from scientific materialism. Reality is "the world or the state of things as they actually exist, as opposed to an idealistic or notional idea of them."[21] That implies a "realness" to reality—a solid, material, and inviolable essence to the objects we see all around us. According to this definition, things are actually there, physically present, with every level of reduction discovering more of their physical baseness, unquestioned in their absolute naturality. Reality, as postulated by classical physics, is constructed of solid, material objects that are indisputably real.

Unfortunately, this definition loses validity under scrutiny. As we have seen, reality is composed of things unreal and immaterial—therefore reality is not a "real" entity, not something distinct and tangible. Moreover, since reality is more than can be known through our five senses (the ability to see, hear, touch, taste, and smell), some things exist that we cannot sense such as economic cycles, peak experiences, impending deceit, and first-date chemistry. All of these elude physical confirmation. These aspects of existence are unrelated to the quantum yet are indisputably part of our world. There is thus more to reality than our five senses tell us, both at the material and immaterial levels.

Yet to perceive a reality consisting of more than our five senses, we also must have additional abilities, some type of innate logic or intuition, that is literally "built into us." In short, we know more than our five senses tell us. Philosophically, that is known as *innatism*. This ability transcends any causative physical constituency (the brain) and must be accepted as immaterially based. Competencies such as ESP (extrasensory perception), remote viewing, premonitions, and psychic awareness attest to this innate capability that defies conventional explanation.

Traditional science hates this fact. According to scientific materialism, humans were supposed to be a tabula rasa, a clean slate, with nothing inherent enabling cognition. Intuition should not exist. Nevertheless, support exists that we have "the ability to acquire knowledge without proof, evidence, or conscious reasoning, or without understanding how the knowledge was acquired."[22] For a materialist, actuality was thought to be a wholeness unto itself that required no further identification or explanation. That perspective is fallacious, even before we delve into the atom. Moreover, inherency posits a Creator who placed nonphysical abilities within each and every one of us. Such abilities oppose physicalist explanations and are highly suggestive of Soul.

Yet all of us find comfort in simplification and shared beliefs. Materialists exploit this tendency by controlling information, specifically in education. The result is common ground, what is known as *consensus reality*. Thus, we accept the physical reality we know, the one everyone else accepts. This familiar level of reality, also known as *rudimentary reality,* is easy to understand compared to quantum truths such as the supremacy of Consciousness and is thus also reassuring.

Nevertheless, there are situations where we trust our intuition against consensus reality and choose accordingly. This is rare but commendable. Thus, our perception of reality includes the apparent world, our own individual intuitiveness, and those of the group. The following illustrates this point:

**Physical Existence + Perception +
Consensus = Determined Reality**

Although each individual determines their reality, perhaps we can see how the truths of Quantum Mechanics and their implications are largely unrecognized by the public; they are at once so profound and so threatening that they are best left unknown or ignored. Curiosity gets sublimated to the accustomed and secure. That reinforces the physicalist explanation of reality. Thus, it is incumbent on the proponents of the emerging Consciousness paradigm to consider the sensitivities of humanity when communicating transformational messages regarding the nature of existence.

Levels of Reality

Fortunately, some highly inquisitive minds preceded us and imagined reality as more than rudimentary, instead being stratified. This stratification implies different "levels of reality." The incredible complexity of our world, not to mention a nighttime gaze into the unfathomable heavens, prompted early philosophers to imagine levels of reality far beyond our own. Yet no agreement exists on how best to define or describe these other realms.

Moreover, the concept of levels of reality is contested by scientific materialists who endorse a "single reality" theory of existence. To them, everything around us is part of the same reality, and humans are merely fortuitously present and also rather insignificant participants in this indifferent display. This frame of reference, however, is a Temple of Dagon, complete with collapsible pillars, and is both embarrassingly anachronistic and intellectually corrupt.

To be sure, different levels of reality exist, probably many of them such as a pyramidical or block structure formed from a simple base to ever-increasing degrees of complexity. Logically, each ascent up the pyramid is a derivative of the level below it but more advanced. Another possibility is that levels of reality are contributory, so although not directly contiguous, different levels are accessible and affective of each other. Our preliminary exposure to quantum physics posits at least a double level of reality (absent a unification theory) since the macro and micro worlds are clearly different from one another. Returning to our earlier definition of reality, we can amend it as follows:

Reality is the state of things as they apparently exist on the level discernible to us, recognizing a deeper actuality exists that is layered and increasingly complex.

Particularly relevant to this discussion is the ancient Greek philosopher Plato and his formulation of levels of reality. We will consider his framework here. According to Plato, the first level is *Appearances*, the level perceived by the senses, or the world around us. This is a rudimentary level of its own that is forever changing. The second level is *Forms* where nonphysical forms or ideas represent the more accurate reality. Forms are the purest form of something; for example, the form of a chair is more real than the chair itself, which merely represents the actual form. Thus, Plato suggests the physical world is less real than something deeper or hidden (the realm of the Forms) and that physical reality is a type of illusion. Such was the experience of the first physicists who expected atoms to be solid objects and instead found nearly empty space. Moreover, according to Plato, Mind was a gateway to the Forms, which was remarkably similar to the experimental results of the *Double Slit Experiment* that proved the essentiality of Consciousness. Forms, then, correspond to nonphysical, invisible energy and quantum potential, a type of early inquiry into the secrets of the atom.

Naturally, there had to be a counterweight.

Aristotle challenged Plato by postulating that the ideal reality of Forms was flawed. He insisted that the world was physical and real and could be understood by using our five senses. Aristotle was an *empiricist* (knowledge comes only or primarily through the senses), whereas Plato was an *innatist* (the mind is born with ideas and knowledge, which might be termed "intuition"). Aristotle further argued that all the natural forms on Earth could be understood by utilizing the scientific method that naturally followed from our sensical (of the senses) awareness of the world; as a result, he developed *syllogistic reasoning* whereby an argument can be reasoned more accurately by its structure than by its content.[23] **This is significant because it elevates methodology above findings (if methodology is sacrosanct, then unwelcome experimental results can be subordinated or ignored). Thus, process is institutionalized while results are controlled, as science has often demonstrated.**

Aristotle also believed the rational mind could eventually comprehend everything. This belief proved indispensable to the reign of science beginning in the seventeenth century, also known as the Age of Science and Reason, which has endured and forms our prevailing worldview. In fact, Aristotle championed reason as the source of all knowledge, a power so great that it "unifies & interprets the sense perceptions."[24] The power of Aristotle's ideas is historically enormous, and those ideas essentialized logic as the method whereby humans ultimately discern reality. This "faith in reason" has characterized materialist belief ever since to the point that any alternative methods are invariably condemned. More importantly, Aristotle's conceptualizations formed the "one reality" position so characteristic of scientific materialism.

History, however, provided yet another counterweight.

The next levels of reality discussion concern the work of Nobel Prize–winning physicist Werner Heisenberg, one of the leading theorists in Quantum Mechanics. Heisenberg was famous for his Uncertainty Principle, which demonstrated that the more the position of a particle is known, the less we can be sure of its momentum—and the more we know its momentum, the less we can be sure of its position. This experimentally validated principle stands in absolute opposition to logic, reason, and classical physics. Heisenberg's Uncertainty Principle gave Quantum Mechanics its indeterminate nature in contrast to the typical *determinism* of materialism.

Naturally, that caused Heisenberg to contemplate his discovery in philosophical terms. Obviously, when we are confronted with proof that the micro world of Quantum Mechanics is fundamentally different from the macro world of classical physics, at least two levels of reality position become apparent, which we have noted earlier. Heisenberg went even further. Quoting from physicist Basarab Nicolescu, consider his insight:

> **In fact, Werner Heisenberg came very near, in his philosophical writings, to the concept of "level of Reality." In his famous *Manuscript of the year 1942* (published only in 1984), Heisenberg, who knew well Husserl, introduces the idea of three *regions of reality*, able to give access to the concept of "reality" itself: the first region is that of classical physics, the second – of quantum physics, biology and psychic phenomena and the third – that of the religious, philosophical and artistic experiences. This classification has a subtle ground: the closer and closer connection between the Subject and the Object.**[25]

According to Nicolescu, Heisenberg believed that beyond the macro and micro levels, there is a third level of Soul. Notice our levels of reality are expanding. A closer connection between *Subject* and *Object* can also be viewed as a closer connection between *Observer* and *Observed*. That reminds us, as discussed in Chapter 1, of the *Observer Effect* in Quantum Mechanics whereby Consciousness through observation brings matter and energy into existence (*subject* is Consciousness, *object* is Reality). Thus, the observer or subject "causes" the object or reality to exist, suggesting a potential integration of levels of reality through the powers of Mind.

Here we have used Plato, Aristotle, and Heisenberg to demonstrate both potential levels of reality and the historical contestation between *idealism* and *realism* with insights from the quantum accentuating the conflict between scientific materialism and a new interpretation of reality. Of course, there are other levels of reality philosophies ranging from the "idea" stratifications of René Descartes and William Blake to the rather esoteric arrangements of many contemporary theorists such as Ken Wilber's "domains" or Rupert Sheldrake's "morphic resonance." The point is that many thinkers have pondered universal complexity and were compelled to conclude that different levels of reality are necessary to describe the intricacies of nature. Quantum Mechanics has only added to the enigma. Thus, different levels of reality exist, and we will utilize that fact to eventually construct our megatheory of reality.

Metaphysics and Puzzle Pieces

The previous discussion directs toward the cornerstone of traditional attempts to understand reality known as metaphysics; it is the basis from which all other efforts originated. In fact, levels of reality are encompassed within this larger discipline. The founder of metaphysics was Aristotle who divided it into three main categories: *Ontology*, the study of the nature of being; *Natural Theology*, the study of God and religion; and *Universal Science*, the study of first principles, logic, and reason.[26] Much of this original inquiry into metaphysics remains valid, although large portions of its earliest composition have since been discounted. Currently, metaphysics can encompass as many as one hundred concepts and philosophies, and virtually any academic discipline can be expanded to include metaphysical questions.

Nevertheless, metaphysics attempts to understand first principles and the nature of reality.[27] Metaphysics wants to know the essence of a thing—the true nature of its existence—and is thus the philosophical inquiry into *what is here* and *how it began*. Particularly interesting is that the original metaphysics of Aristotle was considered the first science, comprised of *being, God,* and *reason*. But in our current era, God is largely omitted from these inquiries. Scientific Materialism eliminated a designer due to a false premise of an actual, physical reality, one comprehensible through reductionism and the powers of reason—if man can logically deduce everything by reduction to its constituent parts, who requires God? Thus, many critics, but especially scientific materialists, argue that metaphysics is an abstruse area of knowledge and that metaphysical inquiries are unscientific and unnecessary.

As mentioned, the materialist dismissal of metaphysics depends on a false assumption that only one reality exists and it is fundamentally real. Hence, quantum experimental results are torture to physicalists since those results prove that reality is foundationally unreal. The greatest challenge to scientific materialism comes not from the historical precedence or relevance of metaphysics but rather from quantum truths, specifically the supremacy of Consciousness. Quantum truths change science and metaphysics; they change the entire equation, and both science and metaphysics must adjust accordingly.

Therefore, we are fortunate to be on the cusp of real understanding. Emerging before us is a glimpse of reality through the assemblage of various puzzle pieces, or what is simply known as the duck test—if it looks like a duck, swims like a duck, and quacks like a duck, then it probably is a duck."[28] Certainly this is a highly simplistic approach, but perhaps that proves the more obvious point that quantum truths are glaring indictments against materialism, and although not yet forming an undeniable representation of reality, these pieces are aggregating to a near confirmation of First Mind. Thus, these pieces form a new metaphysics of their own.

Further, it must be remembered that though this study is often disparaging of science that exaggerates its capabilities and proselytizes its virtues instead of encouraging impartial discourse, many of these puzzle pieces are directly attributable to the scientific method. Even when certain discoveries invalidate a previous "scientific" theory, typically it is science that conducts the invalidation. Just as many pieces of the puzzle come from nonscientific avenues such as intuition, meditation, prayer, spiritualism, and expanded consciousness, it is practical to utilize all methods at our disposal since that is true science.

Therefore, any accurate examination of reality must consider all possibilities; in fact, in some areas, advancements may not be realized through any other means. More exciting is that the possibility of using scientific and nonscientific approaches together will assuredly yield greater results than either one working independently or in isolation. We are confronting radically new and enigmatic information that offers not impediment but rather opportunity. Consider the following three quotes from physicists John Gribbin, Neils Bohr, and John Archibald Wheeler. They speak to the surreal nature of reality, a reality that is both illusory and yet wholly dependent on our observations for whatever "realness" it possesses.

> **In the world of the very small, where particle and wave aspects of reality are equally significant, things do not behave in any way that we can understand from our experience in the everyday world. . . . *all* pictures are false, and there is no physical analogy we can make to understand what goes on inside atoms. Atoms behave like atoms, nothing else.**[29]

> **How wonderful that we have met with a paradox. Now we have some hope of making progress.**[30]

> **The universe does not exist "out there," independent of us. We are inescapably involved in bringing about that which appears to be happening.**[31]

We must enlighten humanity to these facts. We all deserve to know the meaningful discoveries of science and their significance for our future. Yet something is impeding the awareness and collective embrace of quantum truths and their implications for reality. Beyond materialist intransigence and its atheistic tendencies, some other systemic factor is causing public ignorance of the truth of existence. So what is it? And how do we eliminate it?

If humans fail to integrate the puzzle pieces of reality into shared wisdom, it is largely due to specialization.[32] We have a natural tendency to specialize, which is culturally reinforced and economically mandated. Specialization undermines awareness by limiting our exposure. **The current system ensures that humans remain uninformed since society rewards those who practice reality instead of exploring it.** What is required is liberation from a delimiting system and an infusion of interdisciplinary thinking.

Rather disappointingly, we certainly cannot expect society to remedially address our collective shortcomings. The educational system, familial structures, economic arrangements, organized religion, and political entities have vested interests in promoting specialization. Time is another limitation; humans rarely have the opportunity to study the nature of reality or the issues of existence. Moreover, it appears that government prefers to avoid the subject, instead prioritizing economic production and consumption—Juvenal's "bread and circuses" in full force with humans easy to govern if food and entertainment are readily provided.[33] The net result is that the standards and values of our culture become our standards and values, producing a routinized and unquestioning society. The single reality worldview is thus promulgated, obscuring Mind as fundamental to nature and levels of reality as fundamental to existence.

Corollary is another philosophically significant point: socially reinforced truth is *ostensible truth* as opposed to *actual truth*. The apparent is proclaimed while the definitive is ignored. Extending this further, we see that actual truth is a derivative form of *subjectivism* as opposed to *objectivism*.[34] Subjectivism believes no objective reality exists; objectivism believes it does. In actuality, subjectivism is correct because our reality is not the definitive reality. The position here, however, is that a type of objective reality exists (material realm) but is a product of foundational Consciousness (subjective realm) that is largely unknown by society. Therefore, *objectivism* is sold to the public as reality, but the actual truth of *subjectivism* evades comprehension.

The issue is further complicated since even within those segments of society that discuss the nature of reality, just as much debate exists as ever existed. In truth, it has never been this contested or conducted with such disdain or acrimony. Virtually every philosophical position, mathematical calculation, metaphysical approach, experimental result, or neurological process has been evaluated, and yet there is no consensus on the fundamental aspects of reality. It is an axiom of philosophical discourse that great minds take ruminated positions and stiffen them. That fact alone would limit the plurality of the puzzle pieces from being pieced together. Include specialization and vested interests, and the truth remains largely obscured. One of our tasks here is to assemble these pieces into a picture that more closely approximates the true nature of existence.

We shall consider these insights next in our study.

CHAPTER 4

Structures of Understanding

Knowledge changes over time. The accrual of truth is best understood through two processes—paradigms and the dialectic—that allow for both accelerated and gradual progression of wisdom. Both are *structures of understanding*. We should think of them as engines that drive the evolution of knowledge and also as guides that further our comprehension. For our first formulation of how knowledge proceeds, we can thank one of the greatest thinkers in history, Thomas Kuhn.

Paradigms

In 1962, Kuhn, a professor of physics and philosophy at the University of California, Berkeley, published a masterpiece of thought, *The Structure of Scientific Revolutions*.[35] It is impossible to overstate the importance of this work. In his magnum opus, Kuhn introduced the concept of *paradigm shift*, a transformation of the foundational aspects of a scientific discipline. A paradigm shift is a revolution of sorts, a rebellion against the status quo, with new discoveries in dramatic contrast to conventional knowledge. Kuhn labeled the current scientific work *normal science*. Science was presumed to proceed in a rather linear fashion with new truths added to existing truths in a steady and cumulative way.[36] Kuhn challenged this by noting that science often proceeds with normal and revolutionary phases. Scientists tend to conduct their activities within an existing and accepted consensus. That state is the current paradigm. Over time, however, new information emerges, and unresolved particularities appear. That causes a crisis since it becomes evident that previous elemental aspects either require revision or are largely invalidated by the new data.

A paradigm shift transforms normal science into a new paradigm because paradigms are largely *incommensurate*. Far from enhancing or reinforcing existing knowledge, new paradigms topple the current state of affairs since they offer greater substantiation of truth. Thus, paradigms are crucial to human progress. Moreover, they are essential to understand how human fallibilities impede our collective advance. Although rarely acknowledged, paradigms are replete with ego involvement, and this insecurity characterizes the defense of paradigms by its existing adherents.

How is this so? Science is supposed to be impartial, is it not?

Typically paradigms have contrasting conceptual frameworks so adherents of each become intransigent in defense of their paradigms. Kuhn saw these advocates form like-minded communities. Any challenge to the existing paradigm (and their community) is refuted on either the inadequacies or conclusions of the competing researcher. Worse, adjacent disciplines are negatively affected. The problem is compounded by advocates who use different terms, approaches, contexts, and methodologies. Kuhn noted that adherents typically talk past each other, and there is little common ground for dispute resolution.

As a result, science is never fully objective. It is subject to the hubris, inadequacies, fallacies, and misperceptions of the human character.

Obviously, worldviews die slowly because of the obstinacy of entrenched interests. Incommensurability ensures theoretical conflicts with a superior paradigm eventually vanquishing a deficient one; nevertheless, such a decisive fight can take hundreds if not thousands of years. Defense of a paradigm includes vicious verbal assaults, reputation smearing, deployment of cronies, and historically even persecution and death. The following are some classic paradigm shifts:

- Classical Physics → Quantum Mechanics
- The world is flat → The world is a sphere
- Bloodletting cures disease → Bloodletting kills
- Divine right of kings → Democracy
- Kynesianism → Monetarism

Following a paradigm shift, the discipline typically returns to normal science, the collection of new data supporting the new paradigm and adherents pursuing their typical accumulation of knowledge. Kuhn moderated his position throughout the years by acknowledging that gradualism (normal science proceeding at its natural rate) works in conjunction with revolutions. Nevertheless, his work was transformative since it proved that progress comes in phases and that rigid communities form in defense of paradigms, stifling advancements. In essence, the scientific method and science itself lost much of its sacrosanctity, which was a paradigm shift in its own right. Scientific dogmatism was questioned, with greater emphasis placed in favor of latitudinarian principles.

That brings us to our next point. Since paradigms die slowly and only after much debate and conflict, we find ourselves currently in a struggle with the ruling paradigm and an emerging one. That strife has been occurring for more than a hundred years. It may require another hundred years before the deficient paradigm is replaced by a competing paradigm that better describes reality. Consider the following paradigm shift that sums up our current situation:

Scientific Materialism ⇒ Consciousness Paradigm

Whether through a revolution or through gradualistic advances, scientific materialism will eventually accede to the Consciousness Paradigm. That is a foregone conclusion. Of course, it is difficult to recognize the paradigm shift as it happens because of the historical timeline required to witness the transformation. The scientific community has largely defended materialism for the same reasons as previous groupings of intellectuals defended other antiquated worldviews. That effort, like so many before it, will prove ineffectual.

The Struggle of Ideas

The second of our processes of knowledge accumulation, one corollary to the above discussion, is the struggle of ideas throughout history. This notion is best understood through a brief examination of the work of German philosopher G. W. F. Hegel, whose work preceded Kuhn's formulation by more than a century. Here, we explore paradigms first because their framework is less elaborate and thus preferable when introducing the concept of knowledge evolution.

The concept for which Hegel is renowned is the *dialectic* where a beginning proposition, a *thesis*, is confronted by its logical opposite, an *antithesis*, and from which a *synthesis* emerges reconciling the two positions. In turn, the synthesis becomes the new thesis, subsequently confronted by yet another antithesis, and the process continues throughout history (although Hegel never used those actual terms, and we have borrowed the formulation from Kant).[37] Each thesis, antithesis, and synthesis arrangement are more refined or advanced than their predecessors. According to Hegel, the dialectic is the engine of growth in all its forms, from the merely physical to the majestically metaphysical.

The Hegelian dialectic can be viewed within the context of paradigms, and paradigms can be viewed within the context of the dialectic. Each is a conflict dynamic. Paradigms that confront each other are dialectical, and the dialectic in turn inspires paradigms. Both can contain degrees of vanquishment or fusion. One can also view them systemically where a change in one produces changes in the other; in effect, there are interdependencies between the two, both concepts equally valid and each contributory to the other.

The point here is that the human past is bound with conflicting ideas. A case can be made that the battle of notions has driven not only philosophical positioning but also experimental results and the direction of science. For example, to conduct an experiment, one usually has a notion of what may or may not happen. The investigator may prejudice the experimental results with previous ideas. That can happen with any scientist in any discipline. Whereas Kuhn believed paradigm shifts applied only in the natural sciences (biology, chemistry, physics), Hegel's formulation allowed for the potential paradigmal effect through the dialectic to the social sciences (sociology, economics, history). Thus, science must better manage its review process in order to ensure objective, experimental results.

Lastly, detractors have actually proved Hegel's formulation by acting as antithetical manifestations (embodiments of antithesis) against his philosophy (thesis). Although much debated, the remediation (synthesis) between his critics and his philosophy has been a general acceptance of his position about the evolution of ideas while denigrating his belief in the actualization of an infinite Consciousness. Moreover, defenders of the scientific paradigm have also proved Kuhn's argument; their intransigence alone validates his point of the fanatical defense of a prevailing worldview.

Theories

We have seen paradigms and the dialectic perform throughout history to forward human progress. At any point in time, scientists, technicians, academicians, and philosophers have originated concepts that impel dialectical or paradigmal advancement. They are known as theories, "a coherent group of tested general propositions, commonly regarded as correct, that can be used as principles of explanation and prediction for a class of phenomena."[38] Theories attempt to describe things, a type of reasoned contemplation about the state of affairs, that form a useful tool to understand reality. In fact, many theories are conceived as impetus to explore a subject further, to challenge the existing state of knowledge, while other theories aggregate thought rather convincingly toward new truths. Moreover, theories engender other theories, challenged by yet more opposing theories, the dialectic progressing as formulated by Hegel.

So *theory progression* is the result of conflict between ideas. But *theory creation* mandates agreement on some basic premises and postulates. Construction of theories typically assumes the following:

- A question is asked regarding some phenomena.

- Research is conducted in related disciplines.

- Hypotheses are developed to describe observable phenomena or relevant facts.

- Experiments are conducted to support or falsify the various hypotheses.

- Searches for correlations in the findings are conducted.

- Theories are developed to unify the experimental results.

- Peer review confirms the research.

- Additional experts build on the theory.

Notice that at no point is an allowance made for personal convictions or individual prejudices. Theory construction should occur in a belief-free environment where the experimental results dictate the direction of the theory. It is considered a violation to intercalate opinions. Moreover, never should results be eliminated or minimized to conform to personal beliefs. Yet the National Academies Press has noted as follows:

> **Other kinds of values also come into play in science. Historians, sociologists, and other students of science have shown that social and personal beliefs—including philosophical, thematic, religious, cultural, political, and economic beliefs—can shape scientific judgment in fundamental ways.**[39]

Perhaps it is only human to interject personal beliefs into science, but such activity removes objectivity. In addition, the peer review process, a supposedly rather impartial undertaking, is fundamentally flawed. A replication of experimental results is often lacking, and reviewers have a tendency to follow accepted knowledge instead of conflicting data. As much as 80% of scientific research may not be published because it doesn't conform to the experimenter's expectations.[40] That much lost information represents an enormous opportunity cost.

Theories are supposedly devised with facts. A fact is "a thing that is known to be true, especially when it can be proved."[41] Theories are initially constructed with facts because facts lend credibility and form rational building blocks. That is good science. The problem arises when facts (and theories based on those facts) conflict with accepted knowledge. Such was the case with the discovery of Quantum Mechanics because it so demonstrably violated scientific materialism. As previously noted, the scientific community exists in a state of disbelief and denial about the mental and spiritual nature of the universe. That is not good science. Consider the words of biochemist Rupert Sheldrake who described leading scientific materialists.

> **I have found that they have no interest in looking at the evidence because they know in advance it must be false. In other words, their position is one of prejudice rather than open-minded scientific enquiry. In that sense, I think they are deeply anti-scientific.**[42]

Theories are woven with facts. The more objective the positioning of these facts, the more legitimate the theory. Dispensing facts undermines the theory. The same applies with the arrangement of facts if such arrangement is meant to deceive or entice. When personal convictions intrude on facts, the resulting theories are invalid and denigrate the scientific process.

Finally, regarding theories, we must determine what can be known through the construction of theories and whether their modification through peer review and peer development can sufficiently describe a phenomenon. Debate about the very knowability of something has raged since antiquity and forms the discipline known as *epistemology*. After all, even mathematics is not infallible.[43] Complete knowability is impossible, but theories are "suggestive" of truth and are thus instrumental to human advancement. Moreover, we have seen that something as enduring as a paradigm (worldview lasting hundreds of years) can be overthrown with superior facts.

Naturally, this has inspired debate about the requirement for something more all encompassing than a single theory, based on the premise that an accumulation of theories into one superstructure better describes a phenomenality. Moreover, any legitimate questioning of knowledge reveals a lack of integration between disciplines since no framework has satisfactorily aggregated everything known and arranged it into a comprehensive whole. This is a massive system failure, so we need something bigger if we are to make sense of it all.

Megatheories

An integration of theories into a larger framework of comprehension is a *mega-theory*, an overarching superstructure of its own. At this level, theoretical efforts are truly interdisciplinary. As with theories, megatheories are subject to revision or supersession, but their appeal lies in their potential to more widely describe a phenomenon. Megatheories not only connect more dots but impart the possibility of tremendous breakthroughs. If, as John Horgan suggested in his seminal work *The End of Science*, scientific advancement and societal progression are diminishing, then megatheories may prove essential to human development because discoveries will happen on the margin.[44] In short, if academic disciplines are nearing their maximums, future advancement will require synthetic approaches in order to advance past points of stagnation.

With respect to the above, we can briefly critique our educational system. Currently, academia offers introductions to numerous subjects but fails to combine them into grand, integrative truths. That results from both the good intentions of educators (to expose students to diverse areas of study) and the limitations of specialization (graduation into a particular expertise). **Thus, we get exposure to disciplines but specialization before integration.** So academia, the assemblage and repository of accumulated knowledge, fails to provide an integrative summation of our collective wisdom. We must develop an entire discipline in order to ameliorate this deficiency with its basic courses a requirement for graduation.

Furthermore, the benefits of megatheories may extend beyond any specific findings or interpretations of the subjects studied; rather, the building of megatheories may cause a cognitive shift for how humans progress intellectually by templating w*holism* instead of *reductionism*. The current system has forced us into specialization, itself a form of reduction, and kept humanity uninformed regarding the larger picture. As a society, we have studied the parts *ad nauseum* when we should be prioritizing the totality. Megatheories offer the possibility that the entirety liberates the truth from the obscurity of disconnected particulars.

This book is such an attempt at a megatheory. We are building toward its conclusions as we proceed. Although our approach is interdisciplinary, perhaps no other academic discipline directs toward a superstructure as much as Quantum Mechanics; its truths are both enlightening and inferential, relevant to virtually every subject. Quantum truths are gateway truths, contextualizing and unifying all that is known regardless of its apparent implausibility or resultant materialist pertinacity. In fact, the resistance to its truths is testament to its paradigmal significance. Next, we will discover the depth of this obstinacy and how this inflexibility distorts the truth of existence.

CHAPTER 5

The Critique of Scientific Materialism

S cience was once a noble quest.

In this chapter, we will examine how science and scientific materialism have devolved into a binge of accumulated status and mountains of privilege. This critique is necessary for a number of reasons. First, a large database of compelling evidence exists that indicts physicalism. Second, scientific materialism is ingrained in our society, vastly exceeding its merits. Third, the elimination of its sacrosanctity is necessary to reveal its hubristic inadequacies. Finally, its interpretations are causal to stagnation and impede our collective advance.

A comparison to the political realm is appropriate.

As governments trend toward bloat and self-indulgence, so too has the scientific community engorged on its own feats and filled itself with its own pomposity. Political structures are notorious for their obsession with extension (preservation of institutions, election of officials, ideological conservation, suppression of opposition), and tragically the scientific community suffers from the same affliction. In fact, science and scientific materialism have progressed to the next stage of hubristic adventure—transforming into its own religion. At exactly the time when pursuit of objective truth is required for human posterity, we rather find science in narcissistic enmity to whatever opposes it.

Foundations

So what exactly is scientific materialism? And what is the lineage of thought that brings us to its current interpretation?

"Scientific materialism is the belief that physical reality, as made available to the natural sciences, is all that truly exists."[45] Simple enough, but we have already seen that physical reality is comprised of immaterial and incorporeal Consciousness, with no material reality as such. Quantum Mechanics proves it. So scientific materialism as an explanation of reality is groundless and positions us improperly in our search for truth since physicalism fails to account for the metaphysical nature of being.

As noted earlier, scientific materialism posits that eventually everything will be understood by associations between matter and energy; but if matter and energy are immaterial at their core, what we witness are the physical *effects* of their interconnection, not their authentic base. As we have noted, scientists were deceived by the visible universe, things appearing real even when comprised of unreal things, which was understandable considering our physical senses. **Yet the enigma remains that an immaterial essence is somehow manifesting a physical universe.** Quantum actualities suggest that this immaterial essence is Mind, although to physicalists a reality constructed of Consciousness was unfathomable since Mind has no physical properties.[46] We cannot see it, and we cannot touch it. For materialists, Consciousness is not a real element in a real world.[47] Mind is a property indescribable through physicalist interpretations, and because of its "invisible" nature, it was missed until reductionism took us to the atom.

History demonstrates that the first materialists were *atomists* (those who philosophized that nature was comprised of small, indestructible pieces of matter), including the ancients Democritus and Epicurus. Materialism was furthered in the early modern era by Thomas Hobbes and Pierre Gassendi who espoused the material nature of things in their arguments against the dualism of René Descartes, which suggested a Consciousness apart from the physical body. Then came Francis Bacon, the father of the scientific method, who advocated that truth resulted from observing nature through the senses, and Galileo added sophisticated measurement. They were followed by Isaac Newton who solidified such thought with mathematically confirmed classical mechanics and foundational physics. Charles Darwin added biological processes to the scientific observation of nature through his Theory of Evolution, and Albert Einstein added commonality to all frames of reference, viewing the fundamental laws of nature as universal. In aggregate, these formulations reinforced each other and caused materialist rigidity in the sciences. The larger point is that the scientific method became synonymous with the quest for truth, devoid of exterior approaches or contrary opinions.

Thus, since the Age of Enlightenment, science has promoted a deterministically physical universe elucidated by conformist experimentation and selective mathematics. Everything would eventually be understood through the powers of reason, resulting in a belief system known as scientific materialism. To scientific materialists, science had proved the physical nature of reality, and Consciousness was simply a function of chemical exchanges in a physical brain. Mind was accidental, a random assortment of matter and energy, and the universe was nothing more than an indifferent, emotionless space devoid of any inherent value and personal meaning.

Unfortunately for scientific materialism, science proceeded to make further advancements, and the dialectic and paradigms proceeded as expected. The biggest advancement, of course, was the *Double Slit Experiment* that proved the primacy of Consciousness. The universe was suddenly full of self-awareness, intention, will, and desire. It was a monumental reveal—the single greatest scientific achievement in history—that discovered the causal connection between foundational Consciousness and manifested physical reality. With this discovery came an enormous implication: Mind came first, *ab initio*; everything in nature is a product of the Great Consciousness.

And what was the result of such a revelation?

Scientific Materialism was invalidated. Quantum experiments demonstrated that reality is *idealistic*, a function and

product of Mind, and that physical reality is a type of illusion. The facts are a direct threat to scientific materialism because they eviscerate the physicalism required in order for *realism* to prevail.

Imagine the power of a Great Consciousness generating a physical reality (a universe appearing actual to the senses but immaterial at its core) with nothing more than the force of His Mind. Every law, property, rule, arrangement, and process has been previously invented by a higher power, and humans merely "discover" what was devised before our reality even began.

Dogma and God of the Gaps

Scientific materialism is dogmatic. Dogma is "a fixed, especially religious, belief or set of beliefs that people are expected to accept without any doubts."[48] Obviously, scientific materialism also prefers its authoritarian implications—*do not doubt us*. To question science or its adherents is to question consensus reality and subject one to ridicule and social stigma. The leaders of scientific materialism believe they are "knowledge gods" and above reproach; elitism doesn't even begin to describe the attitude of these increasingly discredited egotists.

Yet consider some basic, contrary facts to their supposed mastery. Nearly all scientific theories have never been proved; science once thought the world was flat; condensed matter physics was going to solve the world's energy problems; software issues crash aircraft and kill trusting passengers; oil spills pollute oceans and destroy wildlife; disintegrating spacecraft kill astronauts; diseases ravage the planet; scientific sophistication caused Chernobyl. We are supposed to trust scientists, have faith in them (sounds like a religion), believe in unproved theories, and never question their abilities. Their failures, however, equal their successes, and society is stagnating because of them.

Laughably, search engine inquiries into dogma will list various religions, philosophies, political parties, dictators, and ideologies as at least partially dogmatic, but the one endlessly missing offender is always science, which **is so dogmatic that it doesn't even recognize its own dogmatic tendencies.** It is caught up in its own delusional grandeur, a modern-day Narcissus appreciating itself in a pond of empiricism. Adherents are like ideological despots, convinced of their own superiority and absolute authority, while the majority of the world's denizens believe in a higher power and secrets of creation far beyond human comprehension. Such arrogance of the scientific materialists is understandable considering the nature of human frailties but unforgivable considering the widespread ineptitude and underperformance of its many professionals.

Consider again the words of Sheldrake:

> **Science is being held back by centuries-old assumptions that have hardened into dogmas. The sciences would be better off without them: freer, more interesting, and more fun. The biggest scientific delusion of all is that science already knows the answers. The details still need working out, but the fundamental questions are settled, in principle. Contemporary science is based on the claim that all reality is material or physical. There is no reality but material reality. Consciousness is a by-product of the physical activity of the brain. Matter is unconscious. Evolution is purposeless. God exists only as an idea in human minds, and hence in human heads. These beliefs are powerful not because scientists think about them critically, but because they do not. The facts of science are real enough, and so are the techniques that scientists use, and so are the technologies based on them. But the belief system that governs conventional scientific thinking is an act of faith, grounded in a nineteenth century ideology.[49]**

Scientific materialism is at least one hundred years out of date. It is rife with obsolescence. Its adherents reject true scientific inquiry in favor of preservation of dogma while their ideological foundations are crumbling. Perhaps like nearly everyone else they grasp their outdated precepts and convictions because of the fear of loss. What type of loss? Loss of status. Loss of income. Loss of privilege. Loss of respect. Moreover, perhaps no territory is defended by scientific materialists as vigorously as those gaps in knowledge that fail to describe the nature of things. In short, these gaps are indictments that materialists prefer to deny.

Typically, however, these voids in knowledge are used to deride detractors of scientific materialism in a phenomenon known as *God of the Gaps*. Although the phrase has a storied history with slightly different interpretations, here *God of the Gaps* means to allot supernatural causes (God) to things currently unknown. Scientific materialism counters these gaps will eventually be understood through scientific advancement. The term is therefore cast pejoratively at critics of science, specifically theists, but also at those who chronicle stagnation with the implication that invoking God to fill in knowledge gaps is desperate and imbecilic.

Interestingly, the *God of the Gaps* argument is actually used more effectively against rather than for scientific materialism as noted by prominent thinker Michael Egnor.[50] Egnor is cited here in a number of quotes because his analysis is particularly astute and convincing. Consider the following discussion of materialism and Consciousness:

> **Any critique of materialist dogma in science from a design or immaterial perspective is derided as a 'God of the Gaps' argument. But the real issue is the gaps, which are plentiful and very wide.[51]**

Science knows less than it thinks it knows. This is especially relevant in the discussion of material or immaterial causes. Egnor goes on to note:

> **[T]he salient characteristics of the mind, such as intentionality, qualia, free will, incorrigibility, restricted access, continuity of self through time, and unity of consciousness (the 'binding problem') seem to be impossible to describe materialistically.... because mental properties are not physical properties. Nothing about matter as understood in our current scientific paradigm invokes subjective mental experience.... Invocation of immaterial causation that incorporates**

subjectivity seems necessary for a satisfactory explanation of the mind.[52]

Huge gaps in scientific knowledge exist. In fact, the more science discovers, the more gaps it reveals. Contrary to consolidating our understanding of reality, science is contributing toward its diffusion by suppressing innovative thinking.

Materialism describes what it can. But the 20th century has been difficult for materialism: creation of the universe *ex nihilo*, the observer effect in Quantum Mechanics, the origin of life, the origin of biological information, the cause of the immaterial mind, all belie materialist reduction. Some philosophers and scientists believe the problem may lie with the limitations dogmatic materialism imposes on natural science. Perhaps design and teleology play a role. To the dogmatic materialist, teleology in nature is a dangerous inference, because it is incompatible with atheism, which is the materialist religion. Acceptance of the obvious evidence for design and teleology in nature would force materialists to rethink their worldview, which never comes easy, especially for fundamentalists.[53]

Briefly, teleology is essentially things having intention in nature, reflecting a central design or a grand purpose. Obviously, scientific materialism despises any type of grand design because it implies a Great Consciousness. The teleological tradition extends from Plato and Aristotle and is a central proposition of Hegel's philosophy. Even the contemporary philosophies of Niklas Bostrom and David Chalmers that emphasize the possibility that we live in a simulation suggest teleology since any simulation must necessarily be designed by some higher intelligence. Moreover, quantum truths (the *Observer Effect*) have shown that Consciousness is intimately connected with matter and energy, even causal to their being. Foundational Consciousness inevitably leads to a First Mind as the causative agent of everything, one complete with a grand purpose—a teleology, if you will. Something as intricate as the universe contains a plan.

Yet against such an edifice of sound reasoning, scientific materialism proceeds in its own self-infatuated quest for ego validation and, dare we say, worship. Adoration is not something inherent in scientific fact but rather in the insecurities of the human psyche. Who does not want to be in the supreme council, the high command, the charmed circle, or the pantheon of the gods? Elitism wears many faces, and one of them is science. Objectivity is always subject to the imperfections of its seekers who, through their personal flaws, ensure their own prejudices. Hence, science is a natural path for mortals who desire the status of gods, objectivity sacrificed for self-glorification. That naturally brings us to how science and its vanguard sought to become its own religion.

The Religion of Science

Perhaps it is natural that ideologies turn into religions of sorts. After all, the objective of all ideologies is to convince individuals to become adherents, to recruit more believers to further the cause. That ranges from small groups to political parties to nations to the largest religions. If science has an ideology, that ideology eventually seeks to become a religion. Cortical Rider, a biologist with a doctorate in neuroscience, published an excellent article, "Top 10 Reasons Science Is Another Religion," that summarizes how science has transformed itself into a global religion. Below are eight of Rider's ten reasons that reinforce how science has become sacred—a type of religion.

1. **Science Thinks Humans Are Special**

2. **It Casts Out Heretics and Persecutes All Other Religions**

3. **Science Reveres Its Own Saints**

4. **Science Makes Up Stories to Describe Our Origins**

5. **Science Has Its Own Code of Ethics**

6. **Science Has Its Own Priesthood**

7. **Science Is Based on Established Dogmas**

8. **Science Requires Faith**[54]

Others have voiced similar opinions, some quite prominent such as Paul Feyerabend and Thomas Kuhn. Studies have proved that extremism runs rampant in the sciences, a fanatical defense of scientific dogma in the same manner as zealots championing their religion.[55] Science aspires to become permanently ingrained, seeking control over its subjects through the power of the system. To further that aim, science crafts its way into ostensibly nomistic structures such as government and academia, seeking virtue to quelch any counterarguments. As the article "Science Is Immensely Important, but It Has a Hubris Problem" notes on Freecology:

> **Science has a serious internal problem. And it's not just that scientists are doing bad science. It's that scientists (and their supporters) are passing off their political opinions as science.[56]**

That is a tragic state of affairs. Science should be devoid of opinions and concerned only with provable facts. As previously noted, scientific success should not exaggerate into its own ideology. Consider the following:

> **Science is useful, but it should make no pretensions to truth. We tend to forget that science is concerned with creating maps of reality — it's a map, not the territory. . . . [M]any scientists have become imbued with a religious fanaticism equalled only by the people they deride.[57]**

A growing number of experts have noticed that many scientists have forsaken their original mission and chosen egomania. That is no doubt exacerbated by the societal tendency toward massive self-absorption; if the average citizen has become narcissistic, imagine the ego heights of those in esteemed positions. It may also be a defense mechanism against increasing scrutiny since stagnation brings its share of criticism. In any case, ego in the sciences is rampant. Regarding this trend, Feyerabend observed:

> **[I]n the colossal conceit of our intellectuals, their belief they know precisely what humanity needs and their relentless efforts to recreate people in their own sorry image.[58]**

Finally, science, like all religions, requires funding, which only engenders moral negligence. Inaccuracies or falsehoods are glossed over so financial support remains without challenge to the orthodoxy.[59] Scandals are minimized. Moreover, science is facing diminishing returns. Replication of experimental results, the foundation of scientific progress, is at a minimum failure rate of 70%; researchers are failing to confirm their own experimental results in the majority of cases.[60] Often many experimental results inspire theories unsupportable by the evidence, leading to scientific dead ends. The amount of wasted dollars is probably incalculable. Thus, a powerful case can be made that science is both enraptured and corrupted in its own religious mania.

Subversion and Trepidation

Admirable things are often subsumed by deplorability; the scientific method, an originally honorable endeavor, has been denigrated by science itself.[61] We should remember that the scientific method is the foundation of science and that method should be sacrosanct. Unfortunately, it has been corrupted. To assist our critique, we should define the scientific method as "a method of research in which a problem is identified, relevant data are gathered, a hypothesis is formulated from these data, and the hypothesis is empirically tested."[62] Objectivity is inherent in this definition. Has science maintained this standard? Is this guideline upheld in every case? How about in the majority of cases? Or has it been abandoned to maintain beliefs and dogmas?

Science was intended to be a system to study nature, from the smallest of the small (atoms) to the largest of the large (the universe). At no point are prejudices allowed to enter the evaluation of the experimental data. The results, according to scientific principles, are to be collected and then verified through further experimentation. Yet science has notoriously violated standard scientific practice to further its ideological aims. Consider the following two examples:

> **[Science assumes] that the universe originated from a quantum fluctuation in nothingness . . . being defined as the temporary appearance of energetic particles out of empty space.**

> Yet no one has ever observed such a fluctuation. . . . It is acceptable to put such ideas forward as philosophical *speculation* but certainly not as scientific fact. Another example of misapplication is supplied by the well-known Darwinian theory of evolution—which is more properly categorized as a hypothesis. This hypothesis is closely tied to the idea of spontaneous generation, which Pasteur disproved. Evolution hypothesizes that life on Earth sprang from inanimate matter some 3.5 billion years ago and has subsequently evolved through a series of genetic mutations and natural selection into the diversity we currently observe. The evidence cited to support this hypothesis is that the fossil record found in the geological column (rock strata) seems to move from less-complex to more-complex organisms. However, no transitional forms (organisms that combine features of two distinct species) have ever been definitely observed in the present or in the fossil record. No experiment to date has been able to produce a living organism from inanimate matter. . . . With no observational or experimental data to back it up, evolution somehow progressed from a suspect hypothesis to scientific fact in less than 50 years.[63]

Considering the fact that many scientists are atheists, it follows that they would extrapolate data into theories and pass them off as laws to validate personal beliefs. But is that science? By that standard, I am the greatest writer who ever lived because I once wrote a sentence. I can also tell the difference between a planet and a star in the nighttime sky. Does that also make me the greatest astronomer?

We can further prove the point by segmenting which political philosophy is more likely to be materialist—liberal or conservative? Liberals tend to be more atheistic than conservatives, which reflects a higher percentage who also are materialists. A recent study of academia found that liberal professors and researchers outnumbered conservative professors by a margin of 12 to 1; in some disciplines and departments, the ratio is 33 to 1. Moreover, nearly 40% of the elite liberal arts colleges have no conservative professors.[64] This "atheistic" partiality not only reinforces the dictums of science and scientific materialism but also perpetuates further stagnation since the liberating implications of First Mind have been ignored. Toynbee has noted that societies stagnate and crumble because a small *creative minority* (e.g., the scientific community) degenerates into a *dominant minority* who refuse to accept new ideas, forcing society into obedience. Naturally, hubris is the culprit.[65]

In addition, there are further criticisms of science than the validation of personal beliefs and political ideology. As cited in *The Economist*, the scientific method is founded on the concept of "trust, but verify."[66] Modern scientists are doing too much trusting and not enough verifying. Throw in economic imperative and career opportunism, and the scientific method is sabotaged for personal and professional advantage. Consider this assessment from the article in *The Economist*:

> **As their [academia] ranks have swelled . . . scientists have lost their taste for self-policing and quality control. The obligation to "publish or perish" has come to rule over academic life. Competition for jobs is cut-throat. Full professors in America earned on average $135,000 in 2012—more than judges did. . . . Nowadays verification (the replication of other people's results) does little to advance a researcher's career. And without verification, dubious findings live on to mislead. Careerism also encourages exaggeration and the cherry-picking of results. In order to safeguard their exclusivity, the leading journals impose high rejection rates: in excess of 90% of submitted manuscripts.[67]**

If the corruption of science is known by an increasing number of intelligent and enlightened members of society, what accounts for the hesitation of our culture to adjust? Where is our leadership? When will the truth be accepted? Since a

Great Consciousness is largely proved, for what reason is science so afraid of a Creator? Perhaps the past can provide an answer.

Throughout history, scientists have lived in fear of persecution from the church and state. Examples range from Servetus to Galileo to Einstein to Turing.[68] The Inquisition is a notoriously famous example of institutionally religious persecution of science and its adherents. Oppression of scientific figures often extended to anyone espousing views outside religious or state doctrine. Imprisonment and death were common. The *conflict thesis* that positions an inherent conflict between religion and science emerged in the 1800s and reigned until the middle of the twentieth century. Although it is currently in disfavor because of a gradually increasing fusion between science and religion (or at least a growing accommodation from both), the concept nevertheless has some noteworthy adherents.[69] Residue from this historical struggle causes hostility. To be equitable, scientists have a valid concern considering the historically significant efforts by the church and state to force compliance to existing religious or political orthodoxy under the penalty of death. Never should science have to face such oppression.

As always, however, there is more to the story. Scientists, whatever their other virtues, have a dubious record defending science and themselves in the face of persecution. Resistance to ideological regimes or oppressive governments has been notoriously deficient.[70] Particularly damning is the case of Nazi scientists who offered little resistance to abhorrent policies, including war crimes and genocide. This can be partially understood by the ostensible neutrality of science with respect to political matters, but it also results from the incessant quest for government funding. Regimes that provide for science and scientific research are typically supported, regardless of ideology. Fear among scientists is obviously a huge factor in their timidity, for it is far better to conduct science in silence than be socially ostracized or imprisoned in a concentration camp. Nevertheless, the historical record clearly shows that scientists have more often shown cowardice than courage in the face of oppressive governments and evil despots. Even the few courageous scientists who have resisted immoral regimes had no official backing from the scientific community.[71] Science has ample reason to be fearful of church and state authority, but it has lost any claim to the moral high ground.

Selective Science

Next, we consider deceitful measures designed to obfuscate contrary facts. Dogmatic science, particularly scientific materialism, is maintained against competing theories through selective methods or outright suppression. No level of accomplishment, credentials, reputation, or standing will deter the materialists from discrimination and repression of those in opposition. Consider the following regarding materialist philosophers of mind:

> Henry Stapp has also consistently pointed out the deeply erroneous and flawed nature of simplistic materialist viewpoints when considered from the perspective of quantum physics. Indeed, he is quite scathing about many philosophers of mind:
>
> > "Philosophers of mind appear to have arrived today at less-than-satisfactory solutions to the mind-brain and free will problems, and the difficulties seem, at least *prima facie*, very closely connected with their acceptance of a known-to-be-false understanding of the nature of the physical world, and of the causal role of our conscious thoughts within it." 'Philosophy of Mind and the Problem of Free Will in the Light of Quantum Mechanics.'
>
> The most interesting phrase here is 'known-to-be-false'. The astonishing fact is that the academic philosophy community has allowed a large number of its members, especially philosophers of mind or science, to flagrantly ignore or misrepresent contemporary physics in order to defend obviously incorrect 'classical' pre quantum positions redolent of the worldview of the late nineteenth century. As Stapp has pointed out:

"the re-bonding [of mind and matter in QM] achieved by physicists during the first half of the twentieth century must be seen as a momentous development: a lifting of the veil. Ignoring this huge and enormously pertinent development in basic science, and proclaiming the validity of materialism on the basis of an inapplicable-in-this-context nineteenth century science, is an irrational act."

The evidence from quantum mechanics for this is now overwhelming. Despite this, hard-headed (a fitting epithet) materialists are regularly allowed the public arena to proclaim their unscientific views in the name of philosophy or science, and in so doing they grievously mislead the public.[72]

The wholesale denial of quantum realities by the scientific community is inexcusable. Their distortion of truth also extends to other disciplines. Consider the following as an example:

The Evolutionary Informatics Lab . . . has published a number of peer-reviewed scientific papers that assess supposed simulations of evolution. Their team developed a methodology for studying so-called "genetic algorithms" — computer programs that are intended to simulate the Darwinian process. These programs incorporate "active information," which is essentially the amount of information smuggled into a search algorithm by an intelligent programmer to help it find a target. Their methodology calculates the amount of active information in a program, showing that intelligence — not Darwinian evolution — is what is finding the targets of these searches. In a new peer-reviewed scientific paper in the journal *BIO-Complexity*, "Time and Information in Evolution," Winston Ewert, Ann Gauger, along with Dembski and Marks, once again show that a mathematical simulation of evolution

doesn't represent biologically realistic processes of Darwinian evolution at all.[73]

These two examples are typical of the materialist attempt to either suppress or ignore other scientifically derived information contradictory to staples of scientific materialism. Contrarian arguments are scorned. This suppression of contradistinctive opinions is widespread and conducted intentionally. The following is a summary of this treachery by Joseph Selbie in his book *The Physics of God*:

> **Even rigorously conducted scientific studies that experiment with nonmaterial notions such as consciousness . . . are granted no credibility by science's high priesthood: the scientists who perform peer reviews, the approvers or rejecters of papers submitted to prestigious scientific journals such as the *Physical Review Letters*, *The New England Journal of Medicine*, or *Proceedings of the National Academy of Sciences*. You would be hard-pressed to find in these journals any papers that stray from the orthodox view of scientific materialism.**[74]

This description of scientific materialism does not conform to what the public expects of science. Next, consider the summation of the situation from *Manifesto for a Post-Materialist Science*:

> **Science is first and foremost a non-dogmatic, open-minded method of acquiring knowledge about nature through the observation, experimental investigation, and theoretical explanation of phenomena. Its methodology is not synonymous with materialism and should not conform to any particular beliefs, dogmas, or ideologies.**
>
> **At the end of the nineteenth century, physicists discovered empirical phenomena that could not be explained by classical physics. This led to the development, during the 1920s and early 1930s, of a revolutionary new branch of physics called**

quantum mechanics (QM). QM has questioned the material foundations of the world by showing that atoms and sub-atomic particles are not really solid objects—they do not exist with certainty at definite spatial locations and definite times. Most importantly, QM explicitly introduced the mind into its basic conceptual structure since it was found that particles being observed and the observer—the physicist and the method used for observation—are linked. According to one interpretation of QM, this phenomenon implies that the consciousness of the observer is vital to the existence of the physical events being observed, and that mental events can affect the physical world. The results of recent experiments support this interpretation. These results suggest that the physical world is no longer the primary or sole component of reality, and that it cannot be fully understood without making reference to mind.[75]

Suppression of scientifically derived contradictory findings to maintain dogma is not science. It is, instead, fascism. Nearly everyone agrees that science is supposed to be objective and welcoming of new data. Yet scientific materialism is conducting its own form of the Inquisition, limiting human advancement through the denial of new empirical discoveries and powerful new theories. We are thus subjected to endless propaganda grounded in baseless interpretations of reality that cause an unprecedented perversion of truth.

Obscurantism with a Purpose

The scientific community is guilty of obscurantism, or "opposition to the increase and spread of knowledge."[76] Perhaps it is human nature, as noted by David Ray Griffin in his book *Religion and Scientific Naturalism: Overcoming the Conflicts*, citing Alfred North Whitehead "(1) to take a given method of obtaining truth as the only valid method, and (2) to exaggerate the truths obtained from that method."[77] Whitehead went further, extending those thoughts:

This obscurantism is rooted in human nature more deeply than any particular subject of interest. It is just as strong among men of science as among the clergy. . . . the obscurantists of any generation are in the main constituted by the greater part of the practitioners of the dominant methodology. Today scientific methods are dominant, and scientists are the obscurantists.[78]

Again, from a human fallibility standpoint, this is quite understandable; humans are an insecure and egotistical group. Nevertheless, we should quit pretending in unassailable scientific objectivity and the impartiality of its scientists.

As discussed earlier, science—as well as political structures—trend toward self-preservation and bloat. Science and society are symbiotic, each benefitting from and perpetuating the other. As a result, science assumes the characteristics of the society from which it emanates, and in advanced nations, one of those attributes is capitalism. As scientist Martin López-Corredoira observed, "Scientific institutions follow the structure of capitalism, so they must continuously grow."[79] Perpetuation and growth should not be the aim of science; the objective should be the truth. To further illustrate this point of scientific and societal integration, López-Corredoira goes on to note:

We have witnessed gargantuan amounts of money invested to support sciences. . . But there are some symptoms which indicate a decline of our scientific culture. First, our society is drowned in huge amounts of knowledge. Most of it is about research of little importance to progress our world view or produces no advances in the basic fundamentals of pure science. Instead, we invent countless technical applications or investigate secondary details. Second, in the few fields where some important aspects of unsolved questions have arisen, powerful groups of administrators of science control the flow of information. They have inherent biases resulting in a preference for consensus truths, rather than having objective

discussions within a scientific methodology. This process gives few guarantees that we are obtaining solid new truths about nature. Finally, should the current scientific process continue the way it is, individual creativity is condemned to disappear.[80]

In turn, society also assumes the characteristics of science since our way of life is linked to scientific breakthroughs. This technology is often indispensable. In fact, virtually all our conveniences, which in our age have become necessities, result from the application of science to personal utility, including commercial aircraft, public highways, air conditioning, heating systems, appliances, computers, smartphones, the Internet, and more. The list is practically endless. Society is infused with science, and science extends itself through the following process:

By playing a major role in shaping cultural worldviews, concepts, and thinking patterns. Sometimes this occurs by the gradual, unorchestrated diffusion of ideas from science into the culture. At other times, however, there is a conscious effort, by scientists or nonscientists, to use "the authority of science" for rhetorical purposes, to claim that scientific theories and evidence support a particular belief system or political program.[81]

We must remember that these individuals are unelected yet exert tremendous influence. The spread of science proceeds undemocratically and without sufficient oversight. Science exceeds its natural bounds and pushes into areas where it was never intended to venture. Worse, it often claims knowledge that is unproved and uses this knowledge to fulfill personal agendas.

That brings us to the concept of *Groupthink*, which occurs as follows:

Groupthink is a phenomenon that occurs when a group of well-intentioned people makes irrational or non-optimal decisions spurred by the urge to conform or the belief that dissent is impossible. The problematic or premature consensus that

is characteristic of groupthink may be fueled by a particular agenda—or it may be due to group members valuing harmony and coherence above critical thought. . . . In the interest of making a decision that furthers their group cause, members may also ignore ethical or moral consequences.[82]

Once dissent is crushed, fanaticism results. Groupthink becomes territorial, guarding its domain in a perceived battle of survival in the ceaseless struggle of ideas, and thus, countervailing beliefs cannot be tolerated and must be destroyed. As Daniel Pouzzner noted in *The Architecture of Modern Political Power*, one of the primary ways in which elites maintain power is through **"ostensible control over the knowable, by marketing institutionally accredited science as the only path to understanding."**[83]

Once the educational system is controlled, the masses can be "taught" to believe anything. Examples include the deluded Soviet citizenry under communism or the fanaticism of the North Koreans. In America, it is known as the rule of the scientific dictatorship.[84] Thus, scientific materialism is a form of indoctrination, promoted by the government and bolstered by sufficient levels of bread and circuses so the public remains unaware of the true nature of reality. Scientific elites benefit, and so does the capitalist economy.

Finally, we should briefly examine the scientific materialist support system known as *peer review*. This process is defined as "the process of someone reading, checking, and giving his or her opinion about something that has been written by another scientist or expert working in the same subject area."[85] Much criticism exists regarding the peer review process, including funding issues and personal favoritisms, but also note that peer review is another form of ideological reinforcement. In addition to the previously discussed hubris and economic reward, the peer review process is characterized by scientific dogmatists silencing minority opinions, typified by comments such as "Does your criticism appear in a peer-reviewed journal?" or that the peer review process is prejudiced against perspectives failing to conform to existing scientific dogma.[86] Moreover, many of these minority positions represent the latest actual *scientific* discoveries, but because they violate existing dogma, they are avoided or censored.

Science is thus its own gatekeeper. Accordant perspectives are allowed entry while dissenters are denied passage. That leads to intellectual authoritarianism. Peer review has also been scandalized by fake reviews, cronyism, conflicts of interest, and ties to commercial entities.[87] The key point is that the peer review process is plagued by illegitimacy in both its structure and its functioning, with the net result being the silencing of dissent and the preservation of scientific orthodoxy. In short, the flawed peer review process not only fails in its mission for objectivity but either purposefully or unwittingly perpetuates a worldview (scientific materialism) that is inaccurate and anachronistic.

Nevertheless, as we have noted earlier, truth emerges over time. Next we will discuss the foundation of the paradigm that is likely to replace scientific materialism in a post-materialist world. This paradigm, like all emerging paradigms, is in its beginning stages, but it is expected to transform our collective worldview in unimaginable ways.

PART II:

A SPIRITUAL UNIVERSE

CHAPTER 6

Consciousness and Unity

We have seen in earlier chapters that the universe is mental and spiritual. Nevertheless, we acknowledge that this is a difficult concept to accept, especially since the vast majority of us have no prior exposure to these truths. Advocates of *idealism*, from Plato to Hegel to Eddington to Sheldrake, would likely sympathize with the reader as they process such counterintuitive premises.

The universe as a construction of Mind appears abstract and even farcical. No doubt, it is revolutionary. Yet we must resolve ourselves to the impossibility of the quantum mechanical world and the primacy of Consciousness because that is the true nature of things. Such is the personal and collective transformation required to construct a Post-Materialist paradigm.

Theories of Consciousness

The quest to understand Mind is an ancient pursuit. Issues have ranged from its existence and definition, its features and nature, its meaning and universal implications, and finally to the quantity of Mind humans possess. These inquiries naturally contributed to grandiose theories of Consciousness in which this study is particularly interested.

The study of Mind typically identifies materialist and dualist theories as basic to the discussion. In the former, Mind is the result of material properties, and in the latter, Mind is its own entity and separate from physical processes.

Extensive subdivisions exist in each, and some conjectures attempt to blend both interpretations into a comprehensive whole. For materialists, the presence of Consciousness independent of the human brain is tortuous; Mind causative of matter and energy, and thus of nature, is excruciatingly difficult to accept because it destroys the worldview. Conversely, the physicalist interpretation of Mind is ridiculous for dualists to accept considering the compelling evidence for Consciousness existing exterior to the body. The subject of Mind is further complicated by the fact that both a material realm and an immaterial realm exist, the latter causative of the former and the former more easily identifiable because it is situated on the latter. Further exploration will eventually confirm the particulars of this deeper realm of Mind.

Consciousness is, however, difficult to place. Experimental results from Quantum Mechanics that proved the primacy of Consciousness also demonstrated that Mind is abstruse. David Chalmers noted the difficulty in ascertaining the conscious experience in sentient beings as the *Hard Problem of Consciousness*.[88] Humans have a sense of being, an awareness of an inner self that cannot be resolved by brain chemistry. These "subjective experiences" defy physical origination. For example, nowhere in any part of the brain is found the sensation of "deep sky" or "profound experience." Simply, the brain is not responsible for our sense of self or subjective experiences.

All of us "feel" things and have subjective components that are uniquely personal to us. They are referred to as *qualia*. Materialism fails to provide any solution to the problem of Consciousness, instead invoking a "Science of the Gaps" argument advocating that materialism will someday fully describe Consciousness through increased understanding of brain functions. That is nonsense. Chalmers argues that a complete mapping and comprehension of all brain processes will nevertheless fail to identify the source of Consciousness, proving that Mind is its own separate entity.

So what is Consciousness and how pervasive is it? And where does it come from?

We have already defined Consciousness as self-awareness, will, intention, and desire. But Consciousness is also an inherent property of the universe.[89] That means Consciousness is designed into the very fabric of reality and transcends time and space.[90] Mind is therefore intrinsic to nature, infused into the totality and actuative of everything visible and comprehendible.

So although the study of Mind has an illustrious and highly contentious past, the issue was best framed by Descartes centuries ago with his belief that Mind and Body are distinct, and Consciousness is immaterial and existing separate from a physical brain. As referenced earlier, that is known as *Mind Body Dualism.* So if Mind is an entity separate from the physical body (which, of course, includes the brain), how does it come to exist? How is Mind able to know itself? *The Hard Problem of Consciousness* is essentially the modern version of these historical questions. Thus, the traditional framing of the problem is shown as follows:

Materialism......Dualism

This polarization presents a number of problems, primarily that with dualism, Mind and Matter are fundamentally different things. That causes an obscure view of nature and the incomprehensibility of both working together. This separation between materialism and dualism naturally leads to a number of Theories of Consciousness, each assigning Mind its proper place within our experience. Theories of Consciousness thus attempt to describe how immaterial Mind can exist in an apparently material universe.

Our framing of the problem actually looks like this:

Materialism...(Theories of Consciousness)...Dualism

Some argue that Quantum Mechanics demonstrates that reality is fully *idealistic*, purely a mental construction, and although that is obviously true at the deepest level, it expedites understanding if we grant the material universe its ostensible physical presence. Later we will examine attempts to unify classical physics with Quantum Mechanics in what are known as Grand Unification Theories (GUTs) and Theories of Everything (TOEs), but at this point note that many Theories of Consciousness are similarly trying to unify materialism with dualism. It is incumbent upon the reader to determine how close the following theories come to achieving this objective.

The first of these Theories of Consciousness is known as *panpsychism* where Mind is dispersed throughout the universe and inherent in all things. This position contends that Mind exists in everything from subatomic particles to the largest living organisms, as well as in planets, stars, galaxies, and the entire universe. It is an ancient philosophy, one with a powerful lineage of thinkers from Parmenides and Plato to Jung and Strawson, and one that has received renewed interest following the revelations of Quantum Mechanics. Subatomic particles and living organisms that demonstrate Consciousness without physical brains suggests that everything has Mind and that Mind is everywhere. More incredible is that the ancients believed that before any experimental data denoted the same. Many prominent contemporary thinkers are advocates of panpsychism, including the previously mentioned David Chalmers.[91]

The second possibility is termed *Conscious Realism*. It is an interesting theory by Donald Hoffman, a professor of cognitive science, who notes that we are conscious agents creating a reality we mutually construct, but that our perceptions do not represent true reality. Due to the *Observer Effect* in Quantum Mechanics, there are no public objects sitting in some objective space.[92] Everything in the universe is a mental construct that describes all subjective perspectives in contrast to conventional science with its preference for material objectivity. Once again, brain fundamentalism is an obstacle to new insights regarding the mind. Consider what Hoffman said regarding the anachronistic nature of materialist thinking as a physical brain function for Consciousness:

> **They'll say openly that quantum physics is not relevant to the aspects of brain function that are causally involved in consciousness. They are certain it's got to be classical properties of neural activity, which exist independent of any observers.... These are all very classical notions under Newtonian physics,**

> where time is absolute and objects exist absolutely. And then
> [neuroscientists] are perplexed as to not making progress.
> They do not avail themselves of the incredible insights and
> breakthroughs that physics has made. Those insights are
> out there for us to use, and yet my field says, "We'll stick
> with Newton, thank you. We'll stay 300 years behind in
> our physics.[93]

The next possible explanation for the universality of Mind is known as the *Quantum Theory of Consciousness.* "According to this theory, our consciousness or mind exists as a sphere or domain of living — or self-aware — energy-information beyond our perceived 3-dimensional reality and cosmos."[94] Our brains are a transceiver of Consciousness that receive energy information transmissions from a central Consciousness in the way a radio receives signals from a broadcast station; we experience these signals as thoughts, feelings, mental images, and other mental activity.[95] We feel these effects originating in our body when, in fact, they come from a source of universal Consciousness.

We can consider this point a little further. The brain as a transceiver of Consciousness is a crucial concept. Scientific materialism made perhaps its biggest mistake when it believed that self-awareness comes from the brain as the generator of mind. Ostensible proof was to crush the brain, and self-awareness ends; but crush a radio, and the announcer also ends. **That leads to this remarkable conclusion: looking inside the brain for Consciousness is like looking inside a radio for the announcer.** The brain does not generate Consciousness, and neither does a radio generate the announcer, yet both work with transmissions produced from a distant source, at least according to this theory. Obviously, this is also a form of panpsychism, for Consciousness is everywhere in the form of emissions. The linkage to our previous discussion in Chapter 2 is patently clear: Mind existed ages before physical brains, before any humans even walked the Earth, as Consciousness has an antecedental lineage to First Mind. Thus, a case can be made that brains are created by a First Source to be transceivers from the origin.

Further, the Quantum Theory of Consciousness may also suggest that the universe exists in a superposition of limitless possibilities, and our Consciousness, through observation, manifests potential into a commonly shared reality. That would mirror the experimental findings of the *Double Slit Experiment* where observation collapses superposition into actually observed particles. Consciousness manifesting a shared reality is similar to the position taken in *Conscious Realism*. Note that the shared reality may not be the ultimate reality but rather one that is mutually experienced. Somehow, perhaps because humans all share the same frequency from the source, we construct and exist in the same experience.

The fourth explanation for the pervasiveness of Consciousness is to identify the whereabouts of this invisible source of Mind in what is known as *protoconsciousness theory*, a type of low-level grounding Consciousness found in the entire universe.[96] It is analogous to the concept of spacetime. It is theorized that we are all connected to this protoconsciousness in a type of unified Consciousness where quantum processes connect matter to it. Our brains are like communication devices connected to this underlying master Consciousness with the possibility of sending information through our experiences back to the source of all Consciousness, as again posited in *Conscious Realism*.

To further the point, a fascinating concept developed by scientist and philosopher Bernardo Kastrup provides one possible explanation for the relationship between protoconsciousness and our own minds. In 2015, a woman with numerous personalities and identities (some blind) was observed through a brain scan when her blind identities were in control. Her brain's visual processing centers shut down, but when her seeing identities were in command, her visual centers were normal.[97] Kastrup noted how this case and other cases might help describe the fundamental question of modern consciousness theory.

We know empirically from DID [dissociative identity disorder] that consciousness can give rise to many operationally distinct centers of concurrent experience, each with its own personality and sense of identity. Therefore, if something

**analogous to DID happens at a universal level, the one uni-
versal consciousness could, as a result, give rise to many alters
with private inner lives like yours and ours.**[98]

We might all have unique personalities because every person is one of the universe's distinct personas, simultaneously existing as an individual and as part of
universal Consciousness. The framework Kastrup considers is a type of universal
template for how Mind could come into individual identities. This is itself a type
of dualism whereby Consciousness has both universal and individual properties.
The more significant possibility is that through some unidentified mechanism
Consciousness is manifesting a physical reality out of an incorporeal essence,
and somehow individual minds are indispensable to the display.

The interface between individuals and universal Consciousness has
resulted in some interesting theories for how this interconnection is achieved.
One prominent theory that investigates the issue is *Orchestrated Objective
Reduction*, or *Orch Or*, as advocated by theoretical physicist Roger Penrose and
psychologist Stuart Hameroff.[99] Essentially a modified physicalist brain theory,
it postulates that mind emerges from quantum processes within the neurons of
the brain as opposed to Consciousness resulting from the connections between
those same neurons. That quantum process is arranged by cellular structures
known as microtubules and places the engine of Consciousness at the quantum
mechanical level where each collapse of the wave function generates a conscious
experience.[100]

The primary criticism is that the theory fails to account for how a warm,
wet, and active brain could host such quantum processes without avoiding
decoherence (itself a desperate theory advocating wave function collapse through
physical processes as opposed to the force of Consciousness). Notice the rather
dismal state of one unproved theory trying to disprove another unproven theory,
Reductio ad Absurdum, which is where materialism ultimately leads. Note again
the question of how Consciousness arises from a physical brain. The answer is
that Mind is not dependent on cellular or quantum structures for its existence
since Mind is immaterial. Hence, the elimination of a physicalist framework

resolves the conflict. Other criticisms exist, specifically debatable postulates and interpretations of axioms contained within the theory, but for our purposes Orchestrated Objective Reduction is an attempt to place Consciousness into physical bodies through the energetic and chemical connections inherent in quantum physics and cellular biology. Although not definitive and possessing erroneous physicalist foundations, the theory is a step forward in examining the integration point of Mind and Matter.

The next explanation for the ubiquity of Consciousness, which no doubt follows from our current Information Age, is known as *Integrated Information Theory* as developed by neuroscientist Giulio Tononi and a number of collaborators. The theory states that a system is conscious if it possesses a requisite amount of measurable integrated information.[101] That includes anything from electrons to plants to humans to computers. Consciousness suffuses the universe through Information, and the interdependence of the parts of the system determines the degree of Consciousness. Synergistic effects occur where the Consciousness of the system is greater than the sum of its parts. Obviously, as a theory it contains elements of panpsychism since any system that demonstrates measurable integrated information is considered conscious; that covers both organic and inorganic matter with Consciousness invariably found everywhere. This theory deserves credit for its emphasis on quantitative measurement, hierarchical structure, and mathematical confirmation. Criticism has focused on the fact that the theory is not falsifiable and that it proposes conditions required for mind insufficient to cause Consciousness.

Integrated Information Theory does, however, lead to another theorization for the ubiquity of Consciousness known as *Emergentism*, another physicalist argument positioned to maintain the disintegrating materialist worldview. Like Integrated Information Theory, it relies heavily on Information as a fundamental force in the universe. The central position of Emergentism is that an entity can have properties its parts do not possess due to exchanges among the parts.[102] If a property is evident and not caused by its constituent parts, it is said to be emergent. That philosophy believes that Consciousness emerged during the course of universal evolution due to sufficient informational complexity.

Although Information is a likely fundamental force in the universe, emergence is simply another word for complexity. Emergentism is convenient when the facts are missing and is another Science of the Gaps argument. Criticism has centered on the fact that emergentism cannot be scientifically verified, that the theory is filled with imprecision, that a higher property results from lower structures yet exerts control over them, and that the theory opposes common sense and observable data. Simply, one cannot propose that parts will work together to *emerge* into a new property of nature with the parts constructing themselves. If they could, we might throw together a fishing pole, a piece of fabric, and a comfortable chair and see an interstellar spacecraft *emerge*. Unfortunately, reality does not work like that.

To its credit, the theory does violate dogmatic *reductionism*, the scientific attempt to define phenomena by reducing them to their constituent parts. Emergentism proposes the opposite, that the level above the parts is the significant level, and this position has drawn the wrath of materialists. Thus, according to Emergentism, Consciousness results from a complex correspondence of neurons in the brain even though the neurons themselves cannot cause mind. Scientific materialism insists that the parts are everything, that neurons must cause Consciousness. Once again, we witness two contrasting and unproved positions that are desperate to maintain some type of physicalist frame while eluding oppositional facts.

The next theory of Consciousness is known as *panexperientialism*, a term coined by David Ray Griffin. It posits that the innate incompatibility of realism and idealism (best exemplified by physical brain versus mind) can be reconciled through the primacy of experience. Consider the following:

If evolution of humans goes all the way down to subatomic particles, then human 'experience' by deduction must have originated at the subatomic level, which implies that not just humans but individual cells, individual molecules, individual

atoms, and even individual subatomic particles, such as photons or electrons, incorporate a capacity for 'feeling' or degree
of subjective interiority.[103]

Note that this is very similar to panpsychism, although it is more *experienced-based*
with diminishing levels of Consciousness occurring as the level of experience
decreases, commensurate with the lessening complexity of the object. A human
has more "experience" than a tree, and a tree has more "experience" than a cell.
So panexperientialism is "having experience," whereas panpsychism is "having
consciousness." The difference is subtle but clear. For panexperientialism, all
matter is capable of experience, whereas for panpsychism, all matter possesses
Mind. Panexperientialism is thus characterized by the belief that reality is comprised of brief events of experience rather than enduring material substances.[104]
The theory is an attempt to proceed past the shortcomings of materialism by
incorporating quantum truths that recognize the immaterial nature of things
and instead substitute experience (*actual entities*) as a unifier of objective and
subjective expositions of Mind.

In short, panexperientialism is a *process philosophy* that fuses objectivity
(physical brain) with subjectivity (Consciousness). Consider the following as a
great summation of the theory:

> **Actual occasions correspond to electrons and sub-atomic
> particles, but also to human persons. The human person is a
> society of billions of these occasions (that is, the body), which
> is organized and coordinated by a single dominant occasion
> (that is, the mind). Thus, process philosophy avoids a strict
> mind-body dualism.[105]**

Panexperientialism emphasizes experience over idealism (everything is mind),
dualism (brain and mind both exist, but are separate things), and materialism
(everything is matter) and posits experience as not only causative to everything
but also as a unifier of the totality of experience known as the universe. To this
theory, experience is everything, and everything is connected through experience.

The next explanation for the pervasiveness of Consciousness is another quantum mind formulation known as Holonomic Brain Theory as advocated by neuroscientist Karl Pribram.[106] It is an interesting theory, advancing that Consciousness is formed by quantum effects residing in or between brain cells. Pribram saw the brain as a holographic storage nexus that stores information like a hologram stores the whole of the information in any part of itself. According to Pribram, both interference waves and nonlocality exist in the brain, which reflects Quantum Mechanics. Memory in the brain is distributed over the entire brain and not in any specific area (a scientific fact), and thus memory is essentially nonlocal in its structure as well as superpositional. In short, the brain assumes the same dynamic as the quantum mechanical world since the brain is comprised of atoms. Materialist criticism notes the excessive complexity necessary for its application and Mind existing exterior to the body.

No doubt, Theories of Consciousness are much to absorb. Perhaps a brief taxonomy can enhance our understanding of their essences, and we can categorize these formulations by type of theory, key feature, and pertinent criticism. Theories can be Mind, Materialism, or a Fusion of both. Key feature and primary criticism are selected for priority and brevity. We have omitted physicalism since it is typically the default Theory of Consciousness and has been referenced throughout this work. Consider the following table:

Theory	Type	Key Feature	Criticism
Panpsychism	Mind	Universality	No Proof of Mind
Conscious Realism	Mind	Conscious Agents	Not Falsifiable
Quantum	Mind	Brain as Transceiver	Immaterialism
Protoconsciousness	Mind	Conscious Source	Unidentified
Objective	Materialism	Quantum Brain	Decoherence
Integrated	Fusion	Information-Based	Not Falsifiable
Emergentism	Materialism	Emergent Mind	Observable Data
Panexperientialism	Fusion	Experience-Based	Conjecture
Holonomic Brain	Materialism	Holographic Brain	Brain Chemistry

The table demonstrates a number of possible hypotheses for Consciousness, ranging from physicalist brain theories to Mind as its own entity. Many thinkers theorize that because of the apparent physical realness of the universe, combined with the primacy of Mind (as confirmed in Quantum Mechanics), a fusion of both best describes reality. According to them, the universe must be a blend of *realism* and *idealism*, although that is rarely acknowledged in their published works. The only remaining question for these thinkers concerns the mechanism whereby this fusion occurs.

The position here is that *realism* is the appearance, and *idealism* is the origin. We can prove the point in the following argument. Consider the process of humans first attempting to understand their world where things appear real. Subsequently, the appearance (*realism*) is analyzed through a number of disciplines, including mathematics, physics, biology, and chemistry, thus "proving" a physical basis for reality. Materialism results. As good science should do, the analysis eventually reduces to the atom, reductionism leading to Quantum Mechanics. There, the primacy of Mind (*idealism*) is discovered, foundational to everything else, with Consciousness acting as the currency of existence. Matter is forced to cede to Mind since the real is found to be made of the unreal. Thus, materialism is disproved with only materialist denialism suppressing the truth of existence.

Unifying Principles

An ostensibly real universe made of immaterial Consciousness requires unifying principles for Mind and Matter since there must be a mechanism for their integration. As previously mentioned, mainstream science is attempting to unify classical physics with Quantum Mechanics through Grand Unification Theories (GUTs) and Theories of Everything (TOEs), but with little success. So here we want to focus on theories that unify Mind and Matter in contradistinction to these ineffectual materialist efforts. As with Theories of Consciousness, none of the following are conclusive, but each contributes additional puzzle pieces, thus providing a more coherent picture of reality (remember the duck test). As before, many of them share common themes and shared characteristics.

The first of these unifying principles is known as the *Anthropic Principle* (relating to human beings), an especially controversial subject since it is human-centric and even selfishly human. Critics are many, including some cited in our study. The principle was first formulated by physicist Brandon Carter and states as follows:

> **The Universe has the fundamental laws that we observe it to have. Also, we exist, and are made of the things we're made of, obeying those same fundamental laws. And therefore, we can construct two very simple statements that would be very difficult to argue against:**
>
> 1. **We must be prepared to take account of the fact that our location in the Universe is necessarily privileged to the extent of being compatible with our existence as observers.**
>
> 2. **The Universe (and hence the fundamental parameters on which it depends) must be as to admit the creation of observers within it at some stage.**[107]

These two statements are known as the Weak Anthropic Principle and the Strong Anthropic Principle, which merely state that humans exist in the Universe, which has certain fundamental parameters, constants, and laws. Thus, our existence is sufficient proof that the Universe allows for us to come into being. That we are here to observe the Universe and that we actively engage in the act of observing imply that the Universe is structured in such a way to allow our existence. This structure is not designed on purpose but rather occurs naturally. We emerge because the physical conditions of the universe naturally lead to sentient beings. That is the essence of the Anthropic Principle.

Quantum Mechanics, however, has proved the necessity of the observer in the construction of reality. Humans are thus significant in the universe since they reflect original Consciousness, not because they merely exist. Our presence is not naturally occurring but rather a result of design. Corollary is the fact that the universe is finely tuned to enable life, which is carbon-based. The universe has very fundamental constants and parameters within a narrow range of values; if any of these constants and parameters were only slightly different, life would be impossible. As John Gribbin and Martin Rees noted in their book *Cosmic Coincidences*:

The conditions in our universe really do seem to be uniquely suitable for life forms like ourselves, and perhaps for any form or organic complexity.[108]

This fine-tuning is so precise that it mandates a Creator. The initial conditions of the universe and the passage of time ensured the development of intelligent life. This inevitability, or what materialists term Natural Evolution, is likely a grand plan designed to fulfill some spiritual purpose. So the Anthropic Principle is disingenuous, attempting to obviate universal fine-tuning, intelligent design, and spiritual purposes by suggesting that the physical universe was materially sufficient to structure life on its own.

For our purposes, what is particularly intriguing about the anthropic principle is an extension of it by John Archibald Wheeler known as the *Participatory Anthropic Principle*. An interpretation of Quantum Mechanics, the principle posits that reality is created by observers and that nothing is real until observed.[109] Not only does the Participatory Anthropic Principle correspond to the results of the *Double Slit Experiment* and the previously discussed *delayed choice experiments*, but it also correctly affirms the essentiality of Consciousness in the establishment of reality. In this theory, the universe might exist as a superposition of states unfolding concurrently in every possible permutation until a conscious observer exists in one of them and makes the first observation, collapsing the superposition into a shared, observable universe.[110]

The Participatory Anthropic Principle presumes a requisite amount of Consciousness (human or extraterrestrial) necessary to collapse the superposition, similar to the previously discussed Integrated Information Theory. Critics argue that this required amount is not only uncorroborated but also self-serving. A further criticism is that organisms on Earth demonstrate Consciousness with rather limited or nonexistent brains (certainly inferior to humans) and thus prove themselves quite capable of making observations. Other challenges concern falsifiability and the fact that observers might occur that are not carbon-based life forms.

Nevertheless, the Participatory Anthropic Principle is a significant advancement over materialist theories because it integrates the findings of Quantum Mechanics and considers the antecedental lineage of Consciousness throughout history. The mistake the theory makes is positioning the first observer as a human being rather than a Great Consciousness. Also, the theory never asks this question: who created the superposition in the first place? Nor does it ask if an initial superposition is even possible. The assumption is that somehow the universe simply came to be, an unsubstantiated materialist interpretation based on quantum fluctuations and designed to avoid the acknowledgment of a Creator. Nature cannot create itself, and there are logical proofs of that.[111]

The next substantial unifying principle to be considered is the possibility that a deeper level of reality (invisible structure) exists below the quantum mechanical level, including the very fabric of spacetime itself. The *Foundation for Mind Being Research* has posted an interesting paper that utilizes a high degree of interdisciplinarity that is rather unique in the synthesis of Mind and Matter.[112] According to this hypothesis, this deeper level of reality generates the shared reality we see, the theory positing some "connector" link atoms with this layer. It is similar to the M Theory in conventional physics where an underlying vibrational dynamic determines the characteristics of subatomic particles and atoms. **The concept of a substructure beneath the atomic one is crucial to our developing megatheory since it provides the basis for how the immaterial becomes the material. We will explore this concept further in subsequent chapters.**

Moreover, this deeper-level connection suggests that the barrier of space-time may not be impenetrable, so human experience is not confined to the material universe. In that way, Mind can transcend the material universe, and the material universe can manifest into Mind. As support for the argument, the theory incorporates such diverse thinkers as Sheldrake, Jung, Einstein, and Jeans. What is fascinating about the theory is the integration of phenomena previously considered separately in the study of Mind and Matter; for instance, synthesizing Quantum Mechanics with psychology and classical physics with teleology. It is a positive advancement over the rather conventional and conformist materialist methodologies that too often dominate the discussion.

The final unifying principle to be examined is *the Mind as a Higher Dimension* where Mind exists in a different dimension than the brain.[113] Here, Mind is a holographically structured phenomenon situated in a space surrounding the physical brain in a fourth spatial dimension but able to access other dimensions external to it. The brain exists in three dimensions, but somehow the fourth dimensional Mind can interact with the physical brain and utilize quantum processes such as *entanglement* and *tunneling* where particles can literally pass through impenetrable barriers. Another consideration is *quantum wave resonance* where a wave structure underlying all the neurons and particles of the brain also passes through the Mind and expedites information transfer. Consider the following from *Uplift* that discusses "the binding problem" (segregation and combination functions in the brain), which is often debated:

The quantum wave resonance of brain and mind field communication can be a clever answer to what is called 'the

binding problem.' Different neural regions and clusters in our brain are responsible for different cognitive functions, say for example, vision, colour, sound or verbal processing. Yet these different signals from different regions in our brain come together collectively *faster* than speed at which they are processed individually, hence giving rise to an observed anomaly known as the binding problem. Now, this is relevant here because it seems that the binding problem arises when we scratch our heads and try to figure out what is happening from just one layer of reality—say from the neural activity of our brain. On the other hand, when we start to view the brain and mind as being many-dimensional manifestations of the same thing and which communicate information at the quantum level through resonance, a better, wider picture starts forming that explains apparent anomalies, such as the binding problem. This also gives more credence to the fact that a flattened and reductionistic view of reality does not work at all. We need a richer, broader and possibly a many-dimensional view of consciousness and reality.[114]

At this point, we should review the above-referenced unifying principles. Key features and primary criticism are summarized. Note the following table:

Principle	Type	Key Feature	Criticism
Anthropic	Unification	Designed Universe	Tautology
Participatory	Unification	Observation	Many Worlds
Deeper Reality	Unification	Hidden Reality	Falsifiability
Dimensional	Unification	Mind as Dimension	Conjecture

Obviously, some mechanism unites Matter and Mind in the universe. Mind is evident, as is Matter, the former causative of the latter. That we know. Matter was considered first and largely understood, at least until Quantum Mechanics proved its basis was Mind. Consciousness is not yet understood; in fact, we are in the preliminary stages of that knowledge. Nevertheless, both Mind and Matter together suggest something larger (core structure) that has eluded our grasp. Could it be that this core structure is responsible for both? Are Mind and Matter simply suggestions of something deeper?

Synthesis

We have seen that Consciousness exists in the universe; both *realism* and *idealism* accept the existence of Consciousness as a property of reality. The argument centers on the origin of this Consciousness, either as a product of brain chemistry or as a separate entity. The uncomfortable divide between the physical obviousness of reality and the causative nature of Mind engendered the Theories of Consciousness and Unification Principles. We have examined some of those, but the great arbiter is Quantum Mechanics, which concludes that Mind is not only separate but foundational. In this manner, quantum truths are an iteration beyond traditional arguments because Consciousness extends past dualism. The following best describes the situation:

Mind is Physical...Mind is Dualistic...Mind is Foundational

Materialists will forever attempt physicalist interpretations of Consciousness; that is to be expected. Many interpretations such as *Enactivism* (cognition results from the interface between an organism and its environment) are obvious attempts to dispense with Mind exterior to Body and maintain a physicalist framework. Others such as many discussed in this chapter may offer legitimate insight. We have progressed from physical Mind to Mind Body Dualism to Mind as foundational. Through science, we have a good understanding of the material realm, but it is through comprehension of the foundational substructure of Mind that we may truly extend ourselves. Gradually, the material is acceding to the immaterial, yet many questions remain. It is against these perplexities that we turn to Post-Materialism.

CHAPTER 7

Post-Materialism

The world is gradually evolving from inveterate materialism to innovative immaterialism. Physicalism fails to account for the *totality of experience* since material processes cannot resolve foundational Mind, quantum behavior, subjective experience, and innate spirituality. The recognition of Consciousness as primary in the universe is compelling humanity into what is known as Post-Materialism.

Post-Materialism is best defined as a paradigm that "grants equal primacy to mind and matter."[115] Note here that Mind is inserted *in addition* to Matter, although homage to physicalism is unnecessary and also disadvantageous, with deference to matter done primarily for tradition and acceptance at a cost of delayed truth. Perhaps such incrementalism (the slow acceptance of Mind as causative of reality) is understandable since science is highly resistant to contrarian views and thus glacially slow. Eventually, though, Consciousness will be viewed as predominant with Matter relegated to its consequence.

The Toppling of Standards

In this part of our study, we will examine some standards of materialism toppled by modern discoveries. Abrading standards eventually crumble, replaced by more factual structures. Four standards have been selected as examples:

- **Reductionism**
- **Darwinism**
- **Statistical Populations Probability and Universal Fine-Tuning**
- **The Many Worlds Interpretation**

We will consider each of these individually. The first of these four, reductionism, is foundational to science and underpins the majority of all scientific approaches.

Reductionism

Reductionism, as we have previously mentioned, is the idea that the whole can be understood by a reduction to its parts. Varadaraja Raman in his article "Reductionism and Holism: Two Sides of the Perception of Reality" noted: "In other words, the world and its workings will be best understood – indeed can only be understood – in terms of the ultimate constituents and forces which give rise to it."[116] According to reductionism, it naturally follows that the parts must also be real and actually exist. Again, from Raman:

> **[I]n the scientific paradigm of the 19th century, ultimately in the world there is only matter and energy in space transforming in time. In other words, every phenomenon can be reduced, in principle, to energy transformations and their impacts of material entities in the arena of space.**[117]

Thus, reductionism extends downward into atoms and molecules that arrange into chemistry and cells, and from there to biology and anthropology, through to society and technology, and finally scaling up to stars, planets, galaxies, and the universe. Everything is causatively linked, micro building to macro. Moreover, to a reductionist, the intricacy of nature necessitates identifying organizing structures within that nature; these complex phenomena should always be described by the simplest underlying principles.[118] That ensures greater verification but also emphasizes the value of reductionism, a consonance where principles conform to parts.

As a result, existence is determined through complicated associations between the smallest to the largest, everything dictated by previous causes and run by simple principles. This is our often noted *determinism* where, with sufficient knowledge, everything can be predicted by understanding how parts configure the whole; thus, reality results from the boundless connections of the material realm, the universe behaving as one tremendous mechanism encompassing the totality of everything we see, with the human brain acting as supreme analyst.

The challenge to reductionism is *holism*. This premise is that a more accurate picture of reality is possible if we view the whole instead of its constituent parts. Everything is a totality. Mind as a whole and causative of Matter violates reductionism because the entirety is responsible for the ingredients. To a materialist, this is physically impossible; the elements necessarily cause the whole with no tolerance for countervailing facts such as foundational Mind. Nevertheless, once you accept that the entirety is more significant than the parts, reductionism (and its close relative, determinism) fails.

But for a materialist, something "whole" enough to cause a universe—say, a Great Consciousness—is completely absurd; an entity devoid of extensible parts simply cannot exist because such an entity is not reducible. Thus, a First Mind is not logically possible because physicalism mandates reduction, and a Being that cannot be reduced cannot be conceived. Yet quantum truths demonstrate the wholeness of Mind. Thus, Consciousness is its own entirety, a destructor of reductionism and, by extension, an annihilator of materialism.

Darwinism

Our next standard to be deposed is rather amusing. If reductionism is contravened by the whole, then the whole of Darwinism is contravened by its reduction. Perhaps we should expect that from a theory that is more than 150 years old. Nonetheless, a third of the American public believes in evolution by natural selection (99% of researchers in the life sciences accept its premise, which proves our earlier point that materialism is dogmatic), and that is quite an accomplishment for such a dated hypothesis.[119] Yet, two-thirds of the public believe that

Darwinism is false, with that number sure to approach 100% if more of its confutations are known.

In fact, a growing movement objects to the provisions of Darwinism, spanning various disciplines and the world's finest colleges and universities.[120] Numerous criticisms exist, and some prove conclusively that the theory is erroneous. We will summarize a few of them shortly, but the reader is directed to various sources such as the Discovery Institute, Access Research Institute, Biologic Institute, and Intelligent Design and Evolution Awareness for a better understanding of these critiques. For a brief summary of the primary arguments against the theory of evolution, see Dina Spector's excellent article, "The 6 Reasons Creationists Think Evolution Isn't a Sure Thing."[121] Humans Are Free also has a wonderful resource detailing nine scientific facts that disprove evolution.[122]

Here is how the parts destroy the whole. The first major denunciation of Darwinism concerns the complexity inherent in human DNA. In the best reductionist tradition, DNA was reduced to its constituent parts and found to contain 3 billion code instructions.[123] Essentially, human DNA is a vast amount of stored information, a type of enormous software program, an instruction manual directing biological necessities, specifically the assembling of proteins. Darwinists claim the engine of evolution creates such complexity through the magnanimous workings of time. Unfortunately, Earth has existed for only a fraction of the time required for the engine of Darwinism to produce such molecular intricacy; thus, it is a fact of existence that such informational complexity must have an intelligent designer. Consider the following from Mario Seiglie:

> **It is hard to fathom, but the amount of information in human DNA is roughly equivalent to 12 sets of *The Encyclopedia Britannica*—an incredible 384 volumes worth of detailed information that would fill 48 feet of library shelves! Yet in their actual size—which is only two millionths of a millimeter thick—a teaspoon of DNA, according to molecular biologist Michael Denton, could contain *all* the information needed to build the proteins for *all* the species of organisms that**

have ever lived on earth, and "there would still be enough room left for all the information in every book ever written" (*Evolution: A Theory in Crisis,* 1996, p. 334).[124]

Too much information is packed into DNA for it to have organized randomly; as mentioned, the genetic code is a highly advanced software program requiring a programmer of incalculable ability. Human DNA is the ultimate indictment against Darwinism. It is preposterous to believe that some single-celled organism adrift in a primordial ocean eventually evolved into such genetic complexity. Physical nature by itself cannot create human beings.

The second indictment against Darwinism concerns the lack of transitional species (missing links) in the fossil record. Even Darwin considered the lack of transitional species to be an extremely valid criticism against his theory (DNA had yet to be discovered). For if all living things are descended from one common ancestor, then there must be transitional species linking every living thing to every other living thing. Unfortunately, they do not exist. Moreover, if they did exist, they would exist in current nature, and we would see them. Instead, what we see is quite different with minimal evidence of transition, and that is limited to variations within species.[125]

The fossil record shows that species evolve, but they do not turn into other species. The base of the tree is missing, with the evolution happening on the branches among types. Materialists fill in the blanks with inferences and assumptions, complete with a list of excuses. According to Darwinists, the lack of fossilized transitional forms results from species being eaten or scavenged. Also, an insufficient number of paleontologists have conducted excavations, so the fossil record is incomplete. Next, isolated, small populations can accelerate evolutionary transformation through "punctuated equilibrium" where species evolve expeditiously into separate species. And finally, these smaller populations do not leave many specimens behind.[126] Notice the *selective science* in their arguments. Whenever some fossil discovery advances their agenda, it is heralded; whenever the fossil record invalidates their arguments, it is ignored. Transitional species do not exist, not because of innumerable excuses but because they do not exist.

Let us take a brief digression regarding selective science since it relates to this discussion. Selective science is akin to *making your own truth*. Once again, a comparison to the political realm is insightful. Governments and societal elites often make their own truths—think Soviet Union, Nazi Germany, Communist Cuba, and North Korea. The public is deceived. Unfortunately, materialism has turned this practice into an art form with academia its prime vanguard and propaganda ministry. All countering perspectives are stifled with debate promptly silenced—no exceptions. The vast majority of humanity rejects Darwinism as the explanation for the origin of life and believes in a higher power. Nevertheless, materialists deny these opinions and the mounting empirical evidence against their position. Simply, denial of truth is not science.

Statistical Populations Probability and Universal Fine-Tuning

Materialism views the world as numbers, specifically statistics and laws of probability. This grounding has both benefits and liabilities. Probability analysis yields a tremendous understanding of the material world but also inclines individuals to see everything as statistical potentiality. Trends, tendencies, extrapolations, ratios, and more are all part of the materialist thought process, *possibility* found not in aspiration or determination but rather in the relationships of numbers. Any exception can be discounted by probability distribution taking the shape of a classic bell curve where the outlier is simply a statistical fluke and thus easily dismissed.

Unfortunately, a probability mindset also causes huge miscalculations since deviations from the standard can be reconciled regardless of how meaningfully significant the variance is. An example is studying a night sky, identifying a wandering point of light, dismissing it as a statistical fluke, and then it becoming an asteroid that destroys the Earth. In other words, such a probabilistic disposition always provides a way out of divergent findings, even if the outlier proves extremely compelling.

The next incrimination against statistical populations probability is our earlier discussion of universal fine-tuning. A number of conditions have been precisely arranged to originate life. Combined, they represent an infinitesimal probability that their alignment happened randomly. No amount of mathematical manipulation can change that fact. Life exists in the universe within fundamental physical constants (speed of light, Planck constant, etc.,) that have a very small range of values; if any of these quantities were only marginally different, life would not occur. A wider selection of values was anticipated, but experimentation demonstrated the narrowness of the range. That implies an extremely precise calibration with intention.

We can expand the point to further our argument. As mentioned, some of the fine-tuning concerns the nature of fundamental physical constants. First, let us look at a brief description. A fundamental physical constant is a "physical quantity with a value that is generally believed to be both universal in nature and to remain unchanged over time."[127] These constants can be used in relation to exchanges between particles and forces, the relative density of the universe, understanding gravitational effects, and the distinct measurements of energy. Fundamental physical constants are thus types of "built-in" structures with values necessary to make the universe work. Consider what Nobel Prize–winning physicist Richard Feynman said about one of these constants:

> **It's one of the greatest damn mysteries of physics: a magic number that comes to us with no understanding by man. You might say the "hand of God" wrote that number, and "we do not know how He pushed his pencil." We know what type of a dance to do experimentally to measure this number very accurately, but we do not know what type of dance to do on the computer to make this number come out, without putting it in secretly!**[128]

These constants are numerical values attributed to phenomena that enable life to begin; this level of intricacy and linkage requires an intelligent designer. With incredibly compelling force, these constants prove a master program designed to ensure the development of life.

Since it also furthers the point, we should consider the issue of carbon-based life. Carbon and oxygen are two elements imperative for biology; they are formed when helium is burned in certain types of stars. Carbon 12 in particular, which is responsible for the preponderance of the carbon in human beings, forms only under very specific circumstances.[129] The excitation of Carbon 12 plays a crucial role in the helium burning of stars and is very dependent on fundamental physical constants for its effect. That creates "life-essential" conditions that are clearly finely tuned. The precise structure of two fundamental forces of nature—the strong nuclear force and the weak nuclear force—also demonstrate fine-tuning since without their meticulous construction they would not allow carbon and other heavy elements to form.[130] These values are not determined randomly but rather designed with purpose.

Lastly, there is the issue of universal ripples resulting from the Big Bang. Consider the following:

> **The ripples in the universe from the original Big Bang event are detectable at one part in 100,000. If this factor were slightly smaller, the universe would exist only as a collection of gas – no planets, no life. If this factor were slightly larger, the universe would consist only of large black holes. Obviously, no life would be possible in such a universe.**[131]

This degree of fine-tuning allowed galaxy formation; it also ensured that galaxies were not excessively dense, causing a universe collapsing into itself where life was impossible. Combined with the other factors mentioned previously, this demonstrates an extreme level of wisdom and planning. Numerous other factors of fine-tuning exist that more dramatically authenticate the exactitude of arrangement. An excellent resource for this is GodandScience.org that lists thirty-four of these factors. Some of them are very unlikely to have occurred without forethought and are virtually mathematically impossible.

So how did the materialists respond to such a convincing case of numbers? They insisted that our universe must be a statistical fluke! Universal fine-tuning without a designer is untenable. Nevertheless, materialists see our universe as an outlier. True to the materialist worldview, we are a mathematical fortuity, existing in the only universe fine-tuned for life. Of course, that explanation requires other universes, an enormous number of them, in fact, to prove our exception. So it is against this level of improbability that we examine the greatest fabrication ever devised as a defense of materialism. What follows can only be described as desperate and embarrassing, a low point for the cognitive abilities of mankind, demonstrating fully the prioritization of dogma over reason and a faith in the ignorance of the masses.

The Many Worlds Interpretation

In Chapter 1, we recounted the *Double Slit Experiment* where Consciousness collapsed the wave function of the atom through observation. That naturally linked matter and energy to Mind. As expected, scientific materialists were dismayed by this finding because it not only appeared nondeterministic, but Consciousness was antecedently traced through history to a First Mind.

So to protect materialist expositions of reality and avoid the theistic nature of quantum truths, Hugh Everett in 1957 developed an interpretation of Quantum Mechanics that denied the collapse of the wave function in direct negation of actual, scientific evidence. He postulated that instead of all possibilities of the superposition collapsing into the one observed state of reality, when an observation is made, the universe branches into a near infinity of other universes where all other outcomes can manifest.[132] The allure of the theory was that it eliminated wave function collapse, randomness, entanglement, and Mind from the experimental results and conformed with the materialist preference for determinism. **To work, however, it came with the laughable conclusion of perpetual universe creation through observation.** That means every time an observation is made by all 8 billion inhabitants of planet Earth, the universe branches into trillions of other universes. Presumably, if extraterrestrials exist, they also make observations and branch our shared universe into trillions more universes. It is theorized that the universe may have billions of other intelligent civilizations whose denizens also make observations as often as we do. That is a tremendous amount of universe creation. If plants and wildlife that have been shown to exhibit Consciousness also make observations, then we have countless numbers of observers creating innumerable universes at an incalculable rate, all to deny the existence of God.

The preposterousness of this hypothesis is best exemplified by the following, a particularly indicting reference that discusses the observation of an electron and the aforementioned branching into other universes:

> **That requires a parallel, identical apparatus for the electron to traverse. More, it requires a parallel you to observe it — for only through the act of measurement does the superposition of states seem to "collapse." Once begun, this process of duplication seems to have no end: you have to erect an entire parallel universe around that one electron, identical in all respects except where the electron went. You avoid the complication of wave function collapse, but at the expense of making another universe. The theory doesn't exactly predict the other universe in the way that scientific theories usually make predictions. It is just a deduction from the hypothesis that the other electron path is real too.**

> **This picture gets really extravagant when you appreciate what a measurement is. In one view, any interaction between one quantum entity and another — a photon of light bouncing off an atom — can produce alternative outcomes, and so demands parallel universes. As Dewitt put it, "Every quantum transition taking place on every star, in every galaxy, in every remote corner of the universe is splitting our local world on earth into myriads of copies." In this "multiverse," says the physicist and many-worlds proponent Max Tegmark, "all**

possible states exist at every instant" — meaning, at least in the popular view, that everything that is physically possible is (or will be) realized in one of the parallel universes. In particular, after a measurement takes place, there are two (or more) versions of the observer where before there was one. "The act of making a decision," says Tegmark — a decision here counting as a measurement, generating a particular outcome from the various possibilities — "causes a person to split into copies." Both copies are in some sense versions of the initial observer, and both of them experience a unique, smoothly changing reality that they are convinced is the "real world." . . . Their universes go their separate ways, launched on a trajectory of continual unraveling.[133]

And this is science? Are we really supposed to believe in endless universe creation instead of a First Mind? Before we discount it as materialist folly, we should note that our tax contributions make theories like this possible. Moreover, such theories either cause or reflect societal stagnation. Although there is a slight difference between the Many Worlds Interpretation and the Alternate Universe Theory (the latter stipulates our universe was created with innumerable other universes without the branching aspects), this is the foundation for the many universes concept so often discussed in modern society.

Moreover, the Many Worlds Interpretation follows from the materialist mindset of Statistical Populations Probability where ours is one of trillions of other universes. Unproven and completely without merit, we are sold this many universe nonsense with its adherents acknowledging that no way exists to test the hypothesis or prove its existence. Of course, these pontificators never believe their own absurdities; since endless copies of them exist in other universes, they should not object if we shoot them in the head. After all, other versions of them will live on. Yet they would be the first ones screaming for security personnel if such an attempt were actually made—in a word, hypocrisy.

Although the Many Worlds Interpretation is a minority interpretation of Quantum Mechanics, it has been growing in acceptance due to a lack of progress in competing theories. That demonstrates the desperation. Hugh Everett believed the Many Worlds Interpretation guaranteed immortality.[134] I suppose that endless copies of yourself is a form of immortality, but it is also a form of eternal punishment if you happen to be supremely deluded. If each of us has the power to create an endless amount of universes through nothing more than observing, then once again, it is time for a new paradigm.

Implications of a Post-Materialist World

Now we must examine the implications of a post-materialist world. Since the 1920s, it has been known that materialism cannot account for the fabric of reality. We have used atomic structures to great advantage, constructing the products and gadgets that define our economy, and society has been greatly forwarded by our understanding of material processes. Material truths are heralded, as they should be, yet when quantum physics points toward *idealistic* and *spiritual* conclusions, these findings are invariably ignored. Materialists seek to delimitate quantum physics "to the operation of these devices, and not to the understanding of the world."[135] That is where science turns pernicious. Materialism chooses what it wants known. Once again, this is selective science and invalidates the essence of scientific endeavor.

Nevertheless, the emerging paradigm of Consciousness must incorporate truths from the previous paradigm. We also have to expand our understanding of the powers of Mind. Consider the following:

> **The new paradigms, both as a worldview and as the basis of the organization of science, are better suited to the character-istics of the world today. There are still important resistances, especially in the intellectual environment, but they will be gradually overcome. The new paradigms accept plurality and validate the idea that in order to better understand reality, several approaches are necessary, several truths can coexist,**

including some defended by the old paradigm, which may continue to be valid.[136]

Two realms exist—the material and the immaterial. We have traversed the planet in commercial aircraft, explored the depths of the oceans, walked on the Moon, and sent probes deep into space. Modern conveniences ranging from ovens, microwaves, cellular phones, and computers make life simpler and more enjoyable. Nevertheless, materialism has failed to provide answers to basic questions of existence and has failed miserably to satisfy our spiritual core. Note the following from Mario Beauregard as an excellent summation of how the emerging Consciousness Paradigm will transcend our current limitations:

Individually and collectively, the PMP [Postmaterialist Paradigm] has far reaching implications. This paradigm re-enchants the world and profoundly alters the vision we have of ourselves, giving us back our dignity and power as human beings. The PMP also fosters positive values such as compassion, respect, care, love, and peace, because it makes us realize that the boundaries between self and others are permeable. In doing so, this paradigm promotes an awareness of the deep interconnection between ourselves and nature at large, including all levels of physical organization. Such interconnection may also encompass non-physical, spiritual realms. . . . [T]he PMP acknowledges spiritual experiences, which relate to a fundamental dimension of human existence and are frequently reported across all cultures: within the postmaterialist framework, these experiences are not considered *a priori* as fantasies or the symptoms of pathological processes. Finally, by emphasizing a deep connection between ourselves and nature, the PMP also promotes environmental awareness and the preservation of our biosphere. In that sense, the template of reality associated with the PMP may

help humanity to create a sustainable civilization and to blossom."[137]

The possibilities of a post-materialist paradigm are enormous. The physical environment may be manipulated in unimaginable ways if we embrace Consciousness. In subsequent chapters, we will explore such mechanisms of transformation. A post-materialist paradigm will also restore true scientific pursuit and reduce dogmatic tendencies based on human insecurity and pride. Humanity, specifically the academic community and those staunch materialists within its domain, must adjust their worldview. Consider this from *Manifesto for a Post-Materialist Science*:

> **Mind (will/intention) can influence the state of the physical world, and operate in a nonlocal (or extended) fashion, i.e. it is not confined to specific points in space, such as brains and bodies, nor to specific points in time, such as the present. Since the mind may nonlocally influence the physical world, the intentions, emotions, and desires of an experimenter may not be completely isolated from experimental outcomes, even in controlled and blinded experimental designs.**[138]

As Imants Baruss noted, there is an element of *inauthenticity* in materialism since the "inauthentic mode of being is characterized by compliance with the expectations of others for our interpretation of reality."[139] This is akin to our discussion of *consensus reality* in Chapter 3 where often-mistaken conceptions of existence are reinforced through a social dynamic. The point is that the erroneous worldview of materialism has been extended to society at large at great cost to verity. Materialists' belief in physicalist foundations is like believing in a forest only to discover that the forest is made of trees and then not believing in the trees. The Consciousness Paradigm of the future will therefore provide a much higher degree of integrity, spirituality, and truth. Consider, for example, the following:

Spiritual intelligence is an ability to access higher meanings, values, abiding purposes, and unconscious aspects of the self and to embed these meanings, values, and purposes in living richer and more creative lives.[140]

Consciousness Paradigm, Post-Materialism, the Paradigm of Mind, Spiritual Intelligence—all are merely different names for the same phenomenon, which is a worldview that transcends materialism. This transilience is not the false boast of *promissory materialism* where everything will eventually be proved by physicalism (already known to be a lie) but rather brisk progress made because previously disparaged areas of interest will suddenly become accessible and accepted. Once materialist obstinacy is removed, an explosion of discovery will follow.

We must get to emancipated science because we are witnessing diminishing returns in nearly all areas of human endeavor. In short, science and technology are stagnating, and we are stifled as a result. Unfortunately, the first efforts of amelioration through the supremacy of Mind were subverted (similar to science itself) by a unique fusion of ideology and unprecedented personal self-absorption; thus was born the New Age Movement, its life course defined by the erroneous interpretation of Consciousness, tribalistic narrowness, eclectic absurdity, factionalistic bellicism, and even religious aspiration. Next, we will explore systemic stagnation and the corruption of Mind through an objective appraisal of what went horribly astray.

CHAPTER 8

Stagnation and Corruption

Stagnation occurs for many reasons. But fundamentally, stagnation results from limits to intelligence, the inability to transcend a certain point of progress. This intelligence, different from Mind, is the more commonly known *brain power*, the acquisition and application of knowledge and skills, especially toward problem-solving. Intelligence is the realm of the physical brain, extended in the modern era to include our devices and technology, including computation and artificial intelligence. It is here we have stagnated. Past this point are the advancing secrets of Mind. So any corruption of the concept of Mind contributes inexorably to stagnation. We will examine that shortly, but first we must consider stagnation and then how the correct identification of Mind could have accelerated our development.

Stagnation

As cited earlier in our study, John Horgan in his best-selling book *The End of Science* suggests that the vast majority of significant scientific discoveries have occurred while the future consists of completing the details.[141] His hypothesis directly contradicts the *scientism* (excessive belief in the power of scientific knowledge) so characteristic of our age. The book was not a rebuke of materialism (Horgan is a physicalist) but rather an observation that science is languishing. According to Horgan, science is stagnating so severely that paradigms themselves may be approaching an end.[142] Horgan is mistaken regarding paradigms (a physicalist views materialism as the only way forward, and if materialism is stagnant, then paradigms cannot advance), but he is correct that the incredible discoveries of the last few centuries are unreproducible.

Perhaps the greatest indictment against scientific and technological progress comes from economist Tyler Cowen who published the small book *The Great Stagnation* in 2011 and whose central premise is that America is stagnating because of falling rates of innovation.[143] Similar to Horgan, Cowen had a common theme of the obvious stagnation in the sciences. As testament to his thesis, he cites the exploitation of the low-hanging fruit in America for initially enabling technological and cultural advancement—free and unused land, the capitalization of the primary materialist scientific discoveries of earlier centuries, the mass education of the citizenry, the relative availability of oil, and the ideological and political structure of the country. These have largely been exploited, and in the case of the latter two are depleting and deteriorating. Further, many economic metrics, including productivity growth, median incomes, returns on labor and capital, and spending efficiency are decreasing and showing few signs of improvement. Advances in health and education have slowed, while the only accelerating sector is information technology.

To the reader, that may appear so implausible as to cause consternation. If so, it exemplifies the massively successful hype campaigns of the scientific and technological communities. Yet the evidence is accumulating that stagnation is real. Consider for effect a few more examples of our collective deterioration: commercial air travel takes the same amount of time as fifty years ago, diseases are endlessly ravaging the planet, public transportation is antiquated and slow, academic test scores are declining, the Internet has provided no improvement in standards of living, and smartphones and social media have degraded the collective work ethic and inspired unprecedented narcissism. We live the same as in the 1960s with only slight improvements, largely in the form of better entertainment options.

Confronted with this observation, how do our elites respond? They suggest further advances in science, which does not address the fundamental problem of entrenched and stagnating scientific materialism. Unless that particular prejudice is removed, we cannot advance since such a solution is like expecting aggregating thunderstorms to stop severe flooding.

The argument also exists that globalization and conformity are causing stagnation because society has less variation than in previous generations and breakthroughs happen because of diversity.[144] The Internet is causing much of this homogeneity, as is the hybridization of cultures. Uniformity spreads in direct correlation to the apex of its advanced countries, and if those cultures are stagnating, the remainder of human civilization (after initially surging) follows them into mediocrity. If those advanced nations are also philosophically materialist, the balance of global society will be limited by physicalist interpretations of reality and never progress to the primacy of Mind.

Another measure of societal stagnation concerns the progress of science through the awarding of Nobel Prizes and the (albeit subjective) ranking of their historical significance. Patrick Collison and Michael Nielsen have noted that expert opinion ranks the first quarter of the twentieth century as the golden age of discovery and that subsequent progress has been more incremental and less notable.[145] Moreover, cost inefficiency is the new standard; it takes researchers much longer and greater expense to achieve the same results as previous scientists who were much younger and required less collaborative environments for success. Consider the analogy that Collison and Nielsen offer:

> **Suppose we think of science—the exploration of nature—as similar to the exploration of a new continent. In the early days, little is known. Explorers set out and discover major new features with ease. But gradually they fill in knowledge of the new continent. To make significant discoveries explorers must go to ever-more-remote areas, under ever-more-difficult conditions. Exploration gets harder. In this view, science is a limited frontier, requiring ever more effort to "fill in the**

map." One day the map will be near complete, and science will largely be exhausted. In this view, any increase in the difficulty of discovery is intrinsic to the structure of scientific knowledge itself.[146]

Naturally, scientific advancement is also subject to the human failings so often referenced in this book. Humans are imperfect, and wherever humans work, in whatever capacity, that undertaking will be subject to our deficiencies. The spillage of flawed character from humans into their various activities is unmistakable and responsible for glaring inefficiencies and delayed progress. As an example, corollary to our earlier references to materialist dogma and groupthink, note the following summation of the problem from a scientist who cites the specific lack of advancement in theoretical physics.

> **Nothing is moving in the foundations of physics. One experiment after the other is returning null results: No new particles, no new dimensions, no new symmetries. . . . They have no clue where new physics may be to find. . . . Some have called it a crisis. . . . It raises the impression that theorists realized the error of their ways, that change is on the way, that they are realizing now and will abandon their flawed methodology. But I see no realization. The self-reflection in the community is zero, zilch, nada, nichts, null. They just keep doing what they've been doing for 40 years, blathering about naturalness and multiverses and shifting their "predictions," once again, to the next larger particle collider.**[147]

This critique extends into all areas. Science and society are stagnating because dogmatic thinkers in a variety of disciplines continue to perpetuate materialism in the face of incontrovertible evidence to the contrary. In fact, it is difficult to even assess the level of stagnation because information is often controlled by materialist extremists. Physicalists hide the truth and deflect metrics that measure their performance. For them, stagnation is an indictment. So instead, we are bombarded with announcements heralding some scientific "discovery," which inevitably is some minor detail as opposed to an actual breakthrough, typically in an effort to secure additional funding and enhanced prestige. As we have noted, scientific materialism accepts only those discoveries that are commensurate with its dogma; if truth lies external to its tenets, it is ignored or disparaged. That is not science, and that is not progress. Advancement originates in truth, and denial of the truth causes degeneration.

History clearly demonstrates that revolutionary progress occurs external to an accepted worldview. Knowledge and advancement are directly correlated to the willingness to change beliefs. Science is based on the concept that facts and statements must comply with the observed state of affairs. That is known as truth. As the facts change, so does the truth. All paradigms are eventually replaced by superior ones, and scientific materialism is no exception. Truth is thus progressive and antithetical to stagnation.

Conceptually, that brings us to the *ingenuity* of society, an adeptness that which is imperative for survival. The research of anthropologist and historian Joseph Tainter revealed that the problem-solving capabilities of societal institutions (basically a measure of ingenuity) are relevant for both sustainability and collapse.[148] As complexity increases, societal institutions must solve problems before encountering diminishing marginal returns. We can extrapolate that institutions naturally reflect the state of knowledge of a civilization, and if these institutions are philosophically materialist and thus incapable of seeking answers exterior to physicalist interpretations, diminishing returns compound, and stagnancy results. Tainter observed that American society is currently facing the same challenges as previous civilizations in decline and, like Horgan and others, notes that innovation is diminishing.[149] Globalization is increasing complexity beyond our ability to manage it, and equally obvious is that materialism cannot provide the framework for solutions.

A more troubling trend is the decline of the average human IQ (intelligence quotient). Since the Victorian Age (1837–1901), the average human IQ has declined from 114 to 100, an astonishing drop of 14 points in less than two hundred years.[150] The average IQ in Antiquity, the time of Socrates, Plato,

Parmenides, and Aristotle, was believed to be higher than 125. In addition, average cranial capacity and brain size have shrunk during the last 10,000 years (another counterargument to Darwinism that suggests natural selection favors increased intelligence).[151] The fact remains that humans are getting less intelligent. Arguments for the cause range from environmental factors to unfavorable population trends, to technology doing more brainwork for us, and to domestication and increasingly urban lifestyles. The educational system in particular has been singled out by experts for abject failures to elevate intelligence since every type of instructional method has been applied with depreciable results. Moreover, dietary and nutritional remedies have proven ineffective. So have psychological enhancements, specifically building self-esteem and confidence-raising. All of these correlate to lower IQ scores in the future and thus more scientific and societal stagnation.

Unfortunately, the fact that humans are in a cognitive regression has consequences beyond anthropological curiosity. Less intelligence is deleterious for both individuals and society. Some examples of our declining intelligence are obvious, such as escalating racism and environmental destruction, with others more surreptitious. These largely unrecognized factors are especially pernicious to societal advancement. Consider the following items, which we will briefly discuss individually:

- **Wealth inequality**
- **Planned obsolescence**
- **Diminished public sector spending**
- **Investment safety**

Wealth Inequality

Wealth inequality is actually becoming notorious and is often noted for its detrimental effects on society because concentration of financial resources results in an elite more interested in accumulating fortune than advancing societal objectives. As financial resources accumulate, expenditures trend toward luxurious lifestyle choices. Future investments are directed at producing greater wealth, leaving fewer funds available for scientific and technological innovation.

Planned Obsolescence

Planned obsolescence is the deliberate design of products to be obsolete in order to require replacement. This tactic is ludicrous and reprehensibly wasteful, but it guarantees perpetual markets, thus enabling the financial elite to further aggregate resources. The cost to society is that innovation is directed toward slight improvements in existing products and not toward technological breakthroughs.

Diminished Public Sector Spending

Diminished public sector spending occurs when the government delegates spending for scientific and technological projects to free market forces. Many of the greatest breakthroughs of the 1950s and 1960s resulted from government-funded laboratories and research institutes managed through the National Science Foundation (although a scientific elite was created that institutionalized materialism). As research shifted to the private sector, progress has slowed since the aspiration is not innovation but profit maximization.

Investment Safety

Investment safety is the net result of diminished public sector spending. Corporations and venture funding seek investment safety and allocate funds for improvements to existing technologies and products, not true innovation. Such is the current state of affairs. Governments can be more venturesome with financial resources than private companies due to the ability to withstand poor investment decisions through fiscal and monetary policies.

These four aspects speak volumes of the entrenched levels of human ignorance. And these are just a few examples of our collective unintelligence. The result is stagnation and societal collapse. Jared Diamond in his book *Collapse: How Societies Choose to Fail or Succeed* noted many historical similarities in the decline of civilizations that prove our collective incompetence; typically, overpopulation and environmental factors contribute significantly to such collapse.[152] Any society's inability to anticipate potentially destructive phenomena can lead to disaster. America and the vast majority of the world's nations possess poor anticipatory abilities, which may not only result from the homogeneity of economic globalization but also from the deeper scientific materialism on which it depends.

In conclusion, there are a number of factors that contribute to scientific and societal stagnation, and all of them can be traced to a resistance of new ideas. Academia becomes a materialist fortress. Corporations concern themselves with how materialism (technology) can increase their profits, and rare is the corporation (even those employing many scientists) that seeks true scientific breakthroughs. Elites protect privilege by advancing materialist worldviews, which causes society to stagnate and deteriorate. Nevertheless, voices—new voices—are heard, the augurs of a new paradigm demanding systemic reform. The materialist worldview is nearly finished, to be replaced by a paradigm of Mind, the possibilities virtually limitless. Such is the reason the initial corruption of Consciousness has been so detrimental to the human adventure, for it delayed the liberation it sought so desperately to discover.

The Corruption of Consciousness

Unfortunately, the movement to elevate Mind above Matter, what historians term the *New Age*, appropriated Consciousness as a type of "me" experience. The New Age became an egocentric extension of the individual with the word *Consciousness* considered nothing more than a trendy metaphysical jargon connoting massive self-absorption and introspective absurdity. Where Consciousness could have taken its first substantial step toward its correct place in the hierarchy of nature, it was instead perverted into a societal embarrassment.

Consciousness as a concept has extended from Antiquity into our modern age, as have some rather famous esoteric attempts to describe its nature. The more notorious of these were *Transcendentalism*, the *Theosophical Society*, *Romanticism*, and the *Human Potential Movement*. The latter produced the

New Age, which emphasized spirituality combined with individuality and focused on universal energy as the common thread in all living things. Its philosophy was unique: the goodness of mankind was assumed, evil was ignored, society and its institutions were cast as dubious, and the individual reigned supreme. Everything had to be transcended by increased personal awareness and linkage to a larger universal power.

As a reaction against the spent materialist reliance on logic and reason, also known as *Secular Humanism*, the New Age Movement sought the elevation of inner "essence" or personal Consciousness to discern truth. Spirit energy was the core of an individual and was also considered a fundamental and connective force able to access the universal Mind. Humans were seen as the best hope for themselves and the planet if they could self-actualize; collectively, this self-actualization would transform society on a global scale, inspiring an era of unprecedented social justice and spiritual wisdom.

Another inherent belief was the "oneness" of everything, including a oneness of Mind; central is that increased awareness accelerates evolution to its natural ends. Thus, New Age philosophy is both psychological and teleological; the individual mind is used to advance both personal and universal outcomes. Consider the following:

> **New Age psychology is closely tied to the belief that we can hasten the progress of evolution by achieving a *higher consciousness,* which is the central goal of the New Age movement. Psychology provides the means to achieve this goal.**[153]

Note how Mind is being personalized to fulfill individual agendas. Critics have customarily noted the egotistical nature of any form of *Esotericism* (self-directed access to universal truth) of which the New Age Movement was the latest iteration, but this version commenced an unabashed, historically unprecedented self-centeredness that was simply preposterous. Adherents binged on individual expression. Mind, however, is a fundamental property of nature, not something to be arrogated for personal benefit. Moreover, Consciousness existed way before humans ever walked the Earth, so it is incredibly hubristic to expropriate Mind for individual purposes and claim it as your own.

Curiously, the New Age phenomenon was positioned between traditional religions and scientific materialism, tantamount to a rebellion against both. Hence, it became a dogmatic ideology arrayed against virtually everyone else. Christian fundamentalism was rejected as was scientism. Virtually all forms of progressive spiritualism were welcomed, including astrology, yoga, mediumship, and transpersonal psychology. Facets of materialism were also utilized, especially staples of classical physics such as momentum, energy, motion, and forces, while rejecting the physicalist interpretation of solid matter. Incredibly bizarre was how something as *relativistic* (no absolute truth, only particular truths) as its ideology could also be so absolute. Adherents of the New Age were particularly passionate about their beliefs, causing vociferous condemnation from both religious leaders and social progressives.

The New Age corruption of Consciousness extended beyond the personal realm and into grand conceptual frameworks. Mind required a holistic nature so the individual could anchor to it. In short, Mind had to be a real thing, tangible and authentic, accessible by spirit energy but verified only by individual experience. Thus, Mind became the medium, an access mechanism to the Divine. More importantly, Mind was viewed as a feature of reality and not its ground. Consciousness was seen not as proof of an original Mind but instead as an endless ocean willing to be drawn. Many adherents of the New Age Movement actually believed they were gods, every individual a spiritual authority, allowing them to ascertain superior truths inaccessible to the unenlightened masses.

For this reason, advocates typically dressed a certain way and used common idioms, thereby proving their transformation and "legitimizing" their beliefs. The New Age Movement is eclectic, borrowing from religion, science, history, and philosophy; Mind is replete in all these traditions and easy to appropriate. The "oneness" aspect acted as an all-encompassing blanket able to welcome ideas from anywhere and where suitability became the selector. That not only widened the audience but fashioned Mind into the form of the aspirant.

Consider the following as an example:

> **Ladies and gentlemen, welcome to the New Age, where you can be as ignorant, stupid, vague, ridiculous, foolish, inaccurate, superstitious and open-ended as you like. Feel free to take any bit of any science, religion, philosophy or ancient mystical superstition you like, mix them all together, and create your very own vague spiritual quilt masterpiece with lots of long-sounding words that will make you seem like what you've dreamt up is a profound revelation.[154]**

But as physicalism denies Consciousness for its atheistic purposes, so does the New Age Movement utilize Mind for its conceit. **The New Age Movement discredited the concept of Consciousness, impeding the natural progression and recognition of the primacy of Mind.** As Quantum Mechanics discovered Consciousness in a new and incontrovertible way, so did the New Age Movement regress Mind to its often ambiguous origins.

In conclusion, the New Age Movement and its corruption of Consciousness contribute to societal stagnation by delaying the emergence of a new paradigm. Although the New Age Movement has transformed itself into the *new spiritualism,* its deleterious effects are witnessed throughout society. Consciousness is a word more likely to be ridiculed by the many than embraced by the few. That appears to be the New Age legacy. Regardless, the march of Consciousness as fundamental to reality is inexorable. It is to this progression we next turn our attention.

CHAPTER 9

The Supremacy of Consciousness

As we have seen, history reveals periods where breakthroughs occur and knowledge transforms. Such transformation is invariably agonizing for entrenched interests but enormously necessary for societal advancement. Many significant discoveries violate existing beliefs, arriving in a state of incredulity concomitant with the natural instinct to discount the new information. Consider the words of Thomas Kuhn:

> **In science, . . . novelty emerges only with difficulty, manifested by resistance, against a background provided by expectation.**[155]

When Quantum Mechanics first linked the properties and behavior of the atomic and subatomic worlds to Consciousness, an interesting transformation occurred; where once Mind sought to discover, it now became the discovered. We did not find truth as much as truth found us. Traditional science has renounced this fact because of its revolutionary consequence: Mind is not a product of the physical, but rather the physical is a product of the Mind. Hence, mainstream science exists in a state of denial.

Consciousness over Materialism

The new order is thus the Consciousness Paradigm in which Mind is launched into supremacy and materialism is relegated to the conductor of the physical realm, inventing products and gadgets to improve our lives. Materialists are incapable of the deepest insights into reality because their training and worldview preclude objectivity. For example, only one primary revelation is to be made of Mind, denied by the physicalists but summarized perfectly by physicist Erwin Schrödinger:

The total number of minds in the universe is one.[156]

Only the Mind of God is foundational, the supreme oneness and totality of everything. Materialists will never comprehend this aspect of nature. Worse, they dupe the public with ridiculous interpretations such as *many worlds* and *decoherence* designed to salvage materialist beliefs from their own contradictory discoveries. That will become clearer as we proceed.

After the discoveries of Planck, Einstein, Bohr, and Heisenberg, the scientific community sought to largely ignore the *Consciousness as Primary* aspect of Quantum Mechanics. That was tacitly supported by governments because exploitation of the material realm was in the perceived national interest and also because the inherency of Consciousness prioritizes spiritual questing, diminishing consumerism. This may sound conspiratorial, but consider that governments have a crucial interest in social cohesion; stability results from a strong economy, from producers and consumers obeying the market, and in the words of Karl Marx, "objectifying" themselves as the masses are unconcerned with the larger questions of reality. Elites seek conformity, preferring that humans not think for themselves. History has clearly demonstrated this fact. Thus, Mind as fundamental was sacrificed as a form of societal regulation, a regulation deemed absolutely imperative in an internationally competitive nuclear age. Moreover, spiritual matters were best managed with traditional religion without an official acknowledgement of the *idealistic* nature of reality, faith ensuring conformity and materialism advancing technological society.

Governments should not have worried. The Consciousness Paradigm will not cause social anarchy or replace mainstream science but will rather solidify order and expand possibilities. Where materialism stagnates, Consciousness emerges. This transformation of worldviews will prove more contributive to understanding reality than all the other branches of knowledge combined. The following represents only a partial list of what may be discovered from a prioritization of Mind:

- **Mind and Information form creative power**

- **Energy and Consciousness together form physical reality**

- **Mind as the matrix of all matter**

- **Confirmation of different realms**

- **Singularity as pure Mind**

- **Relationship of Consciousness to Spirit**

We will examine each of these individually, but if Mind is as primary and unitary as experiments demonstrate, they are all interwoven. In fact, the study of Mind might reveal unification principles currently beyond conjecture. In any case, the following represents some of the possibilities.

Mind and Information forming creative power may be recognized as the driver of nature. Some have theorized that Mind and Information (creative power) will be added to the known fundamental forces; in truth, it extends deeper than that. *Creative Power is likely the force behind the forces. Not only is Creative Power evident, but it implies something larger.* Consciousness and Information are their own entities, but unlike the other forces, they are causative of nature, including the other fundamental forces. Something exists behind this Creative Power.

Whereas Mind has been considered primary (to *idealists*, not *realists*), Information has only recently been added to the equation. Like Mind, Information cannot be reduced to a simpler framework (except to the Consciousness that originates it, although it can have nearly endless expressions) and precedes the fundamental forces. Its inherency is obvious, but like Consciousness, it is also contradictory to materialism. Egnor noted this in his article "Is Information the Basis for the Universe?"

> **In the materialist-dominated world of modern science, it is natural to infer that matter (or fields that move matter) is the fundamental reality. But careful consideration of nature, and particularly biology, suggests that information is the basic reality, of which matter is a medium in which information is manifest.**[157]

Information is innate in the universe. Everything contains Information. From the size and mass of the universe to the ordering of galaxies to the particulars of our solar system and down to a 3-billion code instruction human DNA, details and data are everywhere. From the quantum to the universe, everything is filled with Information.

That inspires some questions. What is the relationship between Mind and Information? Does one precede the other? Do they work together? Are they separable or always fused? First, in order for Information to exist, there has to be a *something*. This *something* may be the only thing preceding Information. That sounds like Mind. Thus, some entity existed before the universe, an essence sufficiently creative to "invent" other Information. The inventor of Information could thus use it to construct a physical universe *and* provide Information a place to abound. Logically, Mind creates Information, but Information cannot create Mind. First Mind is paramount, containing all knowledge, including the formation of the properties, constants, fundamental forces, and particulate nature of the universe. Whereas physicalism concerns details, Consciousness concerns sources. Imagine what can be learned by studying foundations instead of derivatives.

Energy and Consciousness together form physical reality is the next possibility. Einstein proved in the Theory of Relativity that matter and energy are equivalent. When matter is analyzed at its deepest levels, it is found to be composed of spinning, vibrating, invisible energy. This matter and its foundational energy are known to be a product of Consciousness. Energy left to its own devices would not form matter. It requires the addition of Mind to construct material substance, the *Observer Effect* in Quantum Mechanics, making electrons actual things out of probabilistic potential. Somehow, energy and Consciousness work together to provide the material nature of our universe.

That also inspires a number of questions. Is energy simply Mind dispersed throughout the universe? Is Mind made of energy? Are energy and Mind separable, or do they always work together? Does energy contain Information?

We can turn to the Laws of Thermodynamics for potential answers to these questions. The first law states that energy can be changed from one form to another, but it cannot be created or destroyed. The second law states that in this transference, a small amount of energy is invariably lost as heat, or what is known as *entropy*, resulting in less energy available for work. Thus, the universe is diminishing. We know the ultimate Mind, the Great Consciousness, is eternal and cannot diminish. As a result, Mind is not made of energy. That means the two are separable; it also means that energy is not the dispersal of Mind throughout the universe. Energy contains Information, but Information is not made of energy. This delineation forms the following hierarchy:

Mind

Information

Energy

Material

First Mind uses Information, of which a certain ordering forms Energy, which ultimately establishes the Material. The physicalism preferred by materialists is actually the result of the informational and energetic processes that precede it, including creative power. Instead of being foundational, Material is actually an outcome of Mind; the Consciousness evident through the experimental results of Quantum Mechanics is merely a remnant of creation, a sign of the handiwork of the Great Consciousness yet powerful enough to act as an adjoining force to everything in existence.

Mind as the matrix of all matter, a phrase attributed to Max Planck, is thus another possibility we must discuss. A matrix is defined as "something that constitutes the place or point from which something else originates, takes form, or develops."[158] Everything in creation is related to everything else, so all Information, Energy, and Material are related to each other with the Great Consciousness as the Source. That means Mind is an underlying connective power, the bonding agent of the universe. The following quote demonstrates how nature reflects this quality:

> **When atoms combine to form molecules they exchange electrons. When an electron goes into an atom (or ion) it somehow knows which orbit it can enter, and which not. This is a fundamental principle that governs the structure of matter. It implies that the electron knows enough about the other electrons that are already there. And no known physical force is responsible for enforcing this behavior. It would seem therefore that elementary particles are in some way interconnected through consciousness.**[159]

Notice the fine-tuning designed into atoms. Mind is everywhere, found even in the minutest particles, and atomic exchanges are specifically structured to allow Material to form. Like DNA, atomic structures are incredible displays of intricacy. That requires a supreme intelligence, nature incapable of this type of elaborate configuration without a designer.

There is one additional point concerning the capacitating nature of Consciousness. Mind is more than just a causative agent; it is imbued in the universe in order for Information to have full utility—a potency, if you will, since sentient beings bring Information to life by observing it. When Consciousness observes, it not only manifests physical reality but also substantiates the value of Information contained within that reality. From this substantiation, we are enabled to use Information to expand ourselves. *Mind is causative, confirmative,* and *creative.* Our mind comes from First Mind, which is the ultimate matrix and source of everything.

Confirmation of different realms is another possibility for the Consciousness Paradigm. It would be anthropocentric to believe our reality is the only reality. We discussed in Chapter 3 the possibility of various levels of reality and reviewed numerous formulations on the subject. Since Mind is a type of creative and unitary power, theoretically it is a common thread throughout all levels of reality. Understanding Consciousness would thus provide access to whatever other realms exist. Consider our previous discussion regarding the dialectic and paradigms. Mind is likely the engine that powers the dialectic (although Hegel believed the dialectic contained its own immanent force), and paradigms themselves are products of Mind, worldviews being an aggregation of ideas and beliefs. Thus, the evolution of Consciousness over time forms new ways to comprehend totality, Mind leading to the eventual identification of various realms.

Singularity as pure Mind is the next concept we must examine. The initial singularity, the thing that existed immediately before the Big Bang, is defined as "a point in space-time where the laws of physics as we know them break down."[160] The materialist premise is that initially all matter and energy in the universe existed in a state of infinite density compressed into something about as big as the human head. Then random quantum fluctuations occurred and caused the Big Bang. This is unproved and even preposterous. Can you imagine hundreds of billions of galaxies, each containing hundreds of billions of stars and planets, all compressed into something the size of a cranium? No.

To be equitable, science is beginning to realize the absurdity of the initial singularity argument and is constructing competing theories. One such theory posits that the universe never had a beginning and instead has existed forever with no origination and no end.[161] Another interpretation is that although there was a Big Bang, there was never a singularity with the universe existing forever as quantum potential.[162] Even mathematics does not support the materialist singularity. Other theories suggest that the Big Bang never happened.[163] Significant is that criticism of the Big Bang and singularity often comes from atheistic scientists who have no theistic axe to grind.[164] Thus, even mainstream science (materialist doctrine) is beginning to disagree with itself.

We can keep with the singularity concept (although, as noted above, the term carries some unproven materialist connotations) in order to make the following points. As we have discussed, the Great Consciousness preceded all existence. Mind was the complete storehouse of all Information. Creation, the Big Bang, and so forth unleashed this creative power, forming the material universe. Consciousness was found to be fundamental. The antecedental history of Consciousness confirms First Mind, preceding and causing the Singularity. It can be illustrated in the following way:

Great Consciousness

Information

Material Universe

Antecedental Consciousness

Great Consciousness

Thus, all existence leads to a Great Consciousness as the source and the conclusion, with God as the singularity. First Mind is responsible for our universe and every level of reality.

Relationship of consciousness to Spirit is the last concept to be discussed. Mind, as we have learned, is not dependent on anything physical; in fact, by its very definition, Mind is ethereal. Hence, if the universe is *idealistic*, comprised of Mind and Spirit, then both are either closely related or extensions of each other. Hegel believed that Spirit is Consciousness and positioned them as one and the same.[165] Often, Consciousness has been compared to Soul, with philosophers arguing that humans have a material nature (Body) and an immaterial nature (Soul and Spirit). In one view, the immaterial nature is comprised of Soul and Spirit together, and in the other, Soul and Spirit are separate.[166] Throughout history, theologians, philosophers, intellectuals, and even scientists have attempted to draw distinctions among Mind, Soul, Spirit, and Body. One of the hopes of the Consciousness Paradigm is that a more thorough and correct understanding of Consciousness and Spirit will emerge.

Soul, which we will examine in much greater detail in Chapter 10, is often portrayed as an intermediary between Mind and Spirit, a quintessence that animates the living so thoughts and emotions are linked from the physical body to the eternal Spirit.[167] Typically, Soul and Spirit are considered commensurately, the difference being that Spirit is an eternal essence and Soul a small piece of that essence placed into humans. In this sense, Soul is derivative from Spirit. This derivative framework also applies to Mind since Consciousness displayed in the universe is derivative from the original Great Consciousness.

A high level of enigmatic interconnection exists among Body, Mind, Soul, and Spirit; their exact configuration and interdependence is currently beyond human comprehension. Obviously, physicalist worldviews will never prove productive enough to understand immaterial essences. The Consciousness Paradigm offers the best hope of exploring the interdependence of these universal essentials and developing a feasible taxonomy. Since our inquiry demonstrates the numinous nature of reality, it is imperative that we more thoroughly examine the concept of Soul. If the universe is incorporeal at its base, Soul assumes extreme importance in the human experience and also links to the larger spiritual essence of the universe. What the body is to *realism*, soul is to *idealism*. Next we will explore the significance of Soul and how it supplants the materialist reliance on a physical frame as primary to human experience.

CHAPTER 10

The Soul

Fundamentally, we are souls.

The concept of a soul appears esoteric and unconfirmable. Yet many circumstances in life suggest that soul and physical corroborations are being witnessed on a nearly daily basis. All are beyond traditional scientific explanation. Whether soul can be definitively verified through our current methodologies is questionable, but it appears we are making progress toward that end. Highly respected academics and courageous scientists are studying the issue and often venturing their reputations in furtherance of objective truth.

Confirmation of the Soul

Historically, Soul has been equated with Mind, specifically the character, intellect, perception, and rationality of a human being. That is true in both religion and philosophy. We can briefly summarize the main positions—everything in the universe has a soul; only humans have souls; only humans have immortal souls; souls are separate from bodies; souls form bodies; and souls and bodies form two distinct aspects of reality.[168] The only unanimity on the subject has, of course, come from the materialists who deny the existence of Soul.

Nevertheless, some new research demonstrates that Soul is either Mind or closely related to Mind, and that Soul represents the actual seat of an individual. Some theories such as *Biocentrism* position life as central to the universe, with

Soul a natural correlate of that life.[169] In fact, an increasing number of materialist scientists are beginning to recognize that Consciousness survives physical death.[170] Many universities study the subject, and academic peer-reviewed journals and published scientific papers have explored the phenomenon in depth. The level of technological sophistication and empirical rigor equals or exceeds all scientific standards, and experimental results are nothing short of incredible.[171]

Other researchers have posited Mind and Soul as likely separate. Their experiments have only obfuscated the issue (such as simply directing subjects to raise their hands and lower them) by demonstrating that the brain reacts to commands from an external source and does not initiate the activity.[172] Apparently, the command is extrinsic to the brain, originating independently of any physical cause. What is this commanding source? Is this Mind or Soul? Perhaps it is both? Could Mind and Soul be separable but act as one? For example, consider the following:

"[S]omething outside of itself" is: the soul, or, more specifically, the consciousness, which is the intrinsic energy of the soul temporarily projected into the body. Modern science offers us strong proof for the existence of the soul.[173]

That demonstrates the complexity of the issue and further frames our discussion. Typically, a distinction is drawn between Mind and Soul, with the Body acting as the impetus for their separability. Before coming into a physical body, the assumption is that both are one essence. A more logical framework will be discussed shortly where both are independently caused and where Soul results from Spirit with mental attributes of Mind, but what matters is that both Mind and Soul cannot be located by materialist science, nor can they be understood in physicalist terms.

In previous chapters, we have seen that Mind defies physical description, yet it is indisputably a fact of existence; Soul is similar, being autonomous, self contained, and immaterially distinct, eluding detection by materialist means but often witnessed. A growing database of evidence exists, demonstrating Soul as separate from Body, especially after physical death. The first of these sensational and well-documented pieces of evidence is the Near-Death Experience (NDE). Interestingly, NDE is a historical phenomenon that affects humans from various socioeconomic and cultural backgrounds, from small children to the elderly, all religious faiths represented and including atheists with virtually all segments of society recounting similar details. Consider the following from the International Association for Near-Death Studies:

> **One of the fascinating aspects of NDEs is "veridical percep-tion," in which the near-death experiencer reports seeing or hearing events during their NDEs that, given the condition and/or position of their physical bodies, should have been impossible to perceive but are nevertheless corroborated as accurate.**[174]

Although dead, experiencers perceive the world around them. This should be impossible, but if we accept that Mind or Soul is a separate entity independent of a physical brain, then the phenomenon makes sense. In fact, it is the only logical explanation. In the classic NDE, the individual dies, travels through a tunnel of light, meets spiritual beings, feels a constant presence of love and peace, and returns to life with details that are simply impossible to know while dead. Some cases concern people who are blind from birth yet report details while dead that require sight, a sense they obviously never possessed in life. Consider the follow-ing that discusses how the blind "see" when they have never experienced vision:

> **In this type of awareness, it is not of course that the eyes see anything; it is rather that the mind itself sees, but more in the sense of "understanding" or "taking in" than of visual perception as such. Or alternatively we might say that it is not the eye that sees, but the "I."**[175]

Blind experiencers recount colors, physical details, building configurations, and spatial relationships that cannot be apprehended by those without sight. Often, their reporting includes details that are only possible from raised vantage points. Even those blessed with sight cannot replicate their visual perspectives. They have no frame of reference for these things and could not invent them in their imaginations, certainly not to the point where they match reality and certainly not while dead. If the NDE is a glimpse of the soul, then soul has panoramic vision and incredible recollective abilities.

Perhaps more interesting is that experiencers often report that when their Consciousness is external to their body, everything is more real. That is known as *Hyper Reality*. It suggests that the level of Mind is more actual than the physical reality we know. Logically, that makes sense because Consciousness is the ground of all being and would thus be experienced as primary and greater in magnitude. The following is a summation of the phenomenon from Charles Paccione's article "Tunnel of Light: Making Sense of Near-Death Experiences" in *Brain World* magazine:

> **[N]ear-death experiences are commonly felt as being "more real than everyday life." Colors, smells, and sensations become fully optimized like never before.**[176]

This adds credibility to the *idealistic* interpretation of the universe where Mind and Spirit are fundamental to reality. NDE is a Consciousness phenomenon, one full of spiritual implications, suggesting that the intrinsic level of existence is one of Spiritual Mind. In this respect, Soul may be a small fusion of Consciousness and Spirit that reflects the nature of the Great Consciousness, the proverbial "man made in the image of God." Logically, the universe would have characteristics of its designer; if the Great Consciousness has mental and spiritual properties, the universe will be filled with Mind and Spirit. That is what we witness in quantum experimentation. Soul is thus the human link to the Divine filled with both mental and spiritual aspects.

NDE also provides additional validation of our previous exploration of levels of reality. The Near-Death Experience provides a glimpse of another level of being that is more abundant, powerful, promising, and delightful. From the reports of experiencers, our reality is subordinate to the *Hyper Reality* and not as glorious. That substantiates our theorization that levels of reality contain a hierarchy. We may never know the extent of this hierarchy, but the physical realm is obviously subsidiary. Therefore, Earth is apparently an intermediate physical location and definitely not our final home.

Other facets of our existence allude to the existence of the soul, although they are not as veridical as in the Near-Death Experience. *Out-of-Body Experiences* (OBEs) and *Astral Projection* are some of these soul-suggestive phenomena. In an OBE, the individual suddenly finds themselves able to perceive the world from a point external to their body.[177] In Astral Projections, this ability is done intentionally with forethought and focus. The Near-Death Experience, however, is survival of Consciousness after physical death. These latter two phenomena are an extension of Mind while physically alive. Often, the individual is able to pass through material structures and travel vast distances. Shifting awareness and vibrational energies are also common. Deep religious histories are associated with these phenomena that are witnessed throughout all societies and demographic groups, even achieving a place of status in various cultures.[178]

If Soul, which is classically related to Consciousness, is the agent in these phenomena, it exhibits similar qualities as Mind. Consciousness is exceptional, capable of collapsing the wave function of an atom and thus possibly extending itself beyond the physical body with quantum nonlocality; Soul is also likely to be as exceptional. Many qualities such as telepathy and psychic abilities suggest a sameness of Mind and Soul, while others such as connection to nature or religious prayer suggest that the two are distinct (as Soul dominates). The point is that humans have immaterial capabilities, albeit rarely observed or utilized, that demonstrates transcendence past material bounds. Mind and Soul act similarly, the former probably more universally and the latter more individually, in what might be termed SoulMind. Thus, SoulMind is a fusion, and until a separability of Mind and Soul can be confirmed through experimentation, we can view them as one entity.

SoulMind is thus superior to the brain and, in fact, to anything physical; it requires no physical structure. As previously noted, science advocates Mind originating in neural and synaptic processes in the brain, although the Great Consciousness did not require a physical brain, and neither do the minds placed in us. Mind works with the brain, the latter likely a transceiver of Consciousness much in the same way that Soul works with Body. The key is the linkage. Somehow, integration occurs, even between material and immaterial forms, an integration for which we have no definitive theories.

Near-Death Experience and mental capabilities such as Astral Projection point toward a reality past materialism. If Soul is the connection to the *Hyper Reality*, Soul exists in both physical and spiritual realms; logically, Soul would have knowledge of both realities. This knowledge implies awareness of a superior realm not experienced on Earth. Yet for existence in our reality, Soul would have to be simplified or made less aware of its grander base. The perfect mechanism for this is a physical body, specifically the brain. Thus, contrary to materialist belief and adoration, the brain is not this wonderful biological computer but rather a basic simplification device. Many NDE experiencers report that the purpose of life is Soul growth, of learning lessons one cannot learn in the Spirit realm. If this is true, then simplification of the Soul is necessary to even participate in this reality. The Soul would have to be made less intelligent, or its knowledge would undermine its purposes here. That might be the reason *Hyper Reality* feels more real since the Soul regains its acuity once it departs the physical frame.

As mentioned, materialists are highly skeptical of the possibility of Soul since for them it defies scientific description and empirical validation. However, there have been scientific attempts to record or scientifically measure the human soul using biological energy and gas discharge technologies.[179] Results suggestive of Soul have also been shown (quite convincingly, according to some) using particle detectors.[180] More scientific attempts will be made in the future. And though the Soul has never been empirically proved by traditional methodologies, presumption of its existence is driving other scientific endeavors such as artificial intelligence.[181]

Soul in the Universe

Soul leads to a metaphysical conclusion about the nature of the universe. Everything points toward an immaterial actuality, a universe comprised of

Consciousness and Spirit as summarized by the following quote from English physicist Sir James Jeans:

> **The stream of knowledge is heading toward a non-mechanical reality; the universe begins to look more like a great thought than like a great machine. . Mind no longer appears to be an accidental intruder into the realm of matter; we ought rather hail it as the creator and governor of the realm of matter. Get over it, and accept the inarguable conclusion. The universe is immaterial, mental and spiritual.**[182]

Although this is informative and even inspirational, Jeans exalts the primacy of Consciousness without specifically relating it to First Mind. He also notes the existent spiritual element without linkage to the source of Spirit. According to Jeans, Mind and Spirit constitute the universe as forces of their own without cause or antecedent. The position here is that he is missing some key interconnections. The correct ordering is as follows:

- **The lineage of Mind leads to a Great Consciousness.**

- **The Great Consciousness is God. He is also a Spirit.**

- **God's nature fills the universe with Consciousness and Spiritual Essence, proving the *idealistic* nature of reality.**

- **Soul is placed into man by God, animating the body. Soul results from Spirit.**

- **Humans are a composite of Mind, Body, Spirit, and Soul.**

- **Soul links the material and spiritual realms.**

Soul is thus an important aspect of the universe. For humans, it is our eternal core with the body nothing more than a physical housing. The following sums it up:

You do not have a soul. You are a soul. You have a body.[183]

Soul incorporates mental and spiritual properties, an integration placed into a physical body. It provides humans with four fundamental aspects of existence, their hierarchy demonstrated as follows:

The Individual

Soul
Spirit
Mind
Body

The Soul is the ultimate self of an individual, a part of Spiritual Essence, with the individual Mind a product of a larger Consciousness and the Body acting as a container. Successful integration of these four fundamental aspects of existence characterize the individual.[184] As the Body degrades, so does the material realm from whence it originates, the former through death and the latter through entropy. Soul, Spirit, and Mind are products of the immaterial realm, thus more expansive and also eternal. Consider the following from Hans-Peter Dürr, former director of the Max Planck Institute for Physics:

> **What we consider the here and now, this world, it is actually just the material level that is comprehensible. The beyond is an infinite reality that is much bigger.**[185]

What we glimpse by our relatively limited knowledge of Soul, Spirit, and Mind is a suggestion of a higher domain. That is the *Hyper Reality* discussed in NDE, a majestic realm far surpassing our familiar material universe. Science should emphasize the study of Soul, Spirit, and Mind since our physical body is a facade. Whether individually or collectively, these facets of life must be examined because nothing is more imperative than the eternal Soul.

We have seen that Soul is a complex issue appearing as an integration of Mind and Spirit but nevertheless ineluctably placed into a physical body. This placement is a fusion of sorts. Could Soul and Body assimilate through energetic properties, quantum entanglement, wave functions, or informational characteristics? Are there as yet undiscovered spiritual atoms and particles that interface with material existence? Is soul analogous to a hologram, there in form but not materially actual? Does an Etheric Body exist, a type of intermediary state between spiritual essence and physical frame? Answers to these questions have significant implications for Soul in our reality, yet they have proved unknowable. The best we can do is speculate on the theoretical positioning of Soul within the universe. The following diagram illustrates the framework:

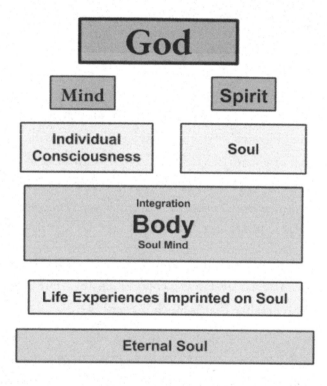

We live in a universe comprised of Mind and Spirit emanating from an original Great Consciousness. Mind generates Individual Consciousness as Spirit generates Soul. Somehow through an undetermined mechanism, both Consciousness and Soul integrate into a physical body, forming SoulMind. As noted, the brain works as a transceiver of Consciousness and simplifies both Mind and Soul so each can exist in material reality. The physical uniqueness of each brain ensures different intelligences, capabilities, interests, and motivations; that, in addition to other factors, secures different choices and experiences, all imprinted on the human soul. Death separates the soul from the body, but the soul transcends as a composite of Mind, Soul, and Experience that lives eternally.

We must remember that Soul animates the Body but results from Spirit, the immaterial bringing life to the material. That provides a key insight into the nature of the designer. The Great Consciousness is alive. It is His essence that originates life into the physical domain. Without First Mind there is no life, no chemistry, no biology, no human beings, no soul, and no hope for life. God provides meaning to existence. In addition, wisdom is imparted to souls through their experience of reality; thus, life is a learning format with an incalculable amount of lessons.

Here is one final point. Throughout our study, when considering how the immaterial constructs the material, indeed how Mind, Body, Soul, and Spirit integrate, we are forced to conclude that physical reality is a type of illusion. Immaterial essence (a nothing of sorts) forming Material reality (a something of sorts) appears impossible. *The real is made of the unreal.* In effect, the universe is fraudulent, and nature is a game of deception perpetrated on us and even on itself. The world is a stage built of nothing but real enough for souls to learn actual lessons. So how can reality so delude? What is the origin of this ruse? Let us explore that next.

CHAPTER 11

The Matrix

I guess we can say the word—*Simulation*. The immaterial nature of the universe points to a type of *Simulation* as the rational explanation for reality. A common theme in science fiction, the word carries some negative connotations. Nevertheless, when something is made of nothing, that suggests simulation. In the ceaseless struggle between *idealism* and *realism*, simulation is assimilative of both. The universe appears material but is made of immaterial essence. This duality reflects the divide between classical physics and Quantum Mechanics. Yet what is the nature of the simulation, and who created it? What is its purpose? We can consider both physicalist and spiritualist perspectives.

The Universe as a Materialist Simulation

A simulation is "a representation of a real activity, created for training purposes or to solve a problem."[186] A simulation can also be defined as "the act of imitating the behavior of some situation or some process by means of something suitably analogous."[187] In short, a simulated reality resembles the real reality in the same way our material reality resembles the *Hyper Reality*. The key point is that only one reality is truly original.

Thus, if our reality is a simulation, then it shares characteristics with all simulations such as the selection of certain attributes, behaviors, assumptions, estimates, anticipations, outcomes, initial conditions, and data evolution. Crucial to the effectiveness of the simulation is a measurement of its accuracy or fidelity. Productive simulations are also managed over time in order to more accurately approach the base reality. This management can entail adjustments, estimations, limitations, and methodizations. Finally, simulations exist for a purpose, typically to see where errors occurred or to measure outcomes.

Many types of simulations exist in a variety of disciplines, including education, manufacturing, economics, flight, robotics, and military planning. **Fundamentally, though, simulations exist so something can be learned.** We should also note that some simulations, known as *interactive simulations*, allow for human participation where the learning is done for the benefit of the participants, not the designer. We can see how this might relate to Souls and First Mind.

It is an axiom of life that philosophical formulations reflect the current state of knowledge. Once quantum experimentation revealed the inherent immateriality of the universe, the possibility of simulation increased. Moreover, the Information Age, specifically vast amounts of computing power, offered the possibility that reality can be simulated using advanced technology. Since our society has indeed made tremendous technological progress, we must explore this possibility. While doing so, we must also consider metaphysical possibilities such as God creating a simulated universe in order to achieve specific objectives.

First, let us look at the technological argument for simulation. Although the computational power to perform a computer-generated simulation as extensive as our universe is currently lacking, it has been hypothesized that such power will exist in the future. A further assumption is that in the next stage of our development, we will transform into "transhumans" by utilizing technology to enhance human capabilities. This is the proverbial blending of man and machine. One common assumption is that transhumans will have an interest in running computer simulations of their ancestors. The leading proponent of this view is philosopher Niklas Bostrom of the University of Oxford who proposes the following possibilities, one of which is nearly certainly true:

1. **The number of human-like civilizations reaching trans-humanity and running ancestor simulations is negligible.**

2. **The number of transhuman civilizations interested in running simulations of their evolutionary history is negligible.**

3. **The number of all humans with our experiences living in a simulation is close to one.**

Bostrom uses a probabilistic approach to argue that these possibilities are equally likely. But if option 1 and option 2 are both false, then some transhumans will run simulations and thereby create more simulated humans than actual transhumans. The number of simulated civilizations will vastly outnumber actual civilizations. Therefore, any civilization, including our own, is probably one of the simulated versions.[188]

According to Bostrom, humans may survive to transhumanism and possibly run advanced computer simulations that prove we exist in a simulation. The criticisms against his argument are replete. We will examine some of them for their relevance to our previous discussions. The following are arguments against a simulated universe:

- **Potential computer simulations will be limited by the computational power of future technology. Miniaturization has been imperative for progress since the number of components on a microchip has expanded over time. This expansion is currently diminishing, forcing a reliance on nanotechnology (the manipulation of matter on an atomic scale). Miniaturization can only proceed to the atomic and subatomic levels, forcing a lower bound, because there is nothing smaller than atoms. Simulations powerful enough to simulate a universe will therefore be impossible.**

- **Simulation requires Consciousness in humans to be a physical process and replicable by machines. Quantum Mechanics has already decimated this notion. Neither brains nor computers cause Mind.**

- **Soul and Spirit are not things replicated with material means such as computers and software. Their existence disproves simulation.**

- **The Simulation Argument is completely unfalsifiable since it is impossible to devise an experiment to test the concept and prove it false.**

- **The Laws of Complexity mandate that whatever is simulating our universe must be larger and more complex than our universe. Humans would not be able to simulate a universe from within a universe.[189]**

Other criticisms of the Simulation Argument exist. The first concerns extraterrestrials running simulations. Consider the following:

> **The one glitch in the simulation argument is that there is nothing to stop the simulation at one super-advanced posthuman (alien) species. It could very well be that our simulators are, for their part, simulated by even more advanced simulators, and those by even more advanced ones, ad infinitum. Who is the first simulator?[190]**

Extraterrestrials running lots of simulations in a universe teeming with lots of extraterrestrials means lots of additional simulated universes. This sounds disappointingly similar to the Many Worlds Interpretation of Quantum Mechanics, which we have previously proved to be farcical.

Second, any simulation replicating an entire universe would mandate being made of the same materials and properties as the base reality and containing the same complexity of information. This complexity of information would prove impossible to replicate. Even if possible, at that point it is no longer a simulation but rather another base reality. That casts doubt on the necessity of running ancestor simulations. What could be learned from a simulation that was no different than base reality? The simulators could simply study the base reality, rendering the simulation unnecessary.

Third, some simulation advocates take a strong anthropocentric view of nature in that transhumans will be the only ones capable of running simulations. Obviously, as previously mentioned, if extraterrestrials exist, their argument is invalidated. As we will see in subsequent chapters, the existence of extraterrestrials (either from other planets, different dimensions, spiritual domains, or supernatural realms) is virtually assured. Claiming universal territoriality for humans is perhaps the height of self-absorption; the possibility of humanity being alone in the universe is miniscule, and the likelihood of our being the dominant intelligence is laughable.

Fourth, researchers from Oxford University have disproved the Simulation Argument because, simply put, "there aren't enough particles in the universe to simulate the particles in the universe."[191] Their research demonstrated that as the number of potentialities increases in the universe (complexity), the computational power required by computers is simply inadequate for successful simulation. They went even further:

> **The researchers calculated that just storing information about a couple of hundred electrons would require a computer memory that would physically require more atoms than exist in the universe.**[192]

The simulation argument is therefore a materialist attempt at "an innovative form of immortality."[193] If transhumans can build their own perfect universe, they can become their own gods. The reader should recognize this theme: humans attempting to become masters of the universe thereby obviate the necessity of a Creator. So in addition to being common, this theme is also tragic and vouches more to human insecurity and conceit than to assurance and ingenuity.

The biggest hole in the technological argument is that base reality has to originate somewhere; simulations might be simulated—created, if you will—by technology-wielding transhumans, but the original universe must be created by First Mind. That, of course, implies the Great Consciousness has a plan, and it is highly unlikely that the plan includes transhumans simulating perfection to create their own version of heaven.

As products of the Information Age, it is expected that Bostrom and others will extrapolate technology into the future and envision universe-generating simulations. This is no disparagement of Bostrom; his work is truly innovative, and his ideas follow quite rationally from our contemporary, technological world. We run simulations in a number of disciplines, and virtual reality is becoming increasingly realistic. In addition, more sophisticated video games and artificial intelligence provide a foundation for the technological simulation argument. Yet more astounding than technological progression and an insight into the prejudicial mind of many materialists is the embrace of something as unlikely as universal simulation while denying the empirically proven supremacy of Mind. The selective science of the physicalists never ends.

The Universe as an Idealistic Simulation

We have substantiated that the universe is mental and spiritual. That means the universe is fundamentally unreal, resembling a simulation. So could the universe be a simulation created by the First Mind? Are there similarities between a technological simulation and a simulation created by a Great Consciousness?

Perhaps the single greatest similarity is that both would contain "design." Consider the following:

> **The notion [a simulation] is inescapably laden with presuppositions of both design and a real substratum from which the 'simulation' arose. Perhaps we could talk of a 'virtual world' to try and escape implications of design. But that still presupposes a real substratum from which it arises. The point is, if we are in what can be properly termed a 'virtual world' or a 'simulation', then there still must be a real world**

from which the virtual world arises, by the very meaning of those terms.[194]

Let us look at a couple of brief points. Any simulated reality would require an original base reality from which it emanated (our reality and the *Hyper Reality*) and would be filled with incalculable design. Such design implies a simulation that is *fine-tuned*. We have previously established in Chapter 7 that the universe is fine-tuned for life. Either this fine-tuning is an aspect of a computer simulation or something crafted by a First Mind. Which is a more likely designer: First Mind or a computer? Since there are a number of incriminating arguments (as proved earlier in this chapter) against a computer-simulated universe, the designer must be God. That is a profound realization. The fallaciousness of the Simulation Argument actually makes a case for Divine causation: the more improbable that the simulation is caused by computer technology, the more probable that it is caused by a Great Consciousness. Despite the evidence, some materialists would rather put their faith (pun intended) in a transhuman computer programmer than an actual God.

The simulation argument gets even more intricate with some thinkers positing that technology can become its own Supreme Being. We reference here Eric Steinhart's article "Theological Implications of the Simulation Argument."[195] One of the fascinating assertions is the concept of "levels" of simulation (i.e., that simulations can generate other simulations). The passage below offers a wonderful summary:

> **For our purposes, the most striking feature of the Simulation Argument is that it justifies the existence of a series of levels of simulation. Our universe is a virtual machine, a machine running on a deeper machine. . . . How deep does the series of simulations go? . . . Any finite number seems arbitrary. For any finite n, why n levels rather than n+1? A more general principle is more reasonable. And any reasoning that applies to our universe surely applies with equal force to any universe that is simulating our universe. So if there is any plausibility**

> **to the thesis that our universe is being simulated by some deeper universe, then there is equal plausibility to the thesis that every universe is being simulated by some deeper universe. The Simulation Argument supports the general thesis that below every level, there is a deeper level. There is an endless series of ever deeper levels.**[196]

This is somewhat similar to the concept of "levels of reality" discussed in Chapter 3. The article furthers the point by noting that there could be a hierarchy of simulations, and at every level, the above simulators would appear as gods.

> **Bostrom writes that in some ways, the posthumans running a simulation are like gods in relation to the people inhabiting the simulation: the posthumans created the world we see; they are of superior intelligence; they are omnipotent in the sense that they can interfere in the workings of our world even in ways that violate its physical laws; and they are omniscient in the sense that they can monitor everything that happens.**[197]

The natural conclusion to this formulation is that eventually the computer becomes so powerful that it is God. At every level, there can be judgment and the recycling of entities into subsequent simulations (analogous to souls in reincarnation), quite similar to Eastern religious traditions. Only in the final simulation would surviving Consciousness (souls) be complete and join with the simulator, the implication being that increasing complexity becomes divine.

As before, this can be easily refuted since something has to cause the base reality from which all simulations originate. Simulations do not just come into existence and cause subsequent simulations. Significant, though, is the attempted fusion of human technological advancement and the spirituality it so often bitterly opposes. Notice the effort to incorporate whatever evidence exists for God into a technological framework since such incorporation maintains physicalist dogma. Materialism is nothing short of disingenuously creative.

The final exploration of a potentially simulated universe concerns the purpose of simulations. Typically, advocates of simulation acknowledge some degree of universal fine-tuning, and this fine-tuning is attributed to the abilities of the initial programmer. Naturally, this computer expert must result from complex physical processes and not be Divine. Thus, fine-tuning exists not for the emergence of life (as that would prove a Divine Plan) but rather due to innate universal complexity. Consider the following physicalist perspective:

> **We now run a Fine Tuning Argument: (1) Our universe is finely tuned for the evolution of complexity. (2) The best explanation for this fine tuning is that our universe was designed by an intelligence that values the evolution of complexity. . . . It can be applied at every level. And it can be applied to the entire hierarchy of levels. . . . [W]e reason backwards analogically from our own simulations. We typically make simulations for two purposes: science and entertainment. By analogy, it is likely that our designers have made our universe either for science, or for entertainment, or for both. If they have made it for science, then everything that goes on in our universe has *epistemic value*. If they have made it for entertainment, then everything that occurs in our universe has *dramatic value*."[198]**

This intelligence is assumed to be transhumans. Notice the anthropocentricity in this argument with humans superimposing their current belief system on future transhumans. These future transhumans possess God-like powers, but they result from our own evolution. To a materialist, universal complexity ensures that life results from inorganic matter and becomes intelligent, that same intelligence producing technology that enables humans to develop into transhumans. From transhumanity, we evolve into Divine status and eventually create advanced computer simulations. Thus, man is not made in the image of God, but rather God is made in the image of man.

This is way past infatuation with computers. It is way past science fiction. The Great Consciousness is comprised of many things, specifically Mind and Spirit, but it is definitely not the result of iterated technology. First Mind knows all scientific knowledge (since He created it) and does not require entertainment; He would have nothing to learn from a simulation nor would He be amused by it. No, this is a level of hubristic projection by man that is both astonishing and appalling. Once again, the reader is reminded of the ceaseless quest by humans to become their own gods.

So if the evidence against a computer-simulated universe is so convincing, as we have hopefully demonstrated, should it even be mentioned in our study? The answer is yes. Below are a number of reasons:

- **Computer-simulated reality provides a theoretical example of simulation, something unreal appearing real.**

- **Simulation is an ideational construct of how God might have made the material realm from an immaterial base.**

- **Simulation also provides a template for how Information could be used by a designer to build the universe.**

- **The concept of simulation encompasses "levels of reality" where the base reality is the spiritual realm and our reality is simulated.**

The position here is that our universe is a simulation but a simulation created by God. It is not a computer simulation because the intricacy and care with which the universe is constructed is beyond any technological means. It can only be the work of an all-knowing, all-powerful Being. What remains is to explore how Consciousness and Soul exist within the simulation and for what purpose they were constructed.

Consciousness and Soul in the Simulation

If the purpose of a simulation is to learn something, then we must ask who is doing the learning. An all-knowing Great Consciousness does not require learning anything. So the learning is for the participants, specifically humans. Extraterrestrials may also learn, but since we cannot confirm or understand their existence, we will confine this inquiry to humans.

In order to grow in understanding, humans must make choices. They must possess free will. We will not explore all the philosophical perspectives regarding free will due to the subject length and space limitations, but free will is often contested by materialists because it violates determinism (only one course of events is possible). Quantum Mechanics, however, has already established that reality is nondeterministic, thus annihilative of materialism and indicative of individual choice. The position is that humans have free will, and it exists even within a Block Universe, which we will subsequently explore in Chapter 12. Soul, the spiritual component placed into humans by God, is integrated with Consciousness as SoulMind and makes choices as well as being a record of them. Note the following:

Since thoughts are immaterial, we have reason to think a mind/soul is a thinking thing that is *other than* nature. That is to say, a soul is an "immaterial thinking thing."[199]

SoulMind is ethereal and placed into material reality, which is actually a type of simulation, apparently designed so souls can exist in physical bodies and integrate with Mind and make choices. Living in material reality mandates learning lessons since life is extremely difficult. We must survive, share the planet with others, and perpetuate our species. It follows that developing moral character and rules of conduct becomes imperative for survival, as does respecting other humans and their decisions, thus ensuring societal progression.

Religious traditions typically postulate that God made the universe for His glorification and satisfaction. From that, we can assume He wanted humans to appreciate both the designer and the creation. If souls are meant to learn, they are meant to learn about their Creator. We have noted many similarities between a computer-generated simulation of the universe and a Great Consciousness designing our reality; both require a certain degree of faith, and both posit a higher power. The difference is that only with God is the base reality possible. Any subsequent realities, including our own, are products of First Mind. We reflect His essence. Consider the following from Carl Feit, a biologist at Yeshiva University who discusses how pure thought penetrates the enigmas of the universe:

> **Something about human consciousness is harmonious with the mind of God.**[200]

With God, there is a numinousness matching the foundation of the universe. Mind comes from His Mind, and Soul comes from His Spirit. Physicalness is a type of intermediary, a medium whereby Mind and Spirit are granted a stage. Behind the apparency of existence is a purpose known only to God. The design in His creation points to meaningfulness, whereas a computer simulation points only to nihility. Thus, nature reveals Divine forethought, and in Divine forethought there is aspiration for us all.

Relevant Reality

Before we conclude this chapter, we must return to the concept of levels of reality. Quantum Mechanics proves that observation creates reality, that Consciousness is the foundation of the universe. **That means observation manifests an observable reality out of invisible potential, the apparent extracted from the abstract.** That transforms the way we view nature. Consider the following:

> **Understanding this requires shifting the way we think of the universe. We can no longer think of the universe as a physical realm in which the things we observe and sense are all that exists.**[201]

Suggested in this quote is that physical reality is one of many realities. How does the concept of simulation conform to this information? How extensive is this abstract potential? How many layers exist? Is there a way to access the other realities? What would be the reason a designer limits us to one reality? Can we manipulate our reality or other potential realities through the powers of Mind? If the universe is a simulation created by God, are the other realities simulations as well? Or is there just our reality and the *Hyper Reality*? And finally, what is the purpose of potentially assorted realities?

We can rely on a specific quantum truth for some further speculation. Inherent in Quantum Mechanics is *Collapse of the Wave Function*. As we have referenced in earlier chapters, observation collapses the wave function and brings into being an actual reality from a superposition of possibilities. That same dynamic may apply at the universal level. Further, a "reality compound" may exist, and our reality, complete with Body, Mind, Spirit and Soul, was chosen by the designer for certain objectives over other realities. Every reality may have different purposes. It is possible that all realities are entangled. It is also possible that they are fully independent and never interface. At this point, it is impossible to know.

Until such time as we derive answers, we must consider the facts. Whether our reality is the only one emerging from the *Hyper Reality* or one of many other realities matters less than existing at all. What we know for certain is our universe and our place within it, living as we do in the *relevant reality*. Logically, we can assume that *Hyper Reality* is the base reality. **Our reality is the realm of questions, while that reality is the realm of answers.** Perhaps as we discussed in Chapter 3, other realities are also deeper than our reality and contain their own answers; they may be arranged in a hierarchy, each level more intricate and advanced than the one below, building on each other. Once again, we can only suppose their order and complexity.

In conclusion, simulation provides a useful, conceptual framework for unifying the material and immaterial elements in our universe since both are contained within its structure. Our physical realm exists but originates from the incorporeal with only scientific materialism insisting that the former is absolute. This simulated universe—our universe—results from spiritual, not material, foundations and disproves physicalism at its core. Nevertheless, our fate is bound with the reality we experience. Next we must consider the possible fates of the universe since they add much to our speculation about the future.

PART III:

UNIVERSAL DESTINY

CHAPTER 12

The Fate of the Universe

W̲e live in a dramatic time.

Humans find themselves in a unique period of history since a transformational and optimistic paradigm (Consciousness) replaces an entrenched and pessimistic one (Materialist). Perspectives regarding the universe are about to change radically. If reality is a simulation created by a First Mind to achieve certain objectives, the universe will have a previously determined fate. This ultimate end may appear "natural" to us, caused by physical laws, interacting forces, and the passage of time, but it will be destined from the beginning. We cannot know its termination date. What we can do is analyze potential fates of the universe and correlate them to potential objectives of the designer.

Universal Structures and Theories

Fate and design are interwoven and speak volumes on the purpose of humans. Our circumstance is bound with universal outcomes and intentions of the First Mind. Unfortunately, there is no consensus on the fate of the universe; in fact, recent discoveries only exacerbate differences of opinion. To demonstrate the complexity of the issue, many interpretations of universal fate depend on the verification of hypothesized matter and energy. From a physical standpoint, the universe is an enigma, and many of its features may never prove detectable.

Nonetheless, the methods used to study the fate of the universe include observation of its shape and structure, the motion of its galaxies, its physical composition, its rate of expansion, its quantum origins, and its total density. Geometry is utilized to determine whether the universe is finite, infinite, flat, open, or closed. Each of these possibilities has huge implications for the ultimate fate of the universe. In defense of materialist science, predictions of universal fates are perhaps some of its finest work; we must remember that the universe is the largest macro and thus extremely difficult to grasp. The distances alone are nearly unfathomable. As knowledge of the incorporeal origins of the universe became known, interpretations of the totality required both physical and metaphysical approaches. Many of the leading theorists have incorporated such divergent perspectives and deserve substantial credit.

It should also be noted that any consideration of universal fates relies greatly on logic and mathematics, which assumes particular significance considering that the structure of the universe often appears counterintuitive and must be mathematically confirmed. Some go even further, considering mathematics fundamentally formative of existence. The following from *The Independent* cites the incredible power of mathematics to effect the universe through an **"ability of nonphysical mathematical constructions to determine the workings of a separate physical world."**[202]

The inference is that mathematics makes the universe function. Others have posited that mathematics is the universe, inferentially making mathematics an actual entity or external reality.[203] That appears unlikely since mathematics is fallible. **Nevertheless, mathematics and logic are the closest that science has come to instruments of proof.**

Here we will have another small digression, although it will provide additional insight into our discussion. The closest that logic and mathematics have come to proving God is known as the *Ontological Proof* formulated by the gifted mathematician Kurt Gödel. The proof (with a number of iterations) was first conceived decades before its actual publication in 1987. The argument is based on specific axioms or self-evident truths that utilize the logic of necessity and possibility and include various assumptions of properties and essences. If the universe results from a First Mind, it proves that Mind is crucial in determining universal fate.

The proof is subject to criticism (including from Gödel's own *Incompleteness Theorems* for which he is more famous, suggesting that mathematics is not completely infallible), and its rightful place assigns a higher probability of God as opposed to any incontrovertibility. The proof is analytically brilliant and precise. It is difficult to argue against its conclusion. Seen this way, the *Ontological Proof* is another significant puzzle piece in the quest to frame the nature of reality. The proof is shown below.

A1	Either a property or its negation is positive, but not both:	$\forall\phi[P(\neg\phi) \leftrightarrow \neg P(\phi)]$
A2	A property necessarily implied by a positive property is positive:	$\forall\phi\forall\psi[(P(\phi) \land \Box\forall x[\phi(x) \rightarrow \psi(x)]) \rightarrow P(\psi)]$
T1	Positive properties are possibly exemplified:	$\forall\phi[P(\phi) \rightarrow \Diamond\exists x\phi(x)]$
D1	A *God-like* being possesses all positive properties:	$G(x) \leftrightarrow \forall\phi[P(\phi) \rightarrow \phi(x)]$
A3	The property of being God-like is positive:	$P(G)$
C	Possibly, God exists:	$\Diamond\exists x G(x)$
A4	Positive properties are necessarily positive:	$\forall\phi[P(\phi) \rightarrow \Box\, P(\phi)]$
D2	An *essence* of an individual is a property possessed by it and necessarily implying any of its properties:	$\phi \text{ ess. } x \leftrightarrow \phi(x) \land \forall\psi(\psi(x) \rightarrow \Box\forall y(\phi(y) \rightarrow \psi(y)))$
T2	Being God-like is an essence of any God-like being:	$\forall x[G(x) \rightarrow G \text{ ess. } x]$
D3	*Necessary existence* of an individual is the necessary exemplification of all its essences:	$NE(x) \leftrightarrow \forall\phi[\phi \text{ ess. } x \rightarrow \Box\exists y\phi(y)]$
A5	Necessary existence is a positive property:	$P(NE)$
T3	Necessarily, God exists:	$\Box\exists x G(x)$

We have used the above proof, **which relies on logic and mathematics**, to lend credibility to universal fates being a construct of God (since the proof goes far to prove His existence, and materialism doesn't get to selectively choose which logic and mathematics are valid), but another contribution is accentuating the gap between the fallibility of mathematics and the structural perfection of the universe. This gap can only be reconciled by a source beyond both mathematics and the universe (the gap perhaps intentionally designed for this exact reason, proving His superiority). Science wants to develop a mathematical representation of the universe that is commensurate with observational facts that have proved elusive and may prove impossible. The hope was that advanced computer programs would accelerate this endeavor. Instead, some scientists have actually used computer programs to substantiate Gödel's framework.[204] In effect, this has added to the tenability of the Great Consciousness.

If we combine what we have learned about the nature of Mind, Spirit, Body, and Soul with interpretations of universal fates, we can compare them for their relevance to His potential purposes.[205] Consider the following summary of possibilities, to be subsequently discussed in greater detail:

Universal Fates	Divine Objectives
Big Bang	Creation of Stage
Heat Death	Completion of Stage
Big Crunch	Cyclic Stages
Universal Collapse	Judgment Day
Universal Uncertainty	Unknown

The Big Bang is not a potential fate, but its existence necessitates considering its contribution to the final outcome of the universe. We will consider it first.

The Big Bang posits an ultimately dense and high-temperature state known as the singularity suddenly exploding outward and inflating, the extreme temperatures eventually cooling and allowing for star and galaxy formation with the universe slowly evolving over time. The laws of classical physics and Quantum Mechanics did not apply in the singularity but were manifest after the Big Bang. Much of this theory depends on many unproved tenets and requires huge leaps of faith, including that the entire universe was originally compressed into the size of a human head. For our purposes, however, it does provide an outcome (physical environment) whereby SoulMind exists and learns lessons such as survival, conflict, understanding, and death.

The second possibility—and the first real potential fate of the universe—is known as Heat Death. In this scenario, the First and Second Laws of Thermodynamics ensure that eventually the universe will run out of the energy available for work. Star, planet, and galaxy formation will cease to exist. The universe expands indefinitely, but at some point, all energy available for work will be spent, and reality will become entropic and lifeless. Obviously, in such an environment, Soul would no longer have a material reality, and Mind and Spirit would have no purpose. It is possible that the Creator might use Heat Death as the end "stage," as it were, but that implies that everything to be accomplished would have been accomplished.

The third possibility is the Big Crunch. In this scenario, universal expansion is slowed by gravity so that eventually gravity forces the universe to recollapse and return to form another singularity. At that point, another Big Bang occurs, and a new universe begins with an explosion outward, leading once again to star, planet, and galaxy formation. That is a cyclic interpretation with the universe an endless series of expansions and contractions. An alternative of the Big Crunch posits that the universe undergoes periods of expansion and contraction, all the while remaining the same universe. For spiritual purposes, cyclic universes appear unnecessary unless the lessons to be learned by souls require many universal cycles in order to accomplish the required learning.

The fourth possibility is Universal Collapse. In this case, the universe just suddenly ceases to exist. The method by which that might happen regards fluctuating energy states. Quantum tunneling could cause a fluctuation whereby the universe transforms from a higher energy state into a lower energy state. Even fundamental properties such as matter and time could be radically transformed. An eviscerated universe is also possible. Although unlikely from a scientific standpoint, God could use Universal Collapse to suddenly terminate existence.

The last possibility is Universal Uncertainty, or tacit acknowledgement that the fate of the universe is unknowable. It is not scientific resignation but rather acceptance of endless layers of baffling complexity; in short, the universe is too naturally complex for full understanding. But it is highly unlikely that a material universe comprised of easily identified atomic structure would not be fully comprehensible unless originally designed for obfuscation. Incalculable complexity achieves this purpose. We have seen this in our own history; every discovery adds to the intricacy of creation. Thus, it appears that the universe was intentionally designed to be a great unknown.

Time and Fates of the Universe

The universe is comprised of four confirmable dimensions: height, width, depth, and time. The combined structure of these four is referred to as spacetime, the first three providing space and the fourth providing time. As we saw in Chapter 2, Quantum Mechanics, specifically *entanglement* and *delayed choice quantum eraser experiments*, prove that time is unified; against logic, the past, present, and future all concurrently exist. The structure of spacetime thus compels questions of how spacetime might affect potential fates of the universe.

How time influences universal outcomes has generally taken the form of three interpretations: *Presentism, Growing Block Universe*, and *Block Universe*. Other interpretations exist but are largely variations of these primary theorizations. We will consider each separately since all have implications for how they might fulfill Divine objectives.

Presentism is the assertion that "only what is present exists."[206] Within this perspective, the past and the future do not exist. Adherents acknowledge that past events happened, but they are lost forever. Presentism claims that everyone and everything exist in current time. Proponents emphasize the inherent "realness" to this interpretation. Yet in 2018, an experiment demonstrated that various observers can experience different realities at the same time.[207] Moreover, Special Relativity proves there is no absolute commonly shared time, so even the "present" is not universally applicable. An interpretation that denies the past and future cannot fulfill the objectives of God since Mind, Spirit, Body, and Soul existed in the past, currently exist, and will exist in the future unless God ends the universe.

Frustration with Presentism as well as its failure to comply with Special Relativity leads to another interpretation known as the Growing Block Universe. In this interpretation, the past and present exist, but the future does not. Consider the following:

The present is an objective property, to be compared with a moving spotlight. By the passage of time more of the world

comes into being; therefore, the block universe is said to be growing. The growth of the block is supposed to happen in the present, a very thin slice of spacetime, where more of spacetime is continually coming into being.[208]

The Growing Block Universe interpretation conforms to common sense because the past is already decided, the present is being constructed, and the future is yet to be determined. That interpretation is in many ways a desperate attempt to maintain materialism since quantum experimentation has already proved that the past, present, and future exist concurrently and are effective of each other. Time in this interpretation is also linear, which is in opposition to the proven counterdirectionality found in Quantum Mechanics; if time is potentially counterdirectional, there must be a reason. Thus, the deficiencies of the Growing Block Universe necessitate another, more compelling interpretation.

The Block Universe, or Eternalism, is the interpretation that naturally follows from both the Theory of Relativity and Quantum Mechanics. It is scientifically validated and asserts that the past, present, and future all exist and are equally real. Hence, the universe exists as a *block* of spacetime, the span of the universe (all activities, processes, lifetimes, and experiences) encoded within this block. Consider the following:

A *block universe* is a four-dimensional block, but instead of being made of cement, it is made of spacetime. And all of the space and time of the Universe are there in that block. . . . From this block time perspective, time, as we experience in the block universe, is an illusion. . . . [O]ur experience of time passing, is only because we are stuck inside the block universe, moving forward along the dimension of time.[209]

The governor of our advancement through the dimension of time is our Consciousness. We notice the forwardness, making reality appear as passing, our mind in a privileged position to witness time. Nevertheless, everything is already determined. A block universe is particularly counterintuitive because it implies that the future has already occurred. John Gribbin in his book *The*

Time Illusion states that even though the world and the universe exist, they do not change. He calls it a block of spacetime that has in it everything that has and will occur. He says the "flow of time is an illusion."[210]

If we also add what we know about the Creator, we get the following:

> **Imagine that I am a God-like being who has decided to design and then create a logically consistent universe with laws of nature similar to those that obtain in our universe. . . . Since the universe will be of the block-variety I will have to create it *as a whole*: the beginning, middle and end will come into being. . . . Well, assume our universe is a static block, even if it never 'came into being', it nonetheless exists (time-lessly) as a coherent whole, containing a globally consistent spread of events.**[211]

That brings us to another astonishing point. To a materialist, the universe is *deterministic*, all events are determined by previously existing causes. But the *Uncertainty Principle* in Quantum Mechanics proves that previously existing causes cannot be precisely measured; they cannot even be fully known. Moreover, they do not exist without Consciousness observing them. That matches the metaphysical foundations of the universe. So how can things be causal and determine future events when they are unknowable and immaterial? The answer is that they cannot. Thus, determinism is a fallacy.

Another staggering implication exists. The universe (and life) does not evolve since everything has already occurred (materialists, specifically Darwinists, hate this fact, which describes their preference for Presentism or the Growing Block Universe since Darwinism cannot inform on how everything happened all at once). All of time (past, present, and future) has already transpired. Nothing truly evolves; it only appears that way. The question, however, is how do humans have free will in a block universe with full eventuation?

To answer that question, we must consider how SoulMind conforms to a Block Universe. The following is highly speculative, but as more data accumulates, its plausibility as an interpretation increases. SoulMind allows us to experience time passing as new events, although these events have already occurred. If SoulMind experiences these new events as original and genuine, free will is ensured. Moreover, if the Block Universe is the correct interpretation of universal fate, then all lives everywhere have existed, are existing, and will exist. Within these lives exists a full panoply of choices made and lessons learned. Souls inserted into these lives thus have an apparatus whereby they can "get an education." NDE experiencers often report that their souls have been inserted into bodies for exactly that purpose, and this dynamic continues with reincarnation into numerous lifetimes. Theoretically, that enables a soul to learn a nearly infinite amount of lessons. A Block Universe is the perfect mechanism for this dynamic since it provides a nearly endless supply of lives and choices.

To further this point, we must briefly examine a concept known as *Superdeterminism*. In its typical understanding, it denies choice and randomness, although as we shall see shortly, it corresponds well with the Block Universe, and we can learn something from it. Consider the following definition of Superdeterminism: **"A generalization of determinism that includes the complete absence of free will."**[212]

Superdeterminism is typically used by some materialists to suggest that the uncomfortable truths of Quantum Mechanics can be superseded by a theory stipulating that everything is determined by natural laws and correlations from the Big Bang forward. All observations and human choices are determined in advance, and therefore free will is an illusion. Without exploring this concept in greater detail (it is too extensive for our purposes and can be adequately summarized here), consider, for example, the case of quantum physicists. The implication is that any experiment lacked choice and every measurement and observation in quantum experimentation was meant to happen that exact way from the beginning of time; that eliminates Consciousness collapsing the wave function (the Observer Effect) and Delayed Choice Quantum Eraser experiments proving the counterdirectionality of time. Naturally, it also eliminates the mental and spiritual nature of the universe. Criticisms against the theory are that it invalidates falsifiability (and thus science itself) and suggests an initial perfect arrangement through some as yet undiscovered process. Even the vast majority of materialists consider it an implausible explanation of reality and quite absurd.

Perhaps, however, we can salvage something of its framework since a Block Universe appears to be constructed through a type of Superdeterminism. Proponents of Superdeterminism posit that the initial conditions of the universe (the Big Bang) determined everything for all of time. That is a physicalist way of describing a Divine Creation with intention. Although Superdeterminism insists on the absence of free will, God in His infinite wisdom constructed a Block Universe whereby SoulMind would experience free will and learn lessons in lives that fully existed. Although superdetermined by God, any individual soul choices made and lessons learned would be experienced as original and authentic. In that way, physical lives are apparatuses for souls, and the Body is expendable and the Soul essential, as many philosophical and religious traditions have espoused for millennia.

To provide further substantiation, we can consider our earlier discussion regarding simulation. A Block Universe is fully designed and wholly self-contained, as is a simulation. Simulations by definition are superdetermined, and the initial conditions are established and the results predicted from this initiality. No greater designer exists to determine the initial conditions of the universe and provide anticipated results than First Mind. Thus, creation is a type of Superdeterminism, one so expertly crafted that it allows for free will in a fully arranged environment. Subsequent chapters demonstrate how free will produces new outcomes in a superdetermined universe; as mentioned, experiments in Quantum Mechanics provide a theoretical foundation for this, revealing concurrently different realities for various observers. This fact is liberating since it means our free will choices are contributory to a grand plan.

This contribution is best defined as creativity. Free will allows us to be creative, so we must explore the concept of creativity. Although the universe, for lack of a better term, is superdetermined (its outcome known only by God), its future is unknown to us. We must therefore live our lives accordingly, constructing the best future possible for ourselves and for posterity since we are fundamentally creative beings. We will turn to this exploration in our next chapter.

CHAPTER 13

Creator and Created

Creativity is fundamental to the universe for its origin and nature. To *create* is to "cause to come into being."[213] *Creative* can be defined as "having the ability or power to create, especially something new or imaginative."[214] The universe certainly came into being, and *someone* had the power to create it. Interwoven into the universe are intricate connections and detailed orderings that defy logical expectation and scientific explanation. This *someone* is a genius beyond compare since this intentioned grandeur cannot result from some random quantum fluctuation.[215] The following shows the causative sequence of creation:

God......Mind......Purpose......
Creativity......Design......Universe

In addition to having a mental and spiritual essence, God is also supremely intelligent and inimitably imaginative. He is the ultimate creative type. Our meager minds will never comprehend His Mind or His magnificent creation. It is simply beyond us. As pond mold cannot understand an orbiting space station, neither can we understand the creative genius of God. Creation therefore is more than just an act of beginning; it is a demonstration of the creative nature and capabilities of the Great Consciousness.

The Universe as a Creation of Mind

With our modern, scientific approach to virtually everything, including a large part of the methodology used in this study, we often fail to notice the majesty of creation. That is our mistake because noticing is proof of His ingenuity. We are part of that creation (the universe) and part of the Great Creativity (His creative thoughts). Consider the following;

> **We are God's creatures; living in the creation, created by the Creator. All of these words point to one of God's most supreme qualities: creativity. Creativity is intimately woven into God's character and makes Him evident to us. To see the works of His hands is to see Him. When we are amazed by the hues of sky at sunset we are experiencing the physical manifestation of His warmth and goodness to us. When unrelenting waves crash against the shoreline we feel His unrelenting power and greatness.... A tree, laden with snow and still in the cold and crisp morning air, sharpens our senses, reminding us of His presence. From soaring mountains to flat deserts our senses experience the terrain of the spiritual world. These are echoes of God's majesty. They all attest to His creativity.[216]**

From atoms scaling to galaxies and from galaxies scaling to the universe, we witness staggering sophistication and execution, God's imaginings coming fully into being, the physical universe obeying laws only He could design. Even prominent physicists realize the handiwork of God through manifest design and the simulation aspect of the universe.[217] With each new discovery comes ever more evidence of His creativity. We are simply astounded. How can anyone, regardless of their powers, invent such incredible details and integrate them into such an incomprehensible whole? What type of Mind is beyond any intelligence range, beyond any classification at all—the type of Mind that knows everything knowable and originates all such knowledge?

Fortunately, we have witness to that Mind. It is the beauty of the *Observer Effect* in Quantum Mechanics whereby we observe the Mind responsible for all creation. Experimentation exposes the master Consciousness of God, our scientific exploration His confirmation. That centralizes the issue of Mind. Consciousness is fundamentally creative, and our minds are only a miniscule fraction of infinite creativity.

Naturally, another scaling results—a comparison between our meager minds and the Mind of God. Unfortunately, in a typically materialist way, the Mind of God is often perceived as a graspable entirety as opposed to an immeasurable infinity. Recognizing Mind is pervasive, and in viewing the universe as a totality, some thinkers such as Philip Goff in his book *Consciousness and the Fundamental Reality* have speculated that the universe is one enormous Consciousness of its own.[218] Others such as Bernardo Kastrup in his book *The Idea of the World* have posited that we are all of one Mind.[219]

Discussing the relative merits of these positions is not our focus; the key point is that the ubiquity of Consciousness has caused many to contemplate the universe as its own Mind, self-aware and self-sufficient, existing without cause, and producing an ontology devoid of God. In this way, even some *idealists* contribute to atheistic materialism because while recognizing the mental nature of reality, they deny its ultimate source, the endlessly creative Mind of God. Perhaps unwittingly, such viewpoints reinforce the notion that Mind is a physical phenomenon when, in fact, Mind is immaterial and spiritual.

These positions, however, are simple to refute. Once again, you cannot get something out of nothing. God—not some random fluctuation—was able to originate the universe in an "explosion of light," the singularity unleashed through nothing more than His will and His power. Consider how Robert Jastrow in his book *God and the Astronomers* explains the Big Bang:

> **The seed of everything that has happened in the Universe was planted in that first instant [the Big Bang]; every star, every planet and every living creature in the Universe came into being as a result of events that were set in motion in the**

moment of the cosmic explosion. It was literally the moment of Creation. . . . the Universe flashed into being, and we cannot find out what caused that to happen.[220]

The Big Bang is highly suggestive of a Creator and is particularly troublesome for materialism that would have preferred a static or steady state universe without origin. Yet discoveries, particularly in the 1960s, invalidated a steady state universe and demonstrated that a Big Bang occurred and thus the universe came into being. Jastrow expounds further on the conundrum that presented for materialism:

For the scientist who has lived by his faith in the power of reason, the story ends like a bad dream. He has scaled the mountains of ignorance; he is about to conquer the highest peak; as he pulls himself over the final rock, he is greeted by a band of theologians who have been sitting there for centuries.[221]

The Big Bang unleashed an unprecedented amount of creativity in an initial explosion of light that contained the origins of incredible complexity, including all known laws of physics, all mathematics, all natural laws, and all known forces in the universe. Before the Big Bang, there was no space or time and certainly no spacetime.[222] Immediately, according to writer Robert Kuhn, host of the television show *Closer to Truth*, Information became ubiquitous in the universe.[223] The creative thoughts of God were the elements, and He used Information to give them actual structure. That is the reason things seem physical yet are made of Mind.

Recent research has made another interesting discovery that offers proof (albeit unintended) that the creative mind of God is responsible for creation. It comes from the European Organization for Nuclear Research (CERN) in Switzerland and is described in Dom Galeon's article "CERN Research Finds 'The Universe Should Not Actually Exist'"—an article beautiful in its exactness:

According to standard physics, the universe had equal amounts of antimatter and matter when it was created. The problem with that is the fact that each antimatter particle should have canceled out its corresponding matter particle, leaving nothing behind. Except they didn't, and here we are left wondering why. . . . [I]ndeed, our universe should never have come into existence.[224]

The difference between an existing universe and one that should not exist can only be solved by supremely creative powers. God can close this disparity. Critics claim this is a "God of the Gaps" argument except it happens with virtually every new scientific discovery, accentuating the gap between our limited grasp and the absolute knowledge of a Creator. The more we learn, the greater our ignorance becomes.

The point is that God's creativity *causes* and yet *confounds*. It *confirms* and yet *complicates*. The Creator of the universe, who has His own plans and purposes, would likely make His creation incomprehensible to its inhabitants. Ambiguity causes both questioning *and* questing. We want to know more than we do. If humans or some other intelligent species understood everything, they would become their own gods. The questing would end. If the objective is to be sought by souls in God's creation, then a knowledge gap must exist between God and man in order to maintain a hierarchy (so the lesser seek the higher). We were meant to seek our Creator.

Hence, the genius of creation also speaks to teleology or "natural ends" of the universe since plans entail purpose and purpose entails desired outcomes. The universe is one enormous design full of intention. So what might be the natural end of the universe, the fulfillment of His ultimate purpose? Are there specific reasons to create such an incredibly intricate reality?

We shall consider a few speculative possibilities, including the following:

- **Reality exists for Soul development and provides endless challenges.**

- **Eternity is forever and is filled with complexity in order to mitigate boredom.**

- **The universe reflects God's nature because He is incomprehensible.**

- **Incomprehensibility creates a desire for absolute knowledge.**

We will briefly expand on these points. If we can believe the accounts of NDE, then Soul development is the reason for creation. Religious traditions also typically posit that life is a process whereby Soul develops. It is further possible that God recognized the length of eternity and created a universe of incredible complexity in order to fill time with challenges to mitigate boredom. If time ceases with a Heat Death universe or when God institutes finality, this point loses credibility. Nevertheless, what follows the end of the universe will certainly fill eternity with something; we can be certain that God will not allow eternity to be tedious. Being incomprehensible, God created a universe that follows from His essence; we cannot understand the secrets of the Creator, and neither can we understand the secrets of creation. Universal incomprehensibility creates questing for more knowledge, exemplified by intelligent species naturally seeking to know everything that exists. That search may take an eternity and may require nearly endless levels of reality.

As we have seen, this questing is a common theme in our study. As mentioned in the works of G. W. F. Hegel and Thomas Kuhn, dialectical progression and paradigmal evolution characterize the universe, and questing is the driver. Contrary to materialist interpretations that postulate the universe as insentient and indifferent, the primacy of Consciousness, the experience of NDE, the history of religious traditions, the emerging domain of psychic abilities, the obviousness of universal fine-tuning, and even Information itself all point to a universe filled with motive. If we were meant to be creative, we must reflect that original intent. Therefore, a link exists between creativity and our own free will.

Human Creativity and Free Will

Creativity extends to Souls in the universe. Since we are made in God's image, we are destined to be creative. Creativity requires free will. Consider the following:

> **God is, first and foremost, a Creator. . . . [T]he fundamental nature of the Divine is to be creative. . . . [H]uman beings are created . . . in the image of God. By linking these two concepts, we formulate the powerful idea that humans are made to be creators. Creativity is inherent in each and every one of us. It is imbued in us from the very beginning. It is a foundational aspect of what it means to be human and an essential pathway to connection with the Divine.**[225]

Or consider this from *New World Encyclopedia* that speaks of creativity and its nature:

> **Creativity, understood as the ability to utilize everything at hand in nature to transform our living environment and beautify our lives, is what distinguishes human beings from all other creatures. This is one way that human beings are said to be in the image of God: they are second creators, acting in a manner analogous to God, the original Creator.**[226]

Creativity, whether the original creativity of God or that granted to us, fills the universe. An excellent summary of this point is found in Imago Arts' article "A Universe of Creativity."

> **The enterprise of human making is inescapable. It is woven into the fabric of what it means to bc human and ultimately – as I see it – draws from the One who has made all things and set them in motion.**[227]

Whether individually driven or through the purposes of God's creation, humans are instrumental in the workings of the universe. What we do matters. The mechanism for these choices is free will, which is necessary for our creativity. Thus, our free will choices determine equally tangible outcomes even within the intractable finality of the Block Universe. That is both conceptually and mathematically provable. The following mathematical discussion can be read lightly since its conclusions are also summarized. For this confirmation, we need mathematics relating all the potential manifestations of free will—x—with nearly endless amounts of equally real outcomes—y—where the latter is a function of the former. All the permutations of free will—x—are known as the domain, while all the equally tangible outcomes—y—are known as the range. Consider the following:

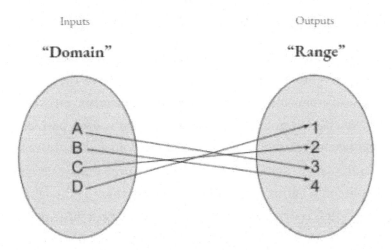

Remember, the Block Universe interpretation contends that there is no separation of past, present, and future. Thus, our formula is $y = f(xn)$ where, as previously mentioned, our domain is n expressions of x, and our range y is all such outputs. Note that the union of these elements (the Block Universe) contains all such inputs and outputs, or all potential combinations of x and y, and as such has the "space available" to accommodate whatever free will choices and equally tangible outcomes might occur. The permutations of all possible free will choices, as well as each potential outcome, can be expressed as:

$$\textbf{Infinity}$$
$$\mathbf{U}(\, x_n,\, f(x_n)\,)$$
$$\mathbf{n \in N}$$

So how can choices that have been made be made again and with different outcomes? How can history be transformed into a new history? We only need to remember *Delayed Choice Quantum Eraser* experiments since they prove that time is revisable. That appears unimaginable, but perhaps totality includes the possibility of impossibility. Likely, all potentialities exist and are made actual by our choices, implying that even a Block Universe has an endless amount of fates. A deterministic universe is increasingly dubious. Consider the following:

> **[T]he notion of scientific determinism is being challenged by the rise of quantum mechanics, which governs the micro world of atoms and particles. According to quantum mechanics, you cannot predict with certainty what route a particle will take to reach a target – even if you know all its initial conditions. All you can do is to calculate a probability, which implies that nature is a lot less predictable than we thought. In fact, it is only when you actually measure a particle's path that it "picks" a specific trajectory – until then it can take several routes at once.**[228]

We should emphasize the final point again—**the universe is made of particles that can take several courses at once.** Perhaps the entire universe follows their lead. An interesting theory known as *Possible States Theory* was recently developed. It posits a universe of unique objects and the unique exchanges among them; the exchanges are designated as possible states. It is quoted here for its relevance to the discussion that different potentialities and outcomes exist in a previously concluded system. Consider the following:

The picture of the universe yielded by the theory differs from the conventional viewpoint in important ways. Past, future and possible states may interact with one another; interactions occur without reference to location in space-time. Given that all possibilities are present, the possible states universe is complete.... Many truths, some contradicting each other, can simultaneously exist.[229]

Might our choices change the trajectory of the universe with differing outcomes equally real? Might God be the only one with advance knowledge of our decisions? In this sense, the universe is an environment in order for various realities to manifest and be evaluated. Reality is a platform for free will and choice and, by extension, for creativity and responsibility. Thus, a certain duty exists for good decisions, an accountability we cannot ignore. We cannot know which of our choices best serve God's plan; all we can do is choose sensibly. Perhaps God has designed a format, the universe, whereby different and equally real outcomes enhance learning opportunities for souls. In any case, the power of choice is the power of creativity, and we must embrace it.

In addition, creativity extends into incredible connections, forming a web of inventiveness where creativity becomes a type of entity unto itself that both characterizes and forwards us. Consider this apt description from Agustin Fuentes' article "Creative Collaboration Is What Humans Do Best":

Creativity is not a private endeavor vested in a single person or a select group of people. It is not solely about genius in the arts or sciences, or actions by prominent artists, celebrities, or politicians. It is not even limited to the work of particularly original thinkers. Creativity emerges from the interconnections of ideas, experiences, and imagination.[230]

Creativity is an opportunity. Much depends on our creative choices, individually and collectively. Our personal and collective free will determines the direction of society and relates to our earlier discussion of cultural advancement or societal stagnation. By definition, stagnation is a diminishment of our collective ingenuity and results from insular thinking. Stagnation is a limit on our creativity, and even incredibly creative individuals are often thwarted by cultural bounds. Thus, we must ensure openmindedness since it creates space for innovation.

As we saw in Chapter 8, academic disciplines are stagnating and require breakthroughs, which in turn require amenability to new ideas and interdisciplinary thinking. Unfortunately, interdisciplinary approaches typically concern only a specific issue or research project, which is a particularly egregious deficiency in our system. Combining disciplines produces higher-level knowledge, which correspondingly produces higher stratums of understanding and creativity. Note the following diagram as a representation of this concept:

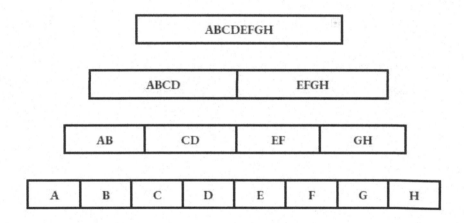

The lowest level represents current academic disciplines. At each level above it, the disciplines combine to produce a higher level of comprehension. For example, AB represents a higher level than A and B individually. As the levels move higher, so too does the stratum of understanding. EFGH provides a higher stratum of understanding than GH, and ABCDEFGH provides a higher stratum of understanding than EFGH.

Note that the higher levels contain less depth than their base disciplines but are more insightful. An oversimplified example would be if discipline A equals Sociology and discipline B equals Biology. AB is Sociobiology (in truth, Sociobiology also contains elements of other disciplines, but the framework applies). Thus, more is known about Sociology and Biology by combining their respective contributions. As C (Quantum Mechanics) and D (Psychology) are added, ABCD might be Sociobiology and Quantumpsychology, an area of study that examines how society might be influenced by not only biological dynamics but also by the random behaviors of its citizens. These higher levels enable new discoveries that surmount stagnation and forward us into new paradigms.

In some ways, this framework is very similar to the Hegelian Dialectic. In fact, it is how knowledge should proceed, through the challenge and incorporation of ideational opposites or ostensibly unrelated disciplines. But as noted in this study, we as a species perform poorly at interdisciplinary thinking. Moreover, our educational institutions fail to communicate both the value added and instructional aspects of the phenomenon. Instead, our system rewards specialization, which worked until the specialties stagnated. Numerous reasons exist for the systemic failure of previous interdisciplinary efforts (although some organizations and academic programs remain), but largely it concerns differing methodologies and defense of established disciplines. As a result, we must integrate disciplines and let their ideas confront one another.

So the future belongs to synthesis if we are to have a future. The more we integrate knowledge, the more we reflect the supreme knowledge of our designer; that allows us to be more capable participants in the construction of reality. For example, we have been living for millennia without the benefit of truly understanding Consciousness and Spirit. Creativity will flourish once we exploit our mental and spiritual foundations. Simply understanding the implications of the quantum mechanical world opens more possibilities than the entirety of classical physics. More knowledge implies more creativity, and more creativity implies more knowledge. Creativity is our destiny, originated and sanctioned by God who has gifted us a significant amount of His creative genius in order to master our world.

Fortunately, there are guides to destiny. These keys have been with us since the beginning of our story. Instituted by the Creator, they are often hidden or ignored by materialists because they do not conform to physicalist interpretations of existence. Our reality is a fusion of the material *and* the immaterial, the universe filled with signs of its design and meaning. These signs direct us toward a deeper appreciation for the entirety of experience, acting as instructions for the fulfillment of universal destiny. It is to these guides that we next turn in our study.

CHAPTER 14

The Management of Destiny

Things happen for a reason.

The universe is filled with *direction* and *destiny*. For our purposes, direction is "the general position a person or thing moves or points towards."[231] Direction in the universe implies a commanding authority, a power responsible for the intricate workings and final outcome of reality. This designer manages the universe to achieve a desired end. As we have established, free will exists, and if the choice agents make poor choices and deviate from God's intent, then adjustment may occur. This adjustment is destiny, "what happens to somebody or what will happen to them in the future, especially things that they cannot change or avoid."[232] Guideposts may be used to direct humans to the proper course in order to achieve divine objectives. Thus, there is active management of the universe—direction, if you will—and the consequence of this direction is destiny.

We have previously discussed free will and tangible outcomes in the context of a Block Universe. We can extend that discussion by including the concept of destiny management. The intricacies involved in the management of destiny are difficult to fathom, but perhaps mathematics provides a framework. Again, if preferred, the reader can read lightly through the mathematics since the points will be summarized.

Function composition is the process of taking outputs of other functions as inputs to new functions. Placed within our context, function composition demonstrates how free will produces outcomes that can be managed (through control mechanisms) to advance Soul development. Once implemented, these control mechanisms act as new, composed functions that originate new free will choices and correspondingly different outcomes. We can use mathematics here to demonstrate the concept.

The standard formula for function composition is $h(x) = g(f(x))$. Consider the following:

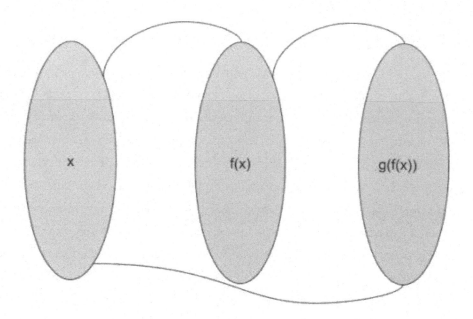

We can also take different inputs and outputs from other functions as inputs to new functions. This is diagrammed below:

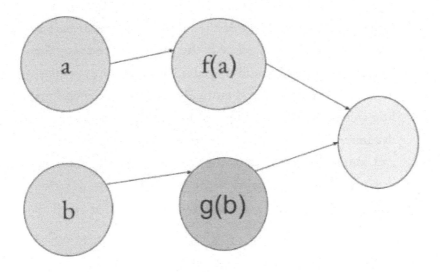

We can use the above conceptual framework to produce the following formula for how the driver of Soul development, free will, wn, forms outcomes that can be managed (through control mechanisms, cm) to produce new free will choices. It is expressed as follows:

$$c_m(w_n) = w_{n+1}$$

The point is that a framework exists whereby free will determines outcomes, and if these outcomes deviate from the plan, then free will is managed through control mechanisms to correct course. At that point, these new outcomes effect further free will choices, and the process proceeds through time. Once again, slight adjustments in behavior and outcomes, even in a previously determined Block Universe, forward God's preferred destiny.

Before we examine the actual guideposts that assist humans in their development, we must first acknowledge that this direction requires a managing intelligence. Some have argued that this intelligence is a fundamental property of the universe and that the human subconscious connects to this intelligence to ascertain certain truths. Consider the following from *Integrative Spirituality*, an organization dedicated to studying this phenomenon:

> **There is more to intelligence than human intelligence. Intelligence is a property of the universe and of all that is in it. Universal Intelligence is the intrinsic tendency for things to self-organize and co-evolve into ever more complex, intricately interwoven and mutually compatible forms. Our human intelligence is but one manifestation of that universal dynamic. The more we are conscious of universal intelligence and connect ourselves to it, the more intelligence (and wisdom) we will have to work with. One might also describe Universal Intelligence as the mind or will of God or Spirit.**[233]

Note the linkage between Mind and Intelligence, both existing without a definitively causative physical brain. Consider this opinion:

> **Some people believe that human intelligence is the pinnacle of natural evolution and can outdo anything nature has to offer – and that there is no God, and that nature has nothing remotely resembling consciousness or intelligence. Others say nature's (or God's) brilliance is greater than any human intelligence – ultimately awesome in its scope and endlessly surprising in its details – and that human intelligence is a small but elegant expression of this larger intelligence and has much to learn from it.**[234]

From the above, we see that Universal Intelligence is First Mind filling the universe, some of which has been granted to us. This intelligence is a form of original Consciousness. Universal Intelligence is different from brain-generated intelligence such as IQ and logical abilities. God uses universal intelligence as a sort of communication mechanism whereby He directs our destiny from His master intelligence. We do not connect to it; rather it connects to us. Within this medium, God also places the aforementioned guideposts designed to advance us toward the appropriate course in order to fulfill His plan. Our intelligence allows us to notice these guideposts as part of exterior reality and recognize their significance in our own minds.

Myths and Archetypes

If universal intelligence is a communication medium and guideposts characterize its nature, forethought is built into reality. Simply, there are distinctive awarenesses placed into human cognition and observable signs assembled into the universe. One of the devices for this communication is *myth*, "a traditional story, especially one concerning the early history of a people or explaining some natural or social phenomenon, and typically involving supernatural beings or events."[235] Another is an archetype, "the most typical or perfect example of a particular kind of person or thing."[236] Note that typical here does not connote average. Both myths and archetypes emphasize a higher standard for humanity in what amounts to aspirational templates compared to common life. In that way, they are similar to the *forms* of Plato where the ideal exceeds the actual. In addition to aspiration, myths and archetypes are meant to provide efficiency since the answers to age-old questions are answered by familiar exemplars of human behavior. According to Carl Jung, these are known as *structuring principles*.

Myths and archetypes are thus essential in order to comprehend our world. Some of the most common myths are the Quest (individual surmounts adversity to learn valuable life lessons), Creation (how the world came into being), Love (romantic and familial love), and Eternity (life, death, and the soul). Common archetypes include the Great Father, the Great Mother, the Mentor, and the Ruler. Obviously, myths contain archetypes, and archetypes contrive myths; together they compel magnificent stories for personal and societal aspiration.

The two greatest thinkers with respect to myths and archetypes are Joseph Campbell, the influential professor of literature and comparative mythologist, and Carl Jung, the founder of analytical psychology. The latter significantly influenced the former. Briefly, we can consider the contributions of each toward the role of myths and archetypes and where they made interpretive mistakes.

Campbell identified the common thread of humanity's truths expressed through mythology and religious tradition and thereby recognized the fundamental unity at the core of nature.[237] In *The Mythic Image*, he argued that the universality of Mind, manifested in our dreams, formed the basis of all mythology.[238] This shared universal Mind, a theme earlier explored by Jung, is the ground from which all myths and archetypes originate, inherent in nature and embedded in human beings. Campbell spent considerable time examining the functions of myth in society and the evolution of myth through the ages. He came to believe that the function of traditional mythology had been replaced by modern philosophers and that humanity desperately required new myths and a universal religion.

Although Campbell's advocacy of universal mind and historical mythology is significant, many of his conclusions are erroneous. Because of his pantheistic views, he has often been considered a founder of the New Age Movement. Consider the following from *The Power of Myth*, which typifies his position:

> **When you see God is the creation, and that you are a creature, you realize God is within you, and in the man or woman with whom you are talking, as well. There's a transcendent energy source. . . . That energy is the informing energy of all things. Mythic worship is addressed to that. . . . [Your life comes] from the ultimate energy that is the life of the universe. . . . You are God, but not in your ego, but in your deepest being, where you are at one with the nondual transcendent.[239]**

Or consider this:

> **I do not have to have faith, I have experience.[240]**

The first mistake Campbell makes is the same one that characterizes other thinkers of the New Age Movement—that because we have spiritual and mental essences, we must be God. Nothing could be further from the truth. A mother gives her DNA to her baby, but that does not make her baby her. The baby is separate. God gave us some of His essence, but that does not mean we are God. God is separate. He is the Creator, and we are the created.

The second mistake is that myths and archetypes do not result from the Universal Mind replacing a Great Consciousness, but rather they are an extension of First Mind. God implemented myths and archetypes as guideposts to assist our development, and both are foundational in human Consciousness. There is precedence for this. The *Innateness Hypothesis* posits that humans possess an innate capacity for language that does not result from environmental exposure or processed learning.[241] Materialists have fought this position because it suggests design, yet the evidence for it is undeniable. For their relationships, humans required language, so the designer ingrained in us innate communication abilities. The same is true of myth and archetype recognition.

At this point, we can turn to Jung. It is this collective world quintessence, including forms of communication and instincts, that precipitated Jung to suggest that archetypes emanate from what he termed the *Objective Psyche*, which is shared from beings of the same species, specifically the inherited structures of the brain. According to Jung, this "database" of human knowledge is the source of archetypes that rise from this database as frequently occurring and extremely important examples in our collective history, thus shaping human behavior. Naturally, any individual manifests some of these characteristics (providing an individuated experience), but they all originate from the same commutuality. For the psychoanalyst Jung, exploring such metaphysical aspects of reality such as religion, mythology, spiritualism, and the supernatural revealed much about the *Objective Psyche* and assisted his efforts in therapy.

The mistake Jung makes is similar to the mistake of Joseph Campbell in that this Universal Mind is a type of entity unto itself, independent of a Creator. Lacking is a satisfactory explanation for its origin other than inherited structures of the brain (a form of materialism). Jung hoped that archetypes could link to a higher power, although he tended to view questions of God within psychological frameworks as opposed to perceiving an all-powerful Creator. For Jung, God was an archetype who was accessible through dreams and visions with humans creating their own unique image of the designer. In this respect, Jung typifies "progressive" scientific approaches that while acknowledging Universal Mind and the possibility of a Great Consciousness nevertheless ground their perspectives in disproved physicalism. Rather, it appears that archetypes and myths result from the mental and spiritual character of the universe, reflecting the nature of God.

Dreams and Visions

Another form of direction and destiny are dreams and visions. Metaphysically, these are assumed to come from the universal mind or supernatural sources. Naturally, materialists ascribe them to residual random brain processes. We can consider some brief definitions in order to frame our discussion. A dream is "a series of thoughts, images, and sensations occurring in a person's mind during sleep.[242] A vision is "an experience of seeing someone or something in a dream or trance, or as a supernatural apparition."[243] Both dreams and visions have been subjects of extensive inquiry, with dream interpretation an especially prominent area of study.

Naturally, studies of both dreams and visions have delineated along *realistic* and *idealistic* lines, the former offering physicalist (brain) explanations and the latter offering more supernatural (spiritual) interpretations. The *Neuroscience of Religion* (materialist, biological causation for religious experience) defines the physicalist position, and *Religious Experience* defines the spiritual perspective. Here, the position is that both are relevant since each may prove actuative on the other, spirit influencing brain activity and the brain providing physical form to interpret spiritual experiences. Only God in His infinite wisdom could integrate the material and the immaterial into a fully functioning biological and spiritual composite (human beings) grounded in physical reality yet receptive to spiritual communication.

Therefore, it appears that both dreams and visions originate from the immaterial realm and are designed to bring awareness to the individual through a combination of physical and incorporeal elements. Because dreams are ubiquitous, they probably result from a more direct layer of Mind and form a steady stream of influence, while visions are less common and also more powerful, suggesting that they result from someplace deeper and are thus utilized for more crucial purposes. In fact, dreams are so customary that there are even "dream dictionaries" that categorize common symbols, images, words, situations, and types, and assign various meanings to them.[244] The analysis of visions has been much less extensive.

Some dreams are more like visions so powerful that they transform. These are known as *numinous* dreams, the term originating with Jung. Consider the following as a succinct summary of the phenomenon:

> **Jung defines a numinous dream as an inner or outer experience that conveys something essential about ourselves that our unconscious wants us to know. That is, numinous dreams explain an aspect of spiritual knowledge that needs to be actualized in our lives. There is always a feeling of fascination about a numinous dream or event.**[245]

These dreams typically expose a deep truth about existence. They feel "more than real" and full of universal wisdom, similar to what experiencers report concerning the *hyper reality* of NDE. It suggests that they originate from a deeper level, likely at the level of visions. Numinous dreams, which cannot be ignored by the experiencer, contain an explanatory power that assists human comprehension, typically remembered and referenced forever. Not only does this suggest direction, but it also implies destiny since it appears that numinous dreams are "sent" from another realm to both enlighten the individual and fulfill some grander purpose.

Visions are similar to dreams, only more powerful and epiphanous. Unlike dreams, they contain some disparaging connotations that are typically viewed by detractors as untenably esoteric or even "new age." Due to the frequency of dreams, materialists are forced to accept them, whereas the infrequency of visions causes physicalists to deny that they exist. Apparently, visions originate from a management realm, ensuring that free will is impacted, direction implemented, course adjusted, and destiny achieved. Visions have even formed the basis for new religions.

The question of utilizing either dreams or visions commensurate with the objectives of destiny management remains. Visions appear to have a greater impact, with dreams less substantial. Hence, visions are more transformational than dreams and may be inserted accordingly. History is filled with famous visions, some being the foundation of new social structures, some forming original philosophies, some expanding existing knowledge, and some leading to incredible scientific discoveries. Visions are thus highly insinuative of both purpose and design, and it may be that dreams are more individually significant and visions more societally consequential. More importantly, both dreams and visions attest to an active management system and suggest another level of intricate design. Even in a Block Universe, the First Mind judiciously inserts dreams and visions in order to guide humans toward a desired end.

Intuition and Recognition

Pertinent to our discussion of dreams and visions, we can briefly summarize the related concepts of intuition and recognition. In Chapter 3, we discussed intuition as an innate human ability that transcends cognitive processes and provides constructive insights. Closely related to intuition is recognition. The difference is that intuition and recognition are typically viewed as *interior-driven* while dreams and visions are typically viewed as *exterior-driven*; the former is within us, and the latter is sent to us.

Intuition is innate knowledge as opposed to something resulting from logic or reasoning. Essentially, it is similar to instinct, requiring no prior experience. Since "life" has instinct, intuition may be an attribute of panpsychism. More importantly, intuition happens before the physical brain has time to process the data. As the brain responds to commands from some deeper part of ourselves, so does this deeper aspect perceive situations before physical cognitive processes begin. It means that intuition comes as an interior messaging system or the sense of the soul.

Unlike intuition, recognition is knowing something from previous knowledge. Two primary types of recognition exist. The first is recognition of things previously learned by our brain, and the second is recognition of things resulting from innate knowledge or intuition. Recognition then results from two inputs, one material and the other immaterial. Since individuals can have different learning capabilities in their physical brains, so too can humans have different recognition capabilities in their souls. The key point is that everyone has material and immaterial capacities that help them negotiate reality, with both physical and incorporeal elements contributing to their choices.

It appears that God placed intuition and recognition as basic guides to influence free will and reserved dreams and visions for more direct forms of management. We should note that humans require many forms of destiny management, probably due to our propensity for bad decisions and moral declination. He has to actively manage what disappoints. As we shall see next in our study, God's direction extends to the grandest example of directed destiny in all existence—the manipulation of objective reality and subjective perception into an unimaginable manifestation of meaning.

Synchronicity

We will spend slightly more time discussing synchronicity than other portions of this chapter due to its fascination and insight. Nearly everyone is familiar with the word, but few understand its meaning. Synchronicity is defined as "the simultaneous occurrence of events which appear significantly related but have no discernible causal connection."[246] The concept was introduced by Jung and is often simply referred to as *meaningful coincidence*. We think this way: **A causes B, and B causes C. In some cases, however, A, B, and C are related not by cause but by meaning to the observer.**

Synchronicity does not replace cause and effect but rather produces another connecting principle for the inherent associations within reality.[247] Synchronicity is a type of perceived togetherness and results from the same source responsible for myths, archetypes, dreams, and visions. Synchronicity is an announcement granted to the experiencer that something larger exists. The level of improbability (events are arranged in statistically impossible ways) ensures its supernatural essence. *It is evidence of a deeper reality.* This deeper reality is often referred to as source, objective psyche, spiritual realm, higher self, or universal mind. Synchronicity is a message system that directs the experiencer toward greater awareness and is proof of arrangement. Consider the following example.

You are considering various movies to watch, and an inner voice guides you to choose a specific title. It is not a genre you prefer. During the movie, you learn a lesson that relates to an issue in your life. Just then you remember that inner voice guiding you to select that particular movie, and mentally you speak the phrase "that must be the reason" for your selection. The protagonist in the movie speaks the phrase "that must be the reason."

The key point is the improbability of the connection. Arranging the two events together appears nearly impossible without supernatural management. Consider another example.

You come into a store and remember that the only other time you were there was with your soul mate. Although the relationship ended, you were connected at the soul level. Both of you knew it was the only such connection in a lifetime. Your mind fills with emotion. How you had wanted that relationship to last forever. The name of your soul mate was exceedingly rare. You wander for a time, oblivious to your surroundings, and the first item you notice has the name of your soul mate on it.

Synchronicity is meaningful coincidence that cannot be rationalized through the laws of probability. In the above examples, none of the events caused one another, but they are related to the experiencer through meaning. Synchronicity proves that everything is connected. Symbolism characterizes synchronicity, and reality is embedded with signs. Objects and events are arranged for synchronistic recognition by a force beyond common experience, the external environment aligned with internal recognition in impossible ways. Synchronicity is thus a form of communication that acts as an advisory, and the more synchronicity is encountered, the more synchronicity appears to the experiencer.

Customarily, synchronicity appears as a sequence of highly inconceivable occurrences that accumulate to the point of undeniability with some circumstances so bizarre that they defy rational explanation. Typically, fewer of them are required for authentication of the phenomenon due to their unmistakable nature. The impossibility of the arrangement is testament to the intricacy of the planning. Someone of incredible knowledge and power is behind this phenomenon.

Not only is synchronicity then an announcement of a larger reality, but it is also a message with particular relevance for the individual. In addition, synchronicity aggregates around impactful and transformative events.[248] We must determine the meaning of the messages. Synchronicity compels a person to a deeper exploration of self and toward a more profound understanding of their motivations and life mission. Synchronicities feel like a mutually contrived fate between the source (deeper realm) and the individual in order to learn specific lessons.

There must be some type of connecting principle rooted in nature (apart from cause and effect) that allows this exchange between an incorporeal source and an individual. In synchronicity, free will is unified with divine direction with the material and immaterial realms linked to reveal meaning. Some process, some method of connectivity, makes this possible. For this, we return to the phenomenon of *entanglement* from our earlier discussion of Quantum Mechanics.

Entanglement is the connection between particles regardless of the distance between them. This linkage is inviolable, a universal level of connectedness fundamental to nature. *Entanglement* provides an underpinning for synchronicity—a mechanism, if you will—for connecting subjective experience and objective reality. Jung believed that synchronicity originated from universal order, from a source responsible for uniting physical events and mental perceptions, and that quantum physics revealed this source. Thus, synchronicities are *entanglement* come to Consciousness.

To its credit, the New Age Movement has been an advocate for the phenomenon. For followers, synchronicities are messages sent by the source to assist someone on the quest for perfection and can be manifested at will. Some have even exceeded this belief by positing that synchronicity is generated by the Higher Self (as opposed to an entirely external source) to educate the base consciousness of the experiencer. That implies that either the Higher Self is a form of God inside an individual, able to manipulate the physical environment (arranging events to be recognized as synchronicity), or the Higher Self recognizes previously arranged events that the base self cannot recognize.

Although the position here is that the New Age interpretation is fallacious, it does focus on whether synchronicity is an interior, exterior, or synthetic phenomenon. We have already established that physical objects are arranged to correspond to mental perceptivity. This arrangement is external to the individual. More importantly, this external arrangement is a complicated endeavor with literally billions of objects and events positioned for recognition, not to mention the complexity of free will. So how is it possible that a thoroughly configured framework (the Block Universe) allows for synchronicity and amended free will choices?

As noted earlier, the Block Universe proves that the past, present, and future have already transpired. That means all possible meaningful coincidences (and slight variations based on free will) are in place. It eliminates the possibility that the physical environment is somehow constructed by the experiencer to reveal synchronicity. It is also unlikely that synchronicity is exclusively a mental projection onto the external world because objects (the environment) have to be arranged in specific ways in order to collaborate with the subjective experience of the individual. That means the following is the likely explanation for the phenomenon:

The Block Universe is designed with synchronicity as a form of communication between source and experiencer. Only God could design a structure fully determined and yet subject to adjustment based on the interjection of synchronicity

and resultant free will. That appears impossible, but as we previously noted, quantum experiments prove that actuality is comprised of many realities. Therefore, synchronicity is utilized to direct destiny, but all the potential destinies may be equally real.

The implication is that the Block Universe contains all possible individual realities, obviating a requirement for various universes to achieve those purposes. If souls are meant to learn lessons, then synchronicity is an instruction manual that directs humans toward their personal destiny in the universe, no doubt also fulfilling the larger purposes of creation. The key point is that an incredible amount of planning is necessary for a synchronistic reality as much as designing atoms, molecules, DNA, star systems, galaxies, and everything else that fills the universe. Synchronicity is perhaps the greatest logistical accomplishment imaginable, managing events through innumerable human and physical connections to reveal meaning to the experiencer. That is only possible with an all-powerful First Mind. The system of synchronicities must also be perpetually updated since circumstances change due to free will. Somehow, God created a Block Universe that is fully formed but nevertheless has flexibility of outcomes, including those outcomes influenced by evolving synchronicities.

Naturally, materialists object to such a system. The typical materialist explanation of synchronicity is *probability theory*, specifically the *law of large numbers*. Essentially, materialists believe synchronicities are those rare occurrences that appear from endless statistical possibilities that eventually manifest; in short, the innumerability of life happenings ensures some situations of synchronicity. Proponents of synchronicity, including Jung, believe its absolute improbability proves the phenomenon and that no amount of statistical probabilities can account for such bizarre connections. Much to materialists' chagrin, Quantum Mechanics has provided a type of foundation for synchronicity with both the connecting principle of *entanglement* and the centrality of Mind highly suggestive of the universal order Jung advocated.

Interestingly, as the recognition of synchronicity has increased, a more scientific approach has been utilized to study the phenomenon. Degrees of both occurrence and improbability appear in synchronicity, a range extending from negligible to sensational. Robert Perry in his book *Signs* has developed empirical criteria that identifies indisputably synchronistic events and in so doing provides further refutation to the materialist argument.[249] His formulation, which defines exactly what constitutes a *sign*, extends the concept of synchronicity to a more provable circumstance as described below.

1. **Events.** Distinct events close in time and notably similar

2. **Parallels.** A list of a number of elements that are shared

3. **Subject Situation.** A situation of personal relevance that the *Sign* is commenting on

4. **Interpretation.** Commentary on the Subject Situation.

Further, according to Perry, a sign is when seemingly random events meet in time in an inconceivable manner. They are parallel with some similarities. Their relationship not only highlights a circumstance in our life but also conveys a definite perspective.[250]

So a *sign* is a more confirmable approach to the phenomenon since it must meet some specific criteria. No doubt the intent is to raise the standard of the identification of the truly synchronistic phenomenon since it is often overestimated by enthusiasts. Typically, familiar coincidences are reported as synchronicity when, in fact, they are merely random happenings. Of course, the separative ingredient is meaning. It is this meaning that so clearly defines the phenomenon, linking subjectivity with the objective world.

Since meaning is subjective, it is doubtful that synchronicity will ever be accepted by materialists since the scientific method cannot capture through experimentation something as anomalous as synchronicity, which cannot be generated in a lab.[251] Neither will experiencers consider statistical probabilities a valid explanation of the phenomenon since they have individually experienced synchronicity, which is impossible to reconcile through numbers. Knowledge is sometimes personal since synchronicity must often be witnessed in order to be believed.

Synchronicity is thus particularly revealing for the experiencer. Like *numinous* dreams, distinct situations of synchronicity provide deep insight and transform affairs. During the point of recognition, existence is magnified, a heightened awareness similar to *hyper reality*. It feels like space and time are distorted. Obvious is the intrusion, with the experiencer sensing a larger force at work. Reality gets shifted. Mind and Matter are briefly unified in actuality. Consider the following from Paul Levy who discusses this unification:

> **In a synchronicity, the conjunction of two cosmic principles, namely psyche and matter, takes place, and in the process a real exchange of attributes occurs as well. In such situations the psyche behaves as if it were material and matter behaves as if it were an expression of the psyche.**[252]

Levy further expresses the belief that the deeper Self cannot only express itself through inner experiences but also attract (manifestation) events in the external world similar to New Age arguments previously cited in Chapter 8. The latter appears dubious. The objection is the same one noted earlier, a desire to elevate humans to supernatural status since manifestation essentially grants to humans the powers of God. Nonetheless, Levy correctly identifies the exchange of attributes between Mind and Matter, which is an enormous step forward in authenticating an *idealistic* universe.

In this chapter, we have reviewed message formats from a deeper level of reality to influence destiny in the universe. Humans are the recipients of myths and archetypes, dreams and visions, intuition and recognition, and directed synchronicity. Yet we must also remember that the universe is a tremendously vast entity. Therefore, universal destiny may also include other intelligent civilizations, which obviously has huge implications for humanity. In short, the management of destiny may include all those who utilize free will, including extraterrestrials. Thus, we may only be experiencing a miniscule amount of managed destiny with the total required for universal direction simply incomprehensible to us, especially if advanced civilizations interact with each other. The more free will that exists in more places and among more intelligences, the more intricate is the management of destiny.

As a result, at least according to a growing number of experts, it is imperative that we colonize space.[253] Human self-perception must accommodate the realization that we may not be alone. Inevitably, we may find ourselves in contact with other intelligent civilizations, so we must be prepared both technologically *and* spiritually. Hence, we must embrace the Consciousness Paradigm since its discoveries will include the exploitation of the immaterial realm, surmount the limitations of classical physics (especially linear space travel), and provide spiritual elevation in order to improve our natures. Finally, our fate is subsumed by universal destiny with God directing us and existing with whatever other sentient beings may exist, and we must appraise ourselves within this larger context. Our leadership will depend on our technological capacities and spiritual credibility. We will consider these subjects next in our study.

CHAPTER 15

Civilizations in the Universe

To a near certainty, we are not alone.

Any reasonable inquiry into the possibility of extraterrestrial life considers a number of important facts and circumstances. Our approach here will be to proceed from a physicalist base but also include spiritual perspectives since much of the subject of extraterrestrial life has obvious metaphysical implications and even potentially supernatural causes. The framework of evaluation is as follows:

1. **Theoretical Underpinnings**

2. **The UFO Phenomenon**

3. **The Absurdity of the UFO Phenomenon**

4. **The Extraterrestrial Hypothesis**

5. **The Interdimensional Hypothesis**

6. **The UFO Phenomenon and the Spiritual Realm**

The confirmation of extraterrestrial life would cause massive ontological and psychological adjustments in our worldview. Virtually every aspect of human existence would be affected, including education, politics, economics, religion, morality, technology—the entire social structure. Anthropocentrism would be discredited, and we would need a new vision of ourselves. Security issues would dominate global discussions. The *Search for Extraterrestrial Intelligence Institute* (SETI) and many other organizations have developed metrics and protocols in the advent of extraterrestrial contact. These measures and recommendations include questions of cultural impacts, technological exchanges, diplomatic relationships, ecological considerations, and the potential malevolence and benevolence of extraterrestrial civilizations.[254] Much forethought has occurred on the subject, especially considering the level of resistance from mainstream media and academia. Before exploring the ramifications of extraterrestrial contact, however, we must first examine the scientific basis for the possibility of other sentient beings.

Theoretical Underpinnings

The single greatest theoretical underpinning for the possibility of extraterrestrial life is known as the *Drake Equation*. Formulated by astronomer Frank Drake, it is a probabilistic calculation that ascertains the number of intelligent civilizations in the galaxy. Intelligence is defined as being technologically communicative. It should be noted that the equation has a wide variance of values since many of the parameters can only be estimated. In fact, the equation is more useful as a consideration of the factors in evaluating the possibility of extraterrestrial life than it is a predictive device. It has been improved over the years by astronomical discoveries and resulting conceptual adjustments. The formulation, taken from the book *The Drake Equation*, is edited slightly from its original form.[255] The equation is as follows:

$$N = R\, f\, n_e\, f_l\, f_i\, f_c\, L \text{ where}$$

N = the number of civilizations in our galaxy
R = the average rate of star formation in our galaxy
f = the fraction of those stars that have planets
n_e = the number of planets supporting life per star that has planets
f_l = the fraction of planets supporting life that develop life at some point
f_i = the fraction of planets that develop intelligent life (civilizations)
f_c = the fraction of civilizations that develop a technological civilization
L = the length of time such civilizations release signals into space

The Drake Equation is a winnowing process, reducing from the total number of stars down to planets with technological civilizations. Although intelligent life is probable, it is likely exceedingly rare. The counterbalance is whether civilizations survive a sufficient time to explore the galaxy without first exterminating themselves through resource depletion, nuclear war, global warming, disease pandemics, or asteroid destruction. Human experience offers little hope for such civilizations to endure. The twentieth century witnessed two world wars, the Great Depression, environmental devastation, and a holocaust. We should remember that all this occurred in the Age of Science and Reason, so scientific and technological progression is no assurance of our future.

In any case, the Drake Equation was formulated within the framework of interstellar communication, specifically transmissions sent into space as the method of detection of intelligent life. It makes no provision for direct contact or other methods of discovery. There is a wide variance in some of the parameters of the Drake Equation, but we can estimate the number of intelligent civilizations in both the galaxy and the universe. In 2010, Italian astronomer Claudio Maccone developed the *Statistical Drake Equation* that utilizes the *Central Limit Theorem*, which states that a sufficient number of independent random variables produce a classic probability distribution.[256] With this method, Maccone calculated that our galaxy contains more than 4,500 intelligent civilizations, whereas the same computation yields about 3,500 for the original Drake Equation. His calculations also deduced the average distance in which the nearest detectable civilization might exist. Remember, his calculations apply only to our galaxy.

To illustrate the magnitude of the possibility of extraterrestrial life in the entire universe, we can perform a simple calculation. We should be conservative—in fact, preposterously so—perhaps ten intelligent civilizations per galaxy. Here is the next question: how many galaxies exist in the universe? The consensus answer is about 400 billion, although an exact number is unknown. So the following equation gives us an extremely conservative number of intelligent civilizations in the universe.

**Ten civilizations per galaxy · 400 billion galaxies
= 4 trillion civilizations in the universe**

That is a huge number of intelligent civilizations. Remember, however, that some experts believe humans are the only intelligent life. Others believe the number of intelligent civilizations exceeds this number by a large margin. So with this much discrepancy, is there another way to determine whether extraterrestrials exist?

The UFO Phenomenon

Humans have been observing unidentified flying objects since we first wandered the Earth. As we will discover, the UFO (unidentified flying object) phenomenon is intricate, exhibiting material and immaterial characteristics, and is both reticent and powerful. It contradicts *consensus reality* and is the greatest unofficially recognized enigma of existence. Nonetheless, it is studied by scientists, academics, intelligence agencies, the military, nongovernmental organizations, defense contractors, technology companies, and individual investigators. Typically, however, the subject is ignored by mainstream media and the culture at large; it takes courage to pursue the UFO phenomenon, and advocates are derided because the concept conflicts with accepted wisdom and governmental pronouncements.

Within the UFO community is widespread disagreement on the phenomenon. It is assumed that the national security apparatus possesses the preponderance of valuable information, but the entire subject is replete with both credible data and obvious disinformation. Even the New Age Movement has contaminated the process with ridiculous theories of extraterrestrial emissaries and universal unity. Perhaps the only area of agreement is that governments have conducted extensive concealment and deception in an effort to obfuscate the truth and control public opinion.

Here, we will examine what is reported about the UFO phenomenon, what can be factually verified, and what makes logical sense. We are especially interested in how the experience relates to other aspects of our study. This comparative approach positions the UFO phenomenon as another puzzle piece of reality. A simple definition of a UFO is "a mysterious object seen in the sky

... for which it is claimed no orthodox scientific explanation can be found."[257] Nearly all UFO sightings are resolved by stars, planets, lights, reflections, aircraft, lighthouses, clouds, and all manner of familiar objects in the sky; nevertheless, a small percentage of sightings remain unidentified and inexplicable. Reports come from commercial and military pilots, ground sightings, tracking and photographic equipment, astronauts in space, and even prominent politicians and government officials.

The attributes of a UFO are astounding. Consider the following characteristics cited by a high-ranking government official and known as these five observables:

1. **Anti-Gravity Lift – ... overcoming the earth's gravity with no visible means of propulsion. ...**

2. **Sudden and Instantaneous Acceleration – The objects may accelerate or change direction so quickly that no human pilot could survive the g-forces. ...**

3. **Hypersonic Velocities without Signatures – If an aircraft travels faster than the speed of sound, it typically leaves "signatures," like vapor trails and sonic booms. ...**

4. **Low Observability, or Cloaking – Even when objects are observed, getting a clear and detailed view of them ... remains difficult. ...**

5. **Trans-Medium Travel – Some UAP have been seen moving easily in and between different environments, such as space, the earth's atmosphere and even water.**[258]

A typical UFO sighting also includes witness testimony citing the craft as under intelligent control, exceeding our current level of technological development, manipulating the physical environment with supernatural capacities, and acting in defiance of spacetime. The Center for UFO Studies has developed basic classification systems regarding the phenomenon.[259] To further our discussion, we will use the following expanded taxonomy that examines some of the more sensational aspects of the UFO phenomenon:

- **Close Encounter 1. Sighting of a UFO**
- **Close Encounter 2. Physical evidence of the UFO**
- **Close Encounter 3. Sighting of the occupants of the UFO**
- **Close Encounter 4. Abduction of humans**
- **Close Encounter 5. Interdependent communication with a UFO**

For critics of the UFO phenomenon, the greater the level of close encounter, the greater the level of implausibility. For advocates, the greater the level of close encounter, the greater the level of comprehension. We can consider each separately for a better understanding of an experience that is comprised of many layers and has both frequently reported incidences and an endless number of questions.

In a Close Encounter 1, the witness discerns details such as the shape of the craft, spatial dimensions, distance from the ground, flight characteristics, lighting and window specifications, emanant sounds, design cuts, exterior edges, and distance travelled. Some reports include reference to engine protrusions, ignition flames, laser or beam activity, shifting structures or shapes, and light transformations.

In a Close Encounter 2, witnesses and researchers report physical evidence such as malfunctions of equipment, indentations in the soil, chemical residue, burned vegetation, damaged trees, broken concrete, and crushed structures. Often there are radioactive readings at the site and surrounding area. Investigators note bizarre atomic and molecular arrangements on recovered metals and alloys, as well as unique chemical signatures and structural properties. Pieces and fragments often cannot be burned or destroyed.

In a Close Encounter 3, witnesses report viewing the occupants of the UFO. These occupants include humanoids, robots, cyborgs, and beings indistinguishable from humans. The humanoids are often described as three to four feet tall with large heads, enormous black eyes, elongated arms, grey skin, and a distinct lack of muscularity. Their facial features are slight, nearly imperceptible. The robots and cyborgs are reported to be more mechanical and usually accompany a humanoid from the craft. The human-appearing extraterrestrials are typically described as tall and blonde with Nordic features. Others are reported wearing spacesuits and flight gear.

In a Close Encounter 4, witnesses report being abducted by extraterrestrials. A standard feature is missing time. These accounts are becoming more common in the exploration of the UFO phenomenon. Typically, the witness reports an examination performed by the extraterrestrials where the human is probed, has their skin scraped, sperm and eggs extracted, fluids injected or removed, tissue sampled, and bodies scrutinized with technical equipment. Often, the extraterrestrial scans the brain of the abducted human, retrieves individual memories, and projects images into the mind. Some humans report being threatened or scoffed at by their abductors. We will return to the subject of abduction to further explore it as an aspect of a much larger UFO phenomenon.

In a Close Encounter 5, there is direct communication between humans and extraterrestrials that involves signaling, messaging, telepathy, meditation, and projection of Consciousness. Pilots often report that a UFO may imitate lighting sequences, aircraft waves, ascents and descents, and flight characteristics of both military and commercial planes in an apparent effort to communicate. Proponents of human-initiated communication advocate various lighting transmissions into the nighttime sky to attract a UFO.

The Absurdity of the UFO Phenomenon

Interestingly, the official acknowledgment of the UFO phenomenon occurred only in 2017 with the release of some UFO videos by the United States Navy.[260] Subsequent government reports have proved inconclusive regarding the nature of the phenomenon. We should note that carefully researched books such as *Clear Intent* and *Above Top Secret* have demonstrated the UFO phenomenon to be real, but the government has taken an inexcusable amount of time to concede the truth.[261] The reason might be the preposterousness of what we will discuss next.

One of the more bizarre aspects of the UFO phenomenon concerns its ability to effect both physical reality and apparent spacetime.[262] It has been noted by a number of prominent UFO researchers, including Jacques Vallée and Jenny Randles, from whom the following paragraphs have utilized much information.[263] For example, witnesses often have a portent that something is about to happen, and their eyes are directed upward to notice the UFO. Randles termed this the "Oz Factor." Remarkably, individuals in the surrounding area (who should see something) often report observing nothing, yet the witnesses in closer proximity observe the craft. Thus, it appears that there is a "sphere of effect" proximate to the UFO. Likely this is caused by either a physical force or a mental projection. In short, does the UFO actually customize the physical environment or insert the image of itself into the mind of the witness? If the former, the UFO has an incredible ability to manipulate the material realm, and if the latter, it has the power to shape the Consciousness of the experiencer. In either case, it exhibits capabilities that far surpass those of human beings.

We can further examine this point to reveal its potential quantum origins. Somehow, the UFO phenomenon is able to connect to the minds of observers while leaving other potential witnesses unaffected. Those under the "sphere of effect" often report telepathic communication with those near them and that time ceases to exist. The UFO controls the situation and secludes the witnesses it prefers. Yet there is often physical evidence of the UFO that suggests it appears in the material realm, not just in the minds of observers. So it follows that the UFO is physically manifest and that part of its reality is its ability to connect to the Consciousness of the observer. This **connection to Consciousness through observation** sounds incredibly similar to the findings of the *Double Slit Experiment*, suggesting the intelligence behind the UFO phenomenon has either learned to exploit the immaterial realm or has ascertained the secrets of Mind.

Perhaps even more bizarre are the particulars of the abduction aspect of the UFO phenomenon. The definitive work in this area was done by Harvard professor John Mack, and his book *Abduction* astonished both believers and critics for its controversial findings.[264] His research examined a diverse representation of society and found no typical demographic or personality type for those who claimed abduction. Some remembered the abduction experience knowingly, and some required hypnotic approaches, although the Beings apparently possess some mechanism to hide or suppress memories. All the individuals were psychologically normal and rational. Mack often utilized findings from other credible researchers and experts to expand his database. That expanded database included case studies from an assortment of countries, with the subjects representing a diverse demographic similar to the United States.

The similarity of accounts is incredible, particularly with respect to the details of the experience. Specifics include descriptions of the Beings, the equipment and instrumentation inside the craft, the conduct of the abductors, the physical design of the UFO, and the methods of abduction. A large number of cases occurred before the Internet. In short, it would be impossible to arrange such similarity of details with no method of communication among experiencers in various countries with different demographic profiles. This adds an enormous amount of credibility to the accounts.

We will examine some of these details to demonstrate the bizarreness of the UFO phenomenon but only after positioning the discussion against the framework of the Materialism and Consciousness debate. Quoting Mack, we note how materialism impedes the search for truth:

> **But something else is called for, I think, which could, over time, exponentially increase our understanding of this subject, namely the recognition of a deep-seated resistance in mainstream Western culture to even considering that there could be phenomena that originate in the unseen or spirit world and cross over and manifest in the material world. For our so-called materialist paradigm, like any worldview, determines what is possible for us to see.[265]**

This critique is crucial in order to understand the anomalous nature of the UFO phenomenon because the details are often supernatural and rejected by mainstream science. The challenge is to construct some method of relating the unconventional to the conventional and the material to the immaterial. Mack utilized a taxonomy that positioned the discussion into categories of information (derived from experiencer accounts) that is relatively familiar to our materialist understanding of reality while allowing for integration of the incorporeal. They are summarized here:

- **The Physical Level: Sightings of a UFO, corresponding lights and tones, physical evidence such as burned vegetation and cuts or skin damage on the experiencers**

- **The Near Technology Level: An extension of current physical laws such as the propulsion system of the UFO and its incredible flight characteristics, the means by which extraterrestrials lift experiencers through solid structures such as buildings and windows, mind control techniques used by the Beings, and the placing of mental images into the minds of witnesses. In effect, this describes a level of technology that humans may achieve in the future.**

- **The Supernatural Level: The Beings have mastered thought travel and telepathy, the distortion of spacetime, the identification of vast realities beyond ours, a connection to Universal Consciousness and a larger totality, and the ability to change physical shapes and structures into other forms.**

Briefly, we can list some other remarkable facets of the UFO phenomenon to demonstrate its apparent ability to integrate the physical and metaphysical realms. That includes aspects of the experience and its effects on the witnesses. It should be noted that the possibility exists that integration may actually be achieved by manipulation of the incorporeal realm in order to effect physical changes in material reality. Such a capability is not integration but rather exploitation of whatever laws govern the metaphysical. In fact, supernaturalism may someday be described by the ability to first understand and then shape immaterial forces to affect the physical world. Other incredible aspects of the UFO phenomenon are as follows:

- **The emission of beams that transport humans to their craft**
- **Witnesses being shown images of the future during abduction**
- **Thoughts expressed as lights and colors yet understood by humans**
- **Past lives uncovered during the abduction experience**
- **Presentation of hybrid (extraterrestrial and human) progeny**
- **Mind manipulation of objects into smaller and larger versions**
- **Messages of environmental destruction and a destroyed Earth**
- **Reduction or cessation of time-structuring reality to fulfill purposes**

These characteristics appear too incredible to believe, far surpassing everything scientifically confirmed. The UFO phenomenon is thus easily denigrated since it appears exceedingly esoteric and even impossible. The capabilities and powers demonstrated by a UFO, including their effects on humans, are beyond this world. Although equating the phenomenon to classical physics and biological frameworks provides some measure of contemplative resonance, the UFO phenomenon eludes conventional comprehension. Yet it is real, and the evidence for its supernatural abilities is increasing with time. For that, we require possible explanations for its origins.

The Extraterrestrial Hypothesis

The Extraterrestrial Hypothesis (ETH) is simply that the UFO phenomenon is entities from other planets. The Drake Equation provides the theoretical underpinnings for the ETH with our galaxy populated by hundreds of billions of stars, each with a number of planets orbiting them. As discussed earlier, the best estimate for intelligent civilizations in our galaxy is about 4,500. Advocates of the ETH posit that intelligent life is a statistically probable outcome with the assumption that extraterrestrials would naturally explore the stars and eventually find us. Since stars in the same galaxy can be billions of years older than other stars, planets that orbit them could be billions of years older than our solar system. Theoretically, then, some advanced civilization could have billions of advanced years on other intelligent life, which could account for the enormous technological gap between extraterrestrials and humans.

Substantial support for the Extraterrestrial Hypothesis exists. As early as 1948, the United States Air Force conducted a study called *Project Sign*, which concluded that the UFO phenomenon was of extraterrestrial origin. Many European countries, including France and Germany, have produced secret documents theorizing that the ETH best explicates unidentified flying objects.[266] Many experts have supported the Extraterrestrial Hypothesis in their public opinions and published works, and a number of prominent citizens, including a number of Presidents of the United States, have witnessed a UFO.[267] Many high-ranking military officers and officials have written books that claim the UFO phenomenon is real and attributable to extraterrestrials.[268] In fact, the preponderant position regarding the UFO phenomenon is that extraterrestrials have been observing life on Earth for millennia. This historical component, dating from ancient Egypt and classical Greece, is confirmatory of the UFO phenomenon since earlier sightings cannot be attributed to modern lighting technology such as aircraft.

So although the theoretical underpinnings for the Extraterrestrial Hypothesis have been established, the question remains how extraterrestrials could travel such vast distances to reach Earth. First, we require some perspective.

It would take more than four years to reach Alpha Centauri, the nearest star other than our Sun, while travelling the speed of light (which humans are nowhere near accomplishing). To reach the same star with current human technology would take 33,000 years. Obviously, no human would survive such a lengthy excursion, and neither could any other life form imaginable. Our galaxy extends 100,000 light years in distance, so linear travel, even at the speed of light, is untenable. Extraterrestrials must have developed some other means to traverse interstellar space.

Does such a means exist? Theoretically, yes. In fact, a number of former government employees have provided fantastic accounts of their work in top-secret programs designed to fabricate faster-than-light technology. We will briefly cite one here, but its authenticity is not our primary concern; its value is the theoretical insight on how nonlinear travel might be possible. Consider the following from Robert Lazar, a nuclear physicist who discussed extraterrestrial propulsion technology:

> **This is accomplished by generating an intense gravitational field and using that field to distort space/time, bringing the destination to the source, and allowing you to cross many light years of space in little time and without traveling in a linear mode near the speed of light.**[269]

Essentially, the UFO can generate its own gravity and pull a desired point of the galaxy toward the craft. At that point, the technology is deactivated, and the universe corrects to its initial position, taking the craft with it. In that way, the travel is nonlinear and accomplished in only the time required to utilize the technology. Scientists are already beginning to lay the theoretical groundwork for gravitational wave, hyper propulsion, spacetime distortion, and quantum entanglement forms of travel.[270]

The larger point is that the Extraterrestrial Hypothesis may describe the bizarre characteristics of the UFO phenomenon because other intelligent species have mastered such technologies. Being older and more advanced, extraterrestrials would logically possess superior, even fantastic technological capabilities that vastly exceed our own. Yet an often referenced criticism to this framework exists; simply that the template for evaluating the possibility of extraterrestrial life is based on our own human experience, beginning with a planet orbiting a star in a habitable zone, eventually producing intelligent life. The question is whether this template is accurate or reflects humans projecting themselves into the experience.

Witness accounts describe extraterrestrials as humanoid yet biologically more advanced than humans, especially their disproportionately larger heads that suggest more highly evolved brains and higher intelligence. Critics have noted this anthropocentrism and suggest that it reflects human prejudice toward our own genotype. Using the Darwinian framework (for the sake of argument) where humans evolved into the dominant life form on Earth and referencing our experience suggests that extraterrestrials would experience similar evolvement. That in itself is quite anthropocentric since nature may be different and evolve differently on other planets. Moreover, this anthropocentrism is not just Darwinian since it also extends to religious traditions. The creation version further supports human essentiality since God created humans in His image, which suggests that any created beings from other worlds would also be humanoid.

The failure in this logic concerning Darwinism is that without the asteroid impact on Earth 65 million years ago, dinosaurs would have evolved into the dominant life form. Humans might not even exist. God can create beings in any image He wants, not necessarily just humanoid. So although our anthropocentrism is natural, it definitely prejudices our perspective; when you have been the only, it is difficult to embrace the many. And though the Extraterrestrial Hypothesis is the leading theorization of the subject, other substantial criticisms exist apart from its anthropocentrism. In fact, these objections form the basis of an alternative explanation for the UFO phenomenon.

The Interdimensional Hypothesis

Opposition to the Extraterrestrial Hypothesis results from two primary factors. One is unconvincing, and the other is quite compelling. The first factor is that extraterrestrials should have made their presence known by public displays or other notable appearances, and since they have not, it proves they do not exist. This objection is ridiculous since there are literally millions of credible sightings and thousands of case studies where the UFO generates physical evidence, complete with reliable witnesses, to say nothing of the abduction phenomenon and its global confirmation. In short, UFOs are making themselves known. Moreover, innumerable government insiders have provided plausible accounts of the UFO presence, and as previously mentioned, the United States Navy has officially acknowledged the UFO Phenomenon as real.

The second factor against the Extraterrestrial Hypothesis is that the characteristics and behaviors of the UFO Phenomenon suggest an origin that is immaterial. As discussed, the UFO Phenomenon appears supernatural, defying any materialist explanations, with the exception that physical evidence often remains at the site. Such evidence may actually be manufactured by the UFO to provide "proof" of the experience, although the causative agent may be esoteric in origin. This description conforms to reality and is extremely plausible. As a result, other interpretations of the UFO Phenomenon are demanded.

The leading alternative interpretation comes from Jacques Vallée, primarily because of its commensurability with the preponderance of evidence. His classic book on the subject, *Passport to Magonia*, originally published in 1969, began to frame his beliefs based on his incredible research.[271] What was especially obvious was that extraterrestrials with superior technology could not account for the absurdity of the facts. The ability to manipulate spacetime and materialize at will defied conventional physics. Often, the physical evidence of the UFO appeared contrived as if to validate the experience of the witness and conflicted with environmental actuality. An element of deception existed. It appeared as though the UFO Phenomenon must be originating in other dimensions, from someplace parallel to us, possibly from the supernatural or spiritual realm. That has become known as the *Interdimensional Hypothesis*.

Beings originating in other dimensions or realms better describe the large number of sightings since no civilization would make millions of excursions through interstellar space to investigate Earth. This position also enlightens us on how a UFO could suddenly manifest, affect similarly located witnesses in different ways, produce conflicting physical evidence, and disappear from view in defiance of conventional physics. To Vallée, the UFO Phenomenon was behaving in an apparently supernatural manner. He also noted that the UFO Phenomenon is historical, including the corollary abduction experience, and is linked to myths and archetypes. Further, his research demonstrated that the UFO Phenomenon is directing humans into their next stage of development, acting as a "control system" over the Earth and guiding society and shaping human belief toward its own ends.

His work inspires a number of questions. As noted, the UFO Phenomenon actualizes in a bizarre manner, existing just past human comprehension and containing a number of familiar elements such as spacecraft, instrumentation, humanoids, and communication; in short, we can relate to it. Nevertheless, the subject is primarily studied by societal elites, specifically those in the national security apparatus. Is this a desired effect of the UFO Phenomenon? Does the UFO Phenomenon take its form for exactly that reason? Although the phenomenon "appears" to a diverse demographic, elites are typically those who investigate and manage the affair. Is that so the public can be gradually desensitized to the phenomenon? Do our leaders trust us enough to know the truth?

Another question is whether the "control system" could be managed by physical extraterrestrials as opposed to beings from a metaphysical realm. If so, what is their objective? What is their reason for secrecy? Vallée never eliminates the possibility the UFO Phenomenon may be extraterrestrial in nature, but it is preposterous that an advanced intelligence would expend so many resources to study us. Such an advanced species would not require huge numbers of abducted humans for examinations or to conduct an extensive hybridization program since their level of scientific and technological progress would make these activities unnecessary. Certainly, they would not venture this far or this often to map the Earth or exploit our natural resources. Invasion and colonization would have happened much before we developed nuclear weapons since they make us more formidable as enemies. Culturally, there is little benefit from knowing us. In short, according to Vallée, the absurdity of the UFO Phenomenon compels conclusions toward a supernatural rather than an extraterrestrial explanation since humans are simply not that interesting.

The UFO Phenomenon and the Spiritual Realm

Since reality is *idealistic* as opposed to *realistic* and everything reflects that nature, the UFO Phenomenon is likely no exception. That provides insight into its essence since it probably originates from an immaterial realm beyond our own, a realm that influences our existence yet remains largely incomprehensible to us. In fact, a stronger case can be made that the UFO Phenomenon is more immaterial than material. Throughout history, the UFO Phenomenon has often been perceived with supernatural or spiritual dimensions, transcending the physical realm.

In our modern era, that is taken to extremes. UFO religions, some of which are so preposterous that they prove either government disinformation or the ridiculousness of man, have appeared positing extraterrestrials as benevolent angels that advance human culture. Environmental messaging is primary. Although there is proof that the UFO Phenomenon is real, there is no evidence of its own divinity or sacred purposes or its occupants as spiritual masters or ethereal emissaries. Whether it is debatable that the UFO Phenomenon is extraterrestrial or interdimensional, the occupants of a UFO cannot be gods since they also were created.

It is possible, however, that the UFO Phenomenon manifests from the same realm as myths, archetypes, dreams, visions, and synchronicity in order to influence society while intentionally obscuring its nature. The metaphysical aspect of the UFO Phenomenon strongly suggests that the spiritual realm is superior and existed much before the creation of our universe. Thus, it can effortlessly interact with our own. Reports of UFO materialization and manipulation of spacetime suggest this supernatural nature since physical beings would lack this ability. Its effects on witnesses are often reported as spiritual, even spiritually transformative.[272] Characteristically, the UFO Phenomenon can impact both physical and spiritual aspects of reality while originating from an immaterial dimension, often changing the physical environment. The question is the mechanism whereby this is accomplished.

Here, we have devised an extremely conjectural possibility for the transformation of physical reality, and it should be viewed primarily as an impetus for further study. We can briefly discuss this mechanism as it pertains to the UFO Phenomenon, but note that its significance in the larger objective of this book is to understand how the properties of the immaterial can potentially arrange material reality to its own choosing. We can use a materialist framework to illustrate the point. The constituents of organic matter are arranged in increasing complexity, from atoms to molecules to chemicals to cells. We know that beneath the level of the atom are subatomic particles made of spinning and vibrating invisible energy. This energy is likely a derivative of Mind. Consciousness, like material forms, may have its own properties arranged in an increasingly intricate way, similar to point particles in classical physics (taking no physical space), yet their arrangement may lead to subatomic and atomic actualization that forms the foundational structure of the material world. That is how Mind and Spirit can become physical reality. Exploitation of the arrangement of Consciousness could theoretically transform everything we know.

Remember, what follows is highly speculative since it is more likely that Consciousness is inseparable due to its foundational nature. Nevertheless, consider the following illustration where parts of Mind or Consciousness Divisions (CDs) can be organized to construct material reality where the various shadings of CDs represent the various components of Consciousness:

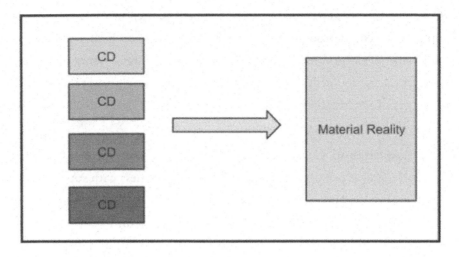

The above may describe how the UFO Phenomenon can distort spacetime and shape reality with apparently supernatural abilities. It is similar to how different atoms form different molecules. In this conceptualization, different Consciousness Divisions would form different subatomic and thus atomic constructions, providing a mechanism whereby foundational Mind becomes material reality. Thus, a different organization of Consciousness Divisions, represented by different shadings as above, could change actuality, represented by another shade as follows:

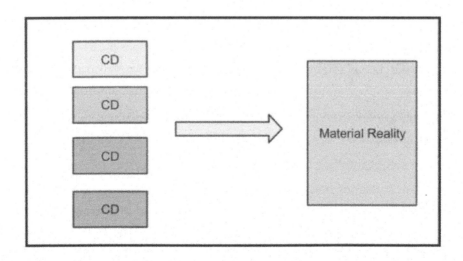

If Consciousness has its own structural properties, then manipulation of its components could produce different material outcomes. If the intelligence behind the UFO Phenomenon has deduced this configuration, they can adjust the physical environment to their choosing. They can also project images into the minds of observers because both material reality and individual minds are comprised of Consciousness Divisions.

As mentioned, Consciousness may be a reality unto itself, inseparable into parts. In this perspective, Consciousness is a oneness with supernatural abilities unlike anything seen in the material realm. It cannot be reduced. Oneness implies simplicity, but Mind is anything but simple; against our tradition of reductionism, its oneness may prove the ultimate complexity. Moreover, perhaps only God can divide Mind. After all, granting us some of His Mind is a division of sorts. More likely, however, He simply manipulates physics according to His will with no divisions required. That suggests that divisions of any nature are manufactured to produce a physical effect when the natural state is immanent and inseparable Consciousness. Quantum physics appears to demonstrate that exact point.

Simply, the UFO Phenomenon may have an in-depth understanding of the properties of Consciousness, its nature, aspects, components, separability, forces, and so on, allowing it to influence humans and the course of society. This competency may have been granted by God or is possibly an aspect of anything originating from the spiritual realm. Or perhaps if extraterrestrials are physical beings, then a natural progression of a species eventually includes a mastery of Consciousness. For us to someday exploit the material realm is an exciting possibility, but with that expertise comes a tremendous responsibility. We must first deserve it.

In conclusion, the UFO Phenomenon is an enigma, but its preliminarily identified aspects are both inspiring and cautionary. Technologically, it offers a tremendous learning opportunity, but unlike other aspects of existence it appears potentially ominous; obviously, it is far more advanced, possessing supernatural powers, and we are in the inferior position. History clearly demonstrates that whenever a technologically inferior civilization comes into contact with a superior one, there are disastrous consequences for the former; typically, the inferior civilization is either destroyed or loses its way of life. But if the UFO Phenomenon is influencing us, it is highly improbable that it seeks our destruction. More likely, it fulfills some grander purpose, and we must further our own expertise in order to learn its secrets. First, though, we must examine how humanity will be affected by the confirmation of extraterrestrial life before we can advance to whatever that particular future offers.

CHAPTER 16

Humanity in the Galaxy

If we venture to the stars, we must be prepared for what we find.

For this discussion, we will assume the Extraterrestrial Hypothesis is accurate and crafts from other worlds are extraterrestrial in origin. Perhaps we should view this chapter as preparedness in case extraterrestrials are actual biological entities as opposed to interdimensional or supernatural beings. It is also possible that the UFO Phenomenon may represent both physical beings and supernatural entities, the latter able to assume the characteristics of the former or the former evolving into the latter. Conceivably, humans may eventually fully interact with both.

Whatever the truth of the UFO Phenomenon, it will transform our world in unimaginable ways; like any intelligent species, we must survive to achieve that transformation. More importantly, we must break through our current stagnation to ensure our survival since our natural resource base is dwindling and the future mandates huge expenditures of energy and materials. Invariably, we must extend ourselves into the solar system and then beyond. The framework of evaluation for that discussion is as follows:

1. **Human Survivability**

2. **Human Advancement and Colonization of Space**

3. **Spiritual Humanity in the Galaxy**

4. **Universal Studies**

We can begin by considering our prospects for survival. Expert opinion is deeply divided on the subject.

Human Survivability

Nature has demonstrated that 99% of all species go extinct. Humans are another species, more intelligent perhaps, but biology proves our vulnerability. Add to that our history. We are a belligerent group. We war and kill each other. Eventually, all weapons are used on a massive scale, with nuclear and biological weapons likely no exception. Thus, a number of issues confront human survival, both in the near and distant future, with the greatest being our own annihilative natures.

Let us consider some other challenges to our survival. In the near term, we have global warming, overpopulation, economic inequality, environmental destruction, and even artificial intelligence. In the distant future are threats such as resource depletion, solar expansion, asteroid impacts, and universal entropy. Of course, we will attempt to extend ourselves to the best of our abilities. That will consist of a number of measures, including managed population reduction, preservation of the Earth, colonization of the solar system, expansion to the stars, and exploitation of sustainable energy sources. Whether we will be successful is subject to widespread debate.

Five mass extinctions have occurred in history. A mass extinction is where a huge number of species die off in a relatively short amount of time. Typically, mass extinctions result from some natural disaster such as asteroid collision or volcanic eruption. Some experts, such as science writer Elizabeth Kolbert, advance the theory that we are headed toward a sixth mass extinction, although this time the transgressor is human beings.[273] Species are disappearing faster than in any period in history, and the oceans of the world are under particular assault.

Advocates for the preservation of the planet typically advise solutions such as limited carbon emissions, water conservation, energy efficiency, and more trees. The *World Economic Forum* advocates increased integration of public, corporate, civil, and personal interests to advance the environmental agenda commensurate with the rise of technological and scientific capability.[274] They term this effort the Fourth Industrial Revolution, which theoretically allows for sustainable economic growth. It should be noted, however, that internationally integrated efforts have thus far failed to achieve the desired reductions in environmental devastation. Moreover, many internationalist organizations use the cover of environmentalism to promote globalist agendas, so each must be evaluated accordingly.

Others posit that our current environmental and species degradation is insignificant compared to previous mass extinctions.[275] The position is rather that humanity is on the precipice of disaster. Research also demonstrates that once a mass extinction begins, nothing can stop it, and a catastrophic event is not required to begin the process. Insidiously, environmental destruction begins gradually, then aggregates, and finally disintegrates the system. According to this perspective, humans have time for corrective measures, but they must begin without hesitation.

An enormous amount of research has been undertaken to ascertain the cause of our rather indifferent depredation of our planet. It is not even definitively proven that humans are causing the next mass extinction since the planet may be warming on its own. Here, however, we will assume human culpability. Thousands of research sources, including books, articles, websites, blogs, and so on, discuss the issue, with notable works listed on *The Environment Show*, but here we will summarize their findings.[276] Following is a list of the typically referenced arguments:

- **Overpopulation – Biology demands reproduction, which eventually drives the population past the carrying capacity of Earth.**

- **Capitalism** – Requires consumption and production to ensure job creation and maintain living standards, thereby neglecting environmental concerns.

- **Globalization** – Advances capitalism on a global scale, exacerbating its destructive tendencies.

- **Economic System Stagnation** – Failure of competing economic systems such as socialism and communism to provide a viable alternative to capitalism.

- **State Dereliction** – Countries around the world have failed to control corporate interests and are often accessories of commercial entities.

Although these findings correctly identify many of the reasons for our failed conservancy of the environment, they all result from something deeper, something more fundamental to life, based in biology and causative of our peril. This is known as the *biological imperative*, the predominant self-preservation mechanism inherent in all living things. Essentially, this is the core of our problems since it causes us to be selfish. Many choose not to reproduce, but virtually everyone chooses to survive. The harshness of nature causes insecurity, all of us seeking safety against adversity to enhance our survival prospects. *The net result is the perception of never having enough.* Thus, we prioritize ourselves, often at the expense of others and certainly at the expense of society. Selfishness is built into us and into the system. The following demonstrates this dynamic:

Harshness of Nature......Insecurity......
Selfishness......Accumulation

Humans strive for additional possessions—to accumulate as it were—a drive firmly established in biology. Our personal relationships, social structures, political arrangements, economic systems, and life philosophies are all based on this drive. Capitalism follows from our form, commensurate with our self-interest, an economic system designed to accumulate possessions to achieve security. Consumerism defines our culture. Even the extremely wealthy strive for more possessions, while on the other end, social justice advocates are married to their tablets and smartphones. This drive to accumulate breeds moral depravity and widespread hypocrisy. Humans are inherently selfish and oblivious to their own culpability, a species that requires vast improvement with little self-awareness of its deficiencies.

So it is extremely dubious that humans will suddenly transform away from self-interest and toward altruism and greater guardianship of the planet. As a result, the overexploitation of Earth will likely progress to inevitable resource depletion and environmental devastation. Initially, materialist technological solutions will be attempted, but they will ultimately fail due to increasing stagnation. Self-interest and economic globalization will eventually decimate whatever innovations and protections are devised, which includes what many consider the next evolution of human economic systems—state-managed capitalism. That, too, will likely fail. China, the leader of state-managed capitalism, pollutes more than any country on Earth. Many experts believe the only viable option at that point will be the colonization of space. According to them, we will simply have to find other worlds in which to sustain ourselves.

Human Advancement and Colonization of Space

In 1964, Soviet astronomer Nikolai Kardashev developed a methodology to measure the technological sophistication of a civilization based on the amount of energy it can exploit.[277] It is known as the Kardashev Scale and serves as a type of prerequisite for colonization since any colonization effort requires a massive expenditure of energy. The Kardashev Scale is as follows:

- **Type I civilization – can exploit all the energy available on its planet**

- **Type II civilization – can exploit energy at the scale of its star**

- **Type III civilization – can exploit energy at the scale of its entire galaxy**

Human civilization is currently a little less than a Type I civilization. A huge presumption in this formulation is that a civilization will endure for the time required for exploitation of advanced energy sources. These energy sources, such as fusion power or space-based solar arrays, have been theorized but remain technological fantasies. Moreover, our current scientific and technological stagnation is a discouraging sign.

So although the Kardashev Scale is a good initial framework for discussions about the energy required for the colonization of space, more relevant is a formulation that recognizes not only the energies required but the full civilizational capabilities necessary to first colonize our own solar system and then the galaxy beyond. We can refer to this capability as the "expertise" of our civilization—the combined energy, informational, scientific, technological, economic, philosophical, and political aspects of human culture. We will not examine here the vast range of technological and logistical issues regarding colonization or the moral implications of whether colonization should be pursued, but we will rather focus on a theoretical framework for its possibility. The feasibility must be presented before the reality can form or the issues be debated.

If it becomes imperative to colonize space, governments must powerfully advocate this framework of feasibility to their citizens and make the benefits of space exploration abundantly clear. Countries in leadership roles, especially the United States, must champion not only the advantages of exploring space but also the opportunity cost of not pursuing colonization, including our own destruction. Moreover, all governments must be truthful about our level of technological stagnation. Consider, for example, the obstacles to the colonization of space:

- **Humans are biologically incompatible with lengthy space travel.**

- **Humans require the physical particulars of Earth for extended survival.**

- **Funding for such adventures exceeds all projected financial resources.**

- **Close proximity planets orbiting proximate stars are adverse to life.**

- **Propulsion system technology is inadequate for extended missions.**

- **Opinion studies have demonstrated public support for domestic priorities.**

With respect to space colonization, a huge gap exists between our ambitions and our limitations. We have little ability to grow nourishment in space or carry sufficient water supplies. We have neither the means to provide the energy requirements for colonization on another world nor a viable method to stop radiation exposure without the protective environment of Earth's atmosphere. We have no method of perpetuating ourselves in space since procreation requires the specifics of Earth's gravity. Simply, our technological sophistication is inadequate to colonize space and is further thwarted by the bounds of classical physics and our current materialist paradigm. Thus, the question becomes whether scientific progress can surpass resource depletion and environmental destruction in sufficient time to extend our species.

Perhaps then it becomes clearer that we must break through materialism and exploit the incredible potential of the Consciousness Paradigm. Our largest obstacle is interstellar distances. We must master nonlinear travel to colonize the galaxy. Transit periods between star systems must be radically reduced since conventional methods are inadequate. We will have to explore many planets before we find suitable ones to colonize, which will require massively efficient surveying and travel. Classical physics cannot exploit the immaterial foundations of the universe since they have different properties and follow different laws; therefore, we must manipulate the fabric of reality to reduce the distances involved. If we do not learn the secrets of foundational Mind, we will never colonize space.

Spiritual Humanity in the Galaxy

If the universe is mental and spiritual, we must master these foundational elements. The exploration and colonization of interstellar space demand more than technological expertise, which also requires a spiritual integrity commensurate with an advanced species. We can refer to this collective spirituality as the *human spirit*. Unfortunately, the history of this term is remarkably materialist and rather limiting. Traditionally, the human spirit is conceived as the end product of an aggregation of distinct human dimensions in the following manner:

**Biological......Psychological......Sociological......
Economic......Informational......Spiritual**

According to this framework, humans are grounded in biology, have impressive psychological abilities, form complex societies, develop economic systems, master information, and eventually advance to spiritual development. Here, the collective human spirit is presumed to be an outcome of the biological and social advancement of our species. This perspective forms the basis for *secular spirituality*, a philosophy emphasizing personal growth and shared universal truth without the requirement of a Creator. Thus, according to secular spirituality, the more time humans spend on Earth, the more advanced becomes their collective spirit.

Any study of history demonstrates the fallacy of this assertion. The collective human spirit has primarily produced inequality and injustice, not to mention war and destruction. So we must change our perspective regarding our natures and recognize how our dispositions affect our futures. We must find a way to surmount the limitations of the *biological imperative* while ensuring our perpetuation through time. In short, humanity requires individual and societal improvement in order to prevail over our self-destructive tendencies.

As we have seen, Spirit is absolute and pure and does not result from some evolutionary and secular process; rather, it is fundamental to reality. Spirit is instilled in us by God; it comes with being human. Once placed in bodies, Spirit is corrupted, and its expression becomes dualistic. That is the reason humans are both good and bad. Our choices either diminish or elevate spirit. *The way to elevate spirit is to recognize its source and act accordingly.* So before we can travel to the stars, we must choose to be exceptional beings who take inspiration from Spirit itself. That will align our spiritual essence with our scientific and technological progression so we virtuously manage our expertise. We must be deserving of colonization by having a spiritually superior culture that serves as an exemplification to other advanced civilizations. In short, we must be better than our past.

Another aspect of a spiritually superior culture is that a causal relationship exists between human achievement and Soul development. In short, the more humanity progresses, the more the soul can learn. This discussion uses some basic mathematics, which the reader can certainly glance over. We can use the concept of moderation from statistics to demonstrate the validity of this argument. Moderation occurs when the relationship between two variables depends on a third variable. Here, the independent aspect is human achievement, and the dependent aspect is soul development. The causal effect, C, acting as a moderator (influences achievement and Soul development), is a function of increasing complexity, time, free will, and destiny management. Consider the following: Let a = achievement, s = soul development, C = causal effect, c = increasing complexity, t = time, w = free will, and dm = destiny management. The formula for this process is the following:

$$C(w, a, c, t, d_m) = s$$

The point is that a huge number of factors contribute to the advancement of society and that in aggregate they also influence soul development. Humans must remember this as they construct their society of the future. We are not only progressing as humans, but we are progressing as Souls.

It should be noted that the preponderance of civilizational studies emphasize the economic, social, legal, and technological advances of a culture without mentioning its spiritual development. Spiritual issues are seen as a lesser or adjunct notion when they should be elevated. Fortunately, some organizations such as the Spiritual Civilization Group aspire toward the development of a "spiritual civilization," which animates other civilizational pursuits with honor and legitimacy.[278] Such civilizations will have transcended inherent biological and cultural selfishness and recognized that individual interests are best forwarded by advances in the collective human spirit.

So what are the qualities of a spiritually advanced culture? Consider the following traits:

- **Intelligence**
- **Creativity**
- **Ethics**
- **Social Justice**
- **Compassion**
- **Environmentalism**
- **Appreciation**
- **Responsibility**
- **Insight**
- **Love**
- **Faith**

No human culture has exhibited these characteristics without countervailing tendencies such as greed, injustice, animosity, devaluation, and selfishness. It is nearly impossible to rate the spiritual stature of a culture because the metrics involved are either unknown, disdained, ignored, or contested. One thing, however, is certain: the materialist tenet of man dominating nature for human benefit is both obviously anachronistic and morally immature. Any extraterrestrial civilization would recognize our environmental indifference and historical malevolence, and determine that we are either primitive or ominous. In truth, it would be sensible for them to subjugate us before we destroy more worlds than our own.

Although it is difficult to measure the spiritualness of a culture, we can start our enhancement by respecting nature and exalting life. We must remember that we are as uncivilized as we are civilized. Our past is atrocious, primarily because we lack *principle*. And what is principle? The term is defined as "a moral rule or standard of good behavior."[279] The term "on principle" can be defined as "because of or in order to demonstrate one's adherence to a particular belief."[280] Humanity often claims to have principle, but seldom do we live principled lives. Hypocrisy characterizes our era. Just look at our leaders. As mentioned, selfishness is absolutely rampant.[281] Globalization and technology have propagated unprecedented narcissism and diminished the possibility of principled unity.

So what is to be done?

Consider the following from David Korten, author of *When Corporations Rule the World*, as a beginning discussion:

1. **Earth Balance**

2. **Equitable Distribution**

3. **Life-Serving Technologies**

4. **Living Communities**

Essentially, Korten recommends sustainability, equal distribution of wealth and power, the development of technologies furthering society, and the construction of social agreements integrating humans and nature to form democratic living communities.[282] The greatest challenge will be equitable distribution since nature is demonstrably hierarchical. Failed economic orders such as communism and capitalism must be replaced with a system that better serves the masses *and* preserves individual aspiration. We must get maximum efficiency from the group while the highly motivated innovate and lead. Aggregation of wealth and corporate interests must be diminished, and living communities must be constructed for ecology and unity. Inherent in such a formulation are human spiritual values such as consideration of others and guardianship of the planet.

For the entire planet to save itself, humans must be unified and dedicated to balancing material and spiritual aspects of existence. About 85% of the world's population is religious.[283] A belief in God is not only pervasive but defines our existence since we are fundamentally spiritual beings. Nevertheless, science has been instrumental to our advance, so the scientific and spiritual domains must be integrated for maximum collective benefit. This fusion will result in shared wisdom and purpose. The Emerging New Civilizations Initiative has an excellent summary of this blending of the physical and the spiritual. Although pursuing the truth is a challenge, we need a common vision in order to make the world what we want it to be and find a balance.[284]

A shared vision for the future begins with us, with the insight spreading from individuals to groups, to localities to states, to nations and alliances, and finally to world civilization. Everyone must participate. If not, increasing scarcity will cause "resource" conflicts with the potential for war and nuclear devastation. Governments (those with powerful militaries) will take all measures against global adversaries to secure adequate resources; as events grow more desperate, they will eliminate personal liberties in order to maintain social control. Survival, as opposed to opportunity, will define human existence.

It is perhaps here that scientific materialism has done its greatest damage, for if scientific materialism impelled a worldview emphasizing "real" things such as resources, products, possessions, wealth, and technologies, then we must shift our perspective toward what accentuates justice, collaboration, unity, community, and destiny. In short, we must prioritize Spirit. In an environment of scarcity, all "real" things are eventually depleted; thus, scientific materialism is a meaningless philosophy since it prioritizes diminishing at the expense of flourishing. Is materialism or spirituality more likely to save planet Earth? The answer is abundantly clear.

Advanced life seeks to perpetuate itself through both biological and cultural processes, but as we have demonstrated, Spirit is fundamental to existence and more fundamental than either Biology or Culture—in fact, causative of both and driven by its own objectives. Thus, complecting occurs among Spirit, Biology, and Culture, with the physical world (and life) inexorably fated with the purposes of Spirit. Soul learning requires both physical bodies and advancing culture to forward spiritual objectives; as we have seen, the more advanced the culture, the more the Soul can learn. Nature, while providing the environment for culture, is, however, eliminative of species. *Thus, we must preserve nature and also transcend it.* Although required to exist in physical form, the individual, community, culture, and species are all bound together with the progression of Spirit, thus ensuring that our fate is a spiritual fate.

If humanity can somehow transform itself into a species with as much spiritual aspiration as scientific proficiency, we may qualify for successful colonization of space. Our conduct may prove instrumental to any potential relationships with extraterrestrials, specifically whether we proceed in peace or war. We can understand this potentiality by examining International Studies, a discipline concerned with relationships between the nations of Earth. This framework extrapolated to space forms Universal Studies, a system of relationships among advanced civilizations that does not concern itself with how space is divided between the nations of Earth (an extension of International Studies). For this next discussion, we will assume that humans are united; if humanity is divided, nations will make separate agreements with extraterrestrials, which will prove disastrous for our species. Therefore, achieving human unity and mastery of Universal Studies will likely prove crucial to our colonization of space.

Universal Studies

On Earth, the discipline of International Studies has produced elaborate theoretical frameworks that define the behavior of the world's nations in global affairs. Included in these perspectives are the activities of nongovernmental organizations, global corporations, religious institutions, ideological factions, interest group associations, and other political and social entities. We will consider only those that are relevant to hypothesized relationships among advanced civilizations in space. Undoubtedly, this analysis is simplistic compared to the vast sum of knowledge existing in the discipline.[285] The basic classifications are below.

Realism – An emphasis on state security, self-interest, rationality, survival, and power. This interpretation parallels biological imperative and economic capitalism. Peace is achieved through forceful militaries balancing power. Morality is less important than state interests.

Liberalism – An emphasis on inherent goodness and interdependence to achieve human objectives. Although the international system is viewed as anarchic, without any dominant organization to enforce law or apply moral codes, self-interest can be exploited for social utility. Common interest and mutual benefit are assumed to mitigate the unethical side of man.

Power – An emphasis on the concept of power, specifically the divisions between military power and cultural power. Both military and cultural power define the influence a nation exerts on the international system. The former describes intimidating force and the latter soft measures such as economics, diplomacy, social incentives, and other cultural aspects.

Polarity – An emphasis on the arrangement of power within the international system. This concept encompasses balance of power, hegemony, interdependence, and the evolution of power. Particularly relevant is the subject of alliances. Polarity has contributed toward innumerable security, trade, defense, environmental, and cultural agreements among nations.

We can extend this framework to intelligent civilizations in the galaxy. Highly developed civilizations will probably combine elements of both realism and liberalism, be cognizant of their relative power, willingly or forcibly participate in alliances, and have spiritual motivations that guide their decisions. Additional characteristics might exist, depending on each culture's place on the Kardashev Scale and its civilizational expertise. Since humanity is relatively primitive, it is difficult to estimate the capabilities, drives, reasons, and justifications of more advanced cultures. We may never know their attributes until they officially establish contact. Even then, effective communication may prove impossible.

An argument exists that extraterrestrial civilizations are secretive and will not announce their presence until humans progress to a sufficient level. The criteria for our qualification is difficult to assess but might include light speed travel, space communication, sustainable development, and international unity.[286] Since extraterrestrials are sure to be more advanced than humans, they will dictate terms.[287] Crucial to humans would be whether extraterrestrials are selfish or universalist, valuing themselves or all sentient life, and whether such considerations drive their decisions.

Perhaps we can attempt an estimate. Although advanced civilizations will be self-interested, reflecting the biological imperative, they are probably more universalist than humans. Advanced extraterrestrial civilizations should have a greater understanding of First Mind, fully incorporating quantum truths into their worldview and thus having a greater appreciation for spiritual matters. In short, they will have surmounted materialism. Thus, we must consider the possibility that extraterrestrial civilizations are more spiritual than humanity.[288] Advanced cultures likely require a fusion of both material and spiritual capabilities in order to extend themselves into the galaxy; as a result, extraterrestrials will presumably be technologically and metaphysically superior to us. That should incentivize us to emphasize enhanced spirituality since our inclusion into a community of advanced species may depend on it.

Further, advanced civilizations may be grouped into similar ethnologies based on genetic similarity or common cultural aspects, including spirituality. Similar species of extraterrestrials may be associated biologically *and* metaphysically, especially if species differentiation results from a history of genetic manipulation or ancient colonization. In such cases, dominant cultures may demand a requisite amount of spiritual development from descendant civilizations. Advanced cultures will likely insist on spiritual unity for security purposes while appreciating slight genetic diversity to enhance survivability; that may prove difficult for humanity to emulate since our slight genetic differences often manifest as racism. Lesser civilizations will probably be similar to us, increasing the potential for conflict. Perhaps there is a large range of civilizational types and vast governances to manage them, but until we advance further, we are unlikely candidates for inclusion.

Leadership will come from the more integrative cultures because such civilizations will have accumulated vast amounts of both scientific and metaphysical knowledge that ensures their cultural security and liberates them to pursue spiritual optimization. Thus, an advanced society should possess innovative technologies and spiritual integrity with its civilization capable of both material self-interest and spiritual universalism. From this we can assume that leadership cultures will be technologically superior, more socially equitable, highly unified, spiritually directed, and imbued with reverence for the Creator and the creation.

Human Expansion and Meaning

As humanity expands into the galaxy, so does our quest for meaning. As noted, the confirmation of extraterrestrials may obliterate our self-perception. In a universe with potentially billions of other civilizations, we must embrace our relatively inferior status. We must see ourselves within the grand panorama of the entire universe, significant as sentient beings but not universally compelling. If we want to ascend into leadership, we must understand the purpose of man and our corresponding role in a glorious, spiritual unfolding.

We can briefly consider a discipline that addresses this issue: Philosophical Anthropology. Originally a metaphysical pursuit, Philosophical Anthropology studied the nature of man, the inference being that his propensities determine his purpose. Subsequently, science got involved, applying its methods and prejudices without definitively accounting for our essence and disposition. Resistance to scientific encroachment formed when many philosophical anthropologists noted the inaccuracies of materialism, specifically how Quantum Mechanics invalidates determinism. Nearly all contributors to the discipline accepted one foundational premise, originally asserted by Aristotle, which in our current age is preposterous—that man was rational. Once again, history has obliterated this notion. Thus, human nature must be managed, cognizant of its deficiencies. It is rational to be moral but illogical to be evil, yet man is both, his nature divided between logic and absurdity, justice and depravity. At his core, man is conflicted.

Many modern philosophical anthropologists have accepted the inherent limitations of human reason in constructing a just society; thus, greater emphasis is placed on man as a choice agent, his will defining his fate, and also his education enabling him to choose more sensibly. In short, reason must be supplemented by instruction since reason alone failed. In this line of thinking, man is not bound by biological disposition or by the influence of society, *but he is limited by his past*. History is thus an indictment against his rationality and proves the contemptibleness in his being.

Here we can contribute our position. The contemptible in man originates with the Body, while his goodness comes from the Soul. The primary problem of man is man. Our natures are defective, and the products of our brain (technology) do not mitigate our obvious behavioral deficiencies. In fact, our inventions often exacerbate our transgressions and place humanity at existential vulnerability.[289] Therefore, the hope of man lies less in the expansion of his intellect and more in the advancement of his spirit. Man must elevate his spirit to raise his benevolence before he destroys his world.

Philosophical Anthropology also extends to questions of culture. Expanding our best cultural attributes may help humans contend with extraterrestrial civilizations. The point is that man is a product of culture, and culture is a product of man. Our self-image becomes decisive since it forms the society from which humanity projects itself into the galaxy. Ultimately, our fate is inexorably bound with the culture we construct. Confronting his past, man has the opportunity to enhance his future.

On Earth, we have obviously failed in our guardianship of the planet. We cannot extend our conduct into space. If extraterrestrial civilizations exist, so will power, and that power will be used to demonstrate hierarchy. Without perspective, our ego could lead to adventurism and imperialism, antagonizing potential adversaries and inciting avoidable conflict. Colonization for survival is understandable; empire-building is egregious. Essentially, we must know ourselves and our place within creation. That mandates a megatheory of our existence and purpose. We can attempt to construct this megatheory after first synthesizing the findings in our study.

CHAPTER 17

The Megatheory

We have examined the concept of reality—our discussion unique and often controversial. Mainstream science disagrees with many of our positions. Prevailing wisdom is in doubt with knowledge diffusing into assorted factions, even within conformist academia. Standards of knowledge are being toppled. Many of the experts cited in our study are often disparaged while grounded in the same empiricism as their numerous critics, simply because they conduct independent research and express contradistinct perspectives. In truth, these men and women are courageous visionaries who are forwarding our future. Criticism of them will likely escalate and become ever more vengeful as the existing paradigm desperately seeks to survive.

Nevertheless, there is a process in which knowledge replaces itself, best described by Thomas Kuhn, with one paradigm supplanting another by offering more explanatory power than its predecessor. That system takes time, especially in our era of intellectual relativism, but this dynamic has characterized the ascent of man throughout history and will determine our collective future. Controversies eventually get resolved.

So what does it mean for us? How are we to benefit? Enough evidence exists to form a more accurate picture of the nature of things. As we have discovered, the universe is made of Mind and Spirit. We are spiritual beings, which prioritizes the development of the eternal Soul and diminishes the meaningless pursuits of the dispensable Body. Acceptance of this fact provides a shared purpose that will transform society into a spiritual community. So we will consolidate our findings, present the megatheory, and then synopsize its philosophical position. Where appropriate, we have divided the following discussion into a number of graphics and commentaries to expedite comprehension.

A Summary of Our Exploration

Summarizing our findings allows us to build the theoretical framework required for a megatheory. More than a listing, it is an integration of our exploration—a type of synthetic architecture, if you will—that promotes a megatheory built on factual analysis and its considerable implications. These conclusions are unimpeded by conformance to materialist ideology and are thus often dissenting to conventional wisdom.

Here is a summary of our findings:

Summary of Findings

- The quest for truth leads to the atom. Quantum Mechanics is the discipline that studies matter and energy at the atomic and subatomic levels. The experimental results of Quantum Mechanics reveal a reality that is contradictory to classical physics and conventional beliefs.

- The Double Slit Experiment demonstrates the Observer Effect, that consciousness creates reality. Observation collapses the wave function, creating physical actuality from immaterial superposition. Mind makes everything real. Antecedently, the First Observer was the Great Consciousness, the source of reality.

- The universe is a mental and spiritual construction proving idealism over realism. The universe cannot be material and real when made of things immaterial and unreal. Consciousness is the ground of all being.

- The supremacy of Mind has universal and ontological implications. Evolution does not produce Consciousness; rather Consciousness produces evolution. Consciousness comes first, and physical reality, including the evolution of life, arises from an initial consciousness.

- The failures of grand unification theories and theories of everything suggest a point of stagnation that must be transcended by the supremacy of Consciousness. The fallacy of materialism must be abandoned. Mind and Spirit are fundamental aspects that must be understood to extend ourselves.

- An idealistic universe mandates new interpretations of reality. The ubiquity of Consciousness and quantum mechanical concepts such as Entanglement and the Uncertainty Principle suggest different levels of reality. One material universe as the only reality is implausible since the universe exists as a product of Mind, an *a priori* reality of its own.

- Recognition of the primacy of Mind and Spirit results from distinct forwarding processes such as the dialectic of Hegel and the paradigm shifts of Kuhn. Currently, the Consciousness Paradigm is replacing the Materialist Paradigm. Humans have advanced through the formulation of theories and megatheories.

- Theories of Consciousness abound, from panpsychism to the Holonomic Brain Theory, but Mind is a fundamental force of nature derivative from First Mind. Energy provides the capacity for work, while Information is the device used to construct Physical Reality. Energy contains information, but Information does not require energy.

- The New Age Movement corrupted the concepts of energy and Consciousness by positioning energy as a transformative force and Mind as an extension of self in a narcissistic attempt to elevate humanity to the level of God. That has perverted the concept of energy and impeded the acceptance of the scientifically derived primacy of Consciousness.

- Humanity is progressing past materialism. A post-materialist worldview accepts a universe that is fine-tuned for life, the failure of Darwinism, the deficiencies of classical physics, the hubristic dogma of traditional science, our current academic and societal stagnation, and the supremacy of Consciousness and Spirit.

- Since the universe is also fundamentally spiritual, humans have souls. God is the ultimate Spirit, and Souls result from the Creator. The near-death experience and the hyper reality are suggestive of Soul.

- An idealistic universe suggests simulation with reality appearing as actual but constructed of immaterial Mind and Spirit. The universe is a simulation created by God for an unknown purpose. Possible objectives of simulation are placement of Souls in physical bodies to learn lessons unavailable as spirits or to fill eternity with endless levels of reality to provide challenge and growth.

- Studies of the universe inspire various interpretations of its fate. Theories abound, but Quantum Mechanics and Einstein's Theory of Relativity substantiate a Block Universe. Past, present, and future are unified, equally accessible, and parallel. Everything that can happen has happened.

- Humans possess free will even in a Block Universe. Choice contributes toward the outcome of the universe. Quantum Mechanics has proved that different, concurrent realities exist. Somehow, God incorporates free will into a determined universe.

- Within this universe exists a tremendous amount of information, including all academic disciplines and all knowledge everywhere. The universe is a vast database. Everything humans discover was invented by the First Mind. The level of complexity is incalculable.

- To achieve His purposes through this incredible complexity, God developed methods to influence human free will. This management of destiny includes myths and archetypes, dreams and visions, intuition and recognition, and perception and synchronicity. More directly, God uses religion, specifically His inspired Word. His objectives form universal destiny.

- Universal destiny includes potential civilizations in the universe. The Drake Equation and the UFO Phenomenon provide the theoretical underpinnings for the possibility of extraterrestrial life and a potential control system over Earth as another form of managed destiny. The UFO Phenomenon appears more supernatural than extraterrestrial, but we must prepare for both possibilities.

- The UFO Phenomenon appears to direct humanity into its next development, including the potential colonization of the galaxy. Colonization may prove necessary for our survival. The Kardashev Scale and universal studies position our advancement into space from energy and cultural perspectives. Humanity must increase its civilizational expertise, both technological and spiritual, for leadership in space.

This summary is a synthesis with the discussion points arranged in an architecture to position our megatheory. In fact, from this point forward everything will combine to build toward the next narrative. That should provide us with additional insight beyond our previous discussions.

Concept Organization

To assist our understanding of the summary of findings, we can delineate them into general categories—**Foundational**, **Societal**, and **Spiritual**. We'll list the pertinent aspects below each category. These categories extend into each other, so Foundational leads to Societal, which leads to Spiritual.

Foundational	Societal	Spiritual
God	The Dialectic	Universal Fates
Mind and Spirit	Paradigms	Block Universe
Consciousness Divisions	Knowledge	Spiritual Purpose
Information	Materialism	Fine-Tuned for Life
Levels of Reality	Stagnation	Soul Placement
Universe	Post-Materialism	Free Will
Simulation	Consciousness Paradigm	Managed Destiny
Immaterial and Material	Exploration of Space	SoulMind
Atomic Structure	UFO Phenomenon	Companionship
Molecules, Cells, Life, Humans	Universal Studies	Fulfillment of Spirit

The categories show the relationships of the concepts and hypotheses to each other, progressing from universal foundations to life and human society, and from society to spiritual purposes. We will use this as a reference as we proceed through this chapter.

The Megatheory

The megatheory of reality consists of five components, which we will explore separately, but together they sequentially encapsulate our philosophical position. Below are the five components:

- **Nature of Reality**
- **Physical Realm**
- **Spiritual Realm**
- **Meaning of Humanity**
- **Universal Destiny**

For each component, we will list the primary attributes followed by a brief discussion. Many of the points were referenced in the summary findings, but we will further integrate them here.

Nature of Reality

- Quantum Mechanics – the gateway to understanding reality
- Idealism – reality is mental and spiritual
- Physical Realm
- Spiritual Realm
- Levels of Reality
- Simulation

Quantum Mechanics, specifically the *Double Slit Experiment,* demonstrates that reality is fundamentally Mental and Spiritual. An obvious physical realm exists, commonly referred to as matter, but underneath it is immaterial essence—mental and spiritual energy, if you will—and observation brings this incorporeal essentiality into material existence. This dichotomy, this division between material and immaterial realms, suggests numerous levels of reality as well as a potentially simulated universe. The primacy of Consciousness and the ubiquity of Spirit mandate an original source capable of extending those essences throughout all creation.

Physical Realm

- Information

- Atoms, Molecules, Chemistry, Cells, Life

- Universe, Galaxies, Stars, Planets, Laws, Properties

- Universal Evolvement, including Time and Thermodynamics

- Physical Life, including all Living Species, Humans, Extraterrestrials

- Advanced Species that form Technological Societies and Civilizations

- Theories of the Universe

- Entropy

In the physical realm, it appears that God used Information to construct the universe. Everything is made of atoms and molecules; chemistry, cells, and life all result from a more complex arrangements of atomic structure. Scaling this structure forms stars, planets, galaxies, and the universe. Functioning results from forces, laws, properties, time, and thermodynamics. Within the universe exists physical life, with survival the imperative. Intelligent species eventually form advanced civilizations where colonization and competition ensues. Various theories exist concerning the final fate of the universe, but entropy is the likely outcome.

Spiritual Realm

- God is a Spirit and the ultimate spiritual source.

- Souls derive from Spirit.

- The universe is fine-tuned for life to generate physical bodies.

- Souls are placed into bodies for spiritual objectives.

- NDE, astral projection, OBE, and hyper reality suggest Souls.

- Spiritual progression is managed through universal destiny.

- Destiny includes the Word of God, myths, archetypes, dreams, visions, intuition, and synchronicity.

The spiritual nature of the universe results from its source: God. Souls result from Spirit and in fact are spiritual essences in themselves; they are placed into physical bodies for a purpose. The necessity of bodies mandated a universe fine-tuned for life. The precision of this universal fine-tuning is proof of a designer. Somehow God was able to successfully entangle spiritual essence into material existence (Souls into Bodies) without definitive detection in order to achieve His objectives.

Consciousness results from First Mind and is dispersed in the universe. Many metaphysical phenomena such as Near Death Experience, Out-of-Body Experience, Astral Projection, and Hyper Reality suggest the existence of Soul. God utilizes assorted forms of destiny management, including His inspired word, myths and archetypes, dreams and visions, and intuition and synchronicity. According to philosopher Hegel, the universe is the evolvement of Spirit, and human free will is instrumental to the process. As the universe reflects its spiritual foundations, so does every human being reflect its foundational Soul. The connection between humans (Souls) and the universe (Spirit) is thus confirmed.

Meaning of Humanity

- Humans are Souls in bodies; free will ensures Soul progression.

- Humanity evolves through the dialectic and paradigms.

- The Physical Realm is largely exploited – scientific stagnation.

- Death of materialism – post-materialism emphasizes Mind and Spirit.

- The next evolution in human progress is the exploitation of Consciousness.

- The Consciousness Paradigm creates the potential for colonization of space.

- End of anthropocentrism – humanity as one of many intelligent species.

- Human positioning in universal destiny.

Humans are containers for Souls, the universe a stage for the evolution of Spirit. Free will ensures that we make choices, and these choices ensure Soul growth. As a result, spiritual advancement is bound with human progression, and our responsibility to Spirit is a responsibility to ourselves. History has demonstrated that societal advancement occurs through the dialectic and through paradigms. Our current paradigm, the Materialist Paradigm, has stagnated and is being replaced by the Consciousness Paradigm, which offers tremendous opportunity for transcendence. As the physical realm has its material construction, so might the spiritual realm have its immaterial construction. Once these constituent parts are discovered, it may prove possible to configure material reality to surmount physical impediments. At that point, we will ascend to the stars, possibly encountering extraterrestrials and causing a transformative assessment of our relative position. If the UFO Phenomenon proves supernatural, we will also discover more of its nature. In either case, our civilization must balance technological progression with spiritual advancement to assume a leadership position in space. We also must recognize our place within the expansion of Spirit and contribute toward its development, accepting our part in the evolution of universal destiny.

Universal Destiny

- God created the universe for His glorification and for sharing His life.

- Creation is filled with Mind and Spirit.

- Block Universe – events and lives with incalculable lessons.

- Choice creates endless possibilities and potentially different fates.

- Souls, derived from Spirit, are designed to spend eternity with the Creator.

- Souls must learn every lesson in order to qualify as viable companions.

- Universal Destiny is the growth of Souls and the fulfillment of Spirit.

God created the universe. Material evolution occurs within the framework of a Block Universe where everything is decided, with a slight variation for free will. What is not decided is spiritual evolution. In fact, souls might be placed into other levels of reality to learn yet more lessons after their own.

Incredibly, the universe integrates free will with determinism so choice is an indispensable component of cause and effect. The Block Universe corresponds with this dynamic where reality is largely determined (including past, present, and future) but subject to adjustment. Even more sensational is that equally real outcomes can occur within the same reality. Thus, the universe is a mutable simulation where free will can produce differing results, yet all are equally real and purposeful. How this is possible is beyond human comprehension but highly suggestive of a Supreme Being with a plan.

Summary of the Megatheory

A summary of the megatheory of reality leads to the final distillation of our investigation. Hopefully, from the facts, data, findings, concepts, premises, arguments, and hypotheses integrated throughout this work we can reduce to a few simple statements that encapsulate our theoretical position. This summary of the megatheory is an assimilation of the previous descriptions in this chapter but fully integrates our ideas. It should be noted that this megatheory is not absolute since the future will certainly bring additional discoveries that augment our formulation. Many points in the summary have been discussed previously but mentioned again for cohesion.

Below is the summary.

Summary of the Megatheory

- The Physical Realm is an illusion; the Spiritual Realm is actual reality.

- The universe is a type of simulation designed for spiritual objectives.

- The Mind of God utilizes information and energy to create atomic structure.

- Atomic structure forms the physical universe, which is fine-tuned for life.

- A universe that is fine-tuned for life ensures that Souls come into bodies.

- Soul development occurs through free will.

- Universal destiny is managed to achieve God's purposes.

- Humanity must extend itself through the galaxy in order to promote Soul development; the more advanced the civilization, the more Soul can learn.

- Humans must assume leadership in space for survival and spiritual advancement.

From our summary, we can make the following speculative argument. Within the Block Universe is an incalculable number of lives, circumstances, choices, and lessons. To God, all the lives within the Block Universe are decided, but to individual souls, these lives would be experienced as new. Recognition of past lives would be erased to ensure freedom of choice. Free will might shift these life courses, but souls could be inserted into lives generally commensurate with the learning required. Hence, physical lives are "choice platforms." Different concurrent realities (proven in quantum experimentation) further suggest free will choices branching into alternative lessons that are equally real.

Much of the following argument is also speculative.

From God, Spirit fills the universe. Religious traditions assert that God created the universe for His glorification and to share His life with others. Souls result from Spirit as part of spiritual essence and reflect the glory of God. Potentially, souls also provide companionship. But from His perspective, souls require spiritual enhancement or eternity cannot be shared. The direct forms of enhancement would be His inspired word and an example of human perfection; humans also required forgiveness, and history is a record of human depravity. Hence, according to Christian tradition, God sent His Son. Other religions have their plans for redemption. Free will also ensures that we have an opportunity to choose God, the greatest choice humans can make. As a result, our learning includes appreciating God and our role within His creation.

Universal destiny, then, is the growth of souls and the fulfillment of Spirit. The world is a proving ground. Life is a game of souls. If extraterrestrials exist, they also fulfill this grand purpose, although appraising them may be impossible for us. Even their nature is highly debatable; they may be expendable or not, they may have souls or not, or they may serve as part of the environment offering additional challenges for our growth as a civilization. Quite possibly, they may come from other dimensions or be entirely supernatural. No one knows for sure. If UFO abduction accounts can be believed, extraterrestrials relate that there is only one God and that everything is under His domain. Therefore, it is reasonable to assume that all life everywhere serves the fulfillment of Spirit. Hence, it appears that **actuality is spiritual evolution in order to advance souls for viable companionship with God.**

We began this study seeking the truth of reality. We have connected some puzzle pieces, but humans are insufficiently advanced both in terms of intelligence and morality to fully comprehend the wonders of creation. We will never have the ability or the integrity to know what God knows. What we do know is that scientific materialism is approaching its end; its reign has been enormous, but a new paradigm is emerging. At this point, the particulars of that paradigm are largely undetermined. But as we begin to see its image, that image—regardless of its obscurity—is imprinted with spiritual signature. Life is a spiritual activity. The universe was designed by Spirit with Spirit as its eventuality. Destiny—our destiny—is inexorably bound with that original Spirit and the fulfillment of its desired ends.

REFERENCES

1. Davisson, C. J., and L. H. Germer. "Reflection of Electrons by a Crystal of Nickel." *Proceedings of the National Academy of Sciences of the United States*, vol. 14, no. 4, 14 Apr., 1928, pp. 317–22, https://www.doi.org/10.1073/pnas.14.4.317.

2. Electrons behave differently if they are being measured (observed) as opposed to unmeasured (unobserved). That is known as the Measurement Problem, the problem of how wave function collapse happens in the first place. Measurement reduces the electron's superposition into one, realized state. Quantum systems evolve deterministically over time through the Schrödinger Equation as a linear superposition of different states, but actual measurements always find the system in a definite state; any future evolution is based on the state the system was discovered and when the measurement was made, which means the measurement did something to the system, which is obviously not a consequence of Schrödinger evolution.

3. *Collective Evolution*, quoted in "Quantum Experiment Shows how the Present Can Change the Past, & That's Not All …" *Intelligence.com*. 20 Jan. 2017. https://iheartintelligence.com/quantum-experiment-present-past/.

4. Deutsch, David. "Comment on Lockwood." *The British Journal for the Philosophy of Science*, vol. 47, no. 2, 1996, pp. 222–28.

5.   Collins Dictionary. "Quantum Mechanics," https://www.collinsdictionary.com/us/dictionary/english/quantum-mechanics. Accessed 26 Aug. 2021.

6.   Planck, Max. *The New Science.* Meridian Books, 1959.

7.   Schrödinger, Erwin. *The Observer,* 11 Jan. 1931. In Michael Silberstein, W. M. Stuckey, and Timothy McDevitt, *Beyond the Dynamical Universe: Unifying Block Universe Physics and Time as Experienced.* Oxford University Press, 2018.

8.   Ibid.

9.   Yiu, Yuen. "Is China the Leader in Quantum Communications?" *Inside Science*, 19 Jan. 2018, https://www.insidescience.org/news/china-leader-quantum-communications. The original Chinese experiment was conducted in September 2017.

10.   Locality simply means that an object is directly influenced by its local surroundings. This rather obvious fact has nevertheless been violated in Quantum Mechanics, further demonstrating the wide gap between classical physics and the quantum world.

11.   Zyga, Lisa. "Physicists Find Extreme Violation of Local Realism in Quantum Hypergraph States." *Phys.Org*, 4 Mar. 2016, https://phys.org/news/2016-03-physicists-extreme-violation-local-realism.html.

12.   Inglis-Arkell, Esther. "An Experiment That Might Let Us Control Events Millions of Years Ago." *Gizmodo*, 19 Feb. 2014, https://gizmodo.com/an-experiment-that-might-let-us-control-events-millions-1525760859.

13.   Australian National University. "Experiment Confirms Quantum Theory Weirdness." *ScienceDaily,* 27 May 2015. https://www.sciencedaily.com/releases/2015/05/150527103110.htm.

14.   Megidish, E., A. Halevy, T. Shaham, T. Dvir, L. Dovrat, and H. S. Eisenberg. "Entanglement Swapping between Photons That Have Never

Coexisted." *American Physical Society,* 3 Jan. 2013, https://journals.aps. org/prl/abstract/10.1103/PhysRevLett.110.210403.

15. "Delayed Choice Quantum Eraser Experiment Explained." *YouTube,* uploaded 26 Aug. 2021. www.youtube.com/watch?v=H6HLjpj4Nt4.

16. This is one of the more bizarre findings in Quantum Mechanics. It is also evidence that panpsychism pervades inanimate objects.

17. *The World,* 10 Jan. 2014, https://www.pri.org/stories/2014-01-09/new-research-plant-intelligence-may-forever-change-how-you-think-about-plants.

18. "New Research on Plant Intelligence May Forever Change How You Think about Plants." *The World,* 10 Jan. 2014, https://www.pri.org/stories/2014-01-09/new-research-plant-intelligence-may-forever-change-how-you-think-about-plants.

19. Kehoe, John. "Do Plants Have Consciousness?" *Mind Power,* 2017, https://www.learnmindpower.com/do-plants-have-consciousness/. Accessed 26 Aug. 2021.

20. Planck, Max. "Interviews with Great Scientists," *The Observer,* 25 Jan. 1931, https://www.newspapers.com/clip/25590070/max-planck-observer-12531/.

21. "Reality." *Encyclopedia.com.*

22. Barzov, Yuri. "The Rise of Conscious Machines." *Above Intelligent,* 27 Apr. 2017, https://aboveintelligent.com/the-rise-of-conscious-machines-601be0d1a9eb.

23. "Aristotle (384 B.C.E.–322 B.C.E.)." *Internet Encyclopedia of Philosophy.*

24. Vardanyan, Vilen. *Panorama of Psychology.* AuthorHouseUK, 2011.

25.   Nicolescu, Basarab. "Transdisciplinarity and Complexity: Levels of Reality as Source of Indeterminacy." *International Center for Transdisciplinary Research*, 15 May 2000.

26.   Aristotle. *The Basic Works of Aristotle*. Modern Library, 2001.

27.   Many definitions of metaphysics exist, but all concern the nature of reality. First principles are things that cannot be deduced from any other principle. A first principle of God would no doubt be challenged by materialists, as would nearly all metaphysical inquiries.

28.   "Duck-Test Meaning." *Your Dictionary*.

29.   Gribbin, John. *In Search of Schrödinger's Cat: Quantum Physics and Reality*. Bantam Books, 1984.

30.   Bohr, Neils. Quoted in "I'm Not Looking, Honest!" *The Economist*, 5 Mar. 2009, https://www.economist.com/science-and-technology/2009/03/05/im-not-looking-honest.

31.   Wheeler, John Archibald. In "Science Quotes by John Wheeler." *Today in Science History,* https://todayinsci.com/W/Wheeler_John/WheelerJohn-Quotations.htm. Accessed 26 Aug. 2021.

32.   Pagel, Mark D. *Wired for Culture: Origins of the Human Social Mind*. W. W. Norton & Company, 2013.

33.   Godwin, John. *Juvenal: Satires Book V*. Liverpool University Press, 2020, p. vii.

34.   Mulder, Dwayne H. "Objectivity." *Internet Encyclopedia of Philosophy*.

35.   Kuhn, Thomas S. *The Structure of Scientific Revolutions*. University of Chicago Press, 1996.

36.   It should be noted that the vast majority of mainstream science believes scientific knowledge proceeds gradually. This belief in gradualism partially

describes the acceptance of stagnation since breakthroughs are seldom anticipated or embraced. Thus, gradualism conceals stagnation.

37. Hegel, G. W. F. *Phenomenology of Spirit*. Cambridge University Press, 2018.

38. "Theory." *Dictionary.com*.

39. Institute of Medicine, National Academy of Engineering, National Academy of Sciences, and Public Policy Committee on Science, Engineering. *On Being a Scientist: A Guide to Responsible Conduct in Research*, Second Edition. National Academies Press, 1995, pp. 6–7.

40. "Rupert Sheldrake Interview." *TheBestSchools*, 20 Mar. 2015, https://thebestschools.org/features/rupert-sheldrake-interview/.

41. "Fact." *Oxford Learner's Dictionaries*.

42. Sheldrake, Rupert, and Michael Shermer. *Arguing Science: A Dialogue on the Future of Science and Spirit*. Monkfish Book Publishing, 2016.

43. Maestre, Nelo, and Ágata Timón. "Thus Ended the Dream of Infallible Mathematics (and Incidentally, Modern Computing Was Born)." *Open Mind*, 20 Sept. 2018.

44. Horgan, John. *The End of Science*. Basic Books, 2015.

45. Bailey, David H. "What is Scientific Materialism?" *ScienceMeetsReligion. org*, 2 Jan. 2021.

46. Goff, Philip. "Science as We Know It Can't Explain Consciousness – But a Revolution Is Coming." *The Conversation*, 1 Nov. 2019, https://theconversation.com/science-as-we-know-it-cant-explain-consciousness-but-a-revolution-is-coming-126143. Goff posits panpsychism as the likely explanation for the phenomenon of Consciousness.

47. Laszlo, Ervin. "What Is Consciousness? From the Material Brain to the Infinite Mind and Beyond." *Conscious Lifestyle Magazine,* https://www.consciouslifestylemag.com/what-is-consciousness-brain-and-mind-2/.

48. "Dogma." *Cambridge Dictionary*.

49. Sheldrake, Rupert. "The Scientific Creed and the Credibility Crunch for Materialism." *Deepak Chopra*, 26 Aug. 2013, https://www.deepakchopra.com/articles/the-scientific-creed-and-the-credibility-crunch-for-materialism/.

50. Egnor, Michael. "Materialism of the Gaps." *Evolution News*, 29 Jan. 2009, https://evolutionnews.org/2009/01/materialism_of_the_gaps/.

51. Ibid.

52. Ibid.

53. Ibid.

54. Rider, Cortical. "Top 10 Reasons Science Is Another Religion." *ListVerse*, 15 Dec. 2012, https://listverse.com/2012/12/15/top-10-reasons-science-is-another-religion/.

55. Lafsky, Melissa. "Are Scientists the Next Religious Zealots?" *Discover*, 4 Aug. 2008, https://www.discovermagazine.com/technology/are-scientists-the-next-religious-zealots.

56. "Science Is Immensely Important, but It Has a Hubris Problem." *Freecology*, 27 Apr. 2017, https://libertarianenvironmentalism.com/2017/04/27/march-for-science/.

57. Butler, Martin. "The Hubris of Science." *Martin Butler*, 25 Nov. 2018, https://martinbutler.eu/the-hubris-of-science/.

58. Horgan, John. "Was Philosopher Paul Feyerabend Really Science's 'Worst Enemy'?" *Scientific American*, 24 Oct. 2016, https://blogs.scientificamerican.com/cross-check/was-philosopher-paul-feyerabend-really-science-s-worst-enemy/.

59. Unzicker, Alexander, and Sheilla Jones. "How Particle Physics Is Eroding the Scientific Method." *EuroScientist*, 5 Sept. 2013, https://www.euro-scientist.com/how-particle-physics-is-eroding-the-scientific-method/.

60. Staddon, John. "Is Science Showing Diminishing Returns?" *Psychology Today*, 4 Apr. 2018, https://www.psychologytoday.com/us/blog/adaptive-behavior/201804/is-science-showing-diminishing-returns.

61. Cupps, Vernon R. "Hijacking the Scientific Method." *Institute for Creation Research*, 31 Jul. 2014, https://www.icr.org/article/hijacking-scientific-method.

62. "Scientific Method." *Dictionary.com*.

63. Ibid.

64. Cooley, Lauren. "Liberalism Is Rampant on Campus and Ruining Academia." *Washington Examiner*, 6 Sept. 2018, https://www.washingtonexaminer.com/red-alert-politics/liberalism-is-rampant-on-campus-and-ruining-academia.

65. Toynbee, Arnold J. *A Study of History*. Oxford University Press, 1945.

66. "How Science Goes Wrong." *The Economist*, 19 Oct. 2013, https://www.economist.com/leaders/2013/10/21/how-science-goes-wrong.

67. Ibid.

68. "Galileo to Turing: The Historical Persecution of Scientists." *Wired*, 22 Jun. 2012, https://www.wired.com/2012/06/famous-persecuted-scientists/#:~:text=Turing%20completed%20his%20year%20of,suicide%20on%207%20June%2C%201954.

69. Guhin, Jeffrey. "The Problem with the 'Conflict Thesis.'" *Mobilizing Ideas*, 1 Apr. 2013.

70. Ball, Philip. "Who Are the Martyrs of Science?" *The Guardian*, 24 Sept. 2014, https://www.theguardian.com/science/the-h-word/2014/sep/24/martyrs-science-history-galileo-nazi.

71. Ibid.

72. Smetham, Graham. "On 'Known-to-Be False' Materialist Philosophies of Mind." *Philosophy* Now, 2012, https://philosophynow.org/issues/93/On_Known-To-Be-False_Materialist_Philosophies_of_Mind.

73. Luskin, Casey. "Peer-Reviewed Science: There Isn't 'Plenty of Time for Evolution.'" *Evolution News*, 13 Dec. 2012, https://evolutionnews.org/2012/12/peer-reviewed_s_1/.

74. Selbie, Joseph. *The Physics of God*. Weiser, 2017.

75. "Manifesto for a Post-Materialist Science." OpenSciences.org, https://opensciences.org/about/manifesto-for-a-post-materialist-science. Accessed 26 Aug. 2021. This manifesto, collaboratively written by many innovative thinkers, is truly an incredible document. A direct challenge to the materialist paradigm, it is a framework for the human future. The authors come from a variety of disciplines, and the manifesto is interdisciplinary in nature, itself a vast improvement on traditional approaches.

76. "Obscurantism." *Dictionary.com*.

77. Griffin, David Ray. *Religion and Scientific Naturalism: Overcoming the Conflicts*. State University of New York Press, 2000, p. 10.

78. Ibid.

79. López-Corredoira, Martin. "Have We Reached the Twilight of the Fundamental Science Era?" *EuroScientist*, 30 Apr. 2014.

80. Ibid.

81. Rusbult, Craig. "Cultural Influences in Science: Causes and Effects." *asa3. org*, https://www.asa3.org/ASA/education/science/cp2.htm. Accessed 26 Aug. 2021.

82. "Groupthink." *Psychology Today*. https://www.psychologytoday.com/ us/basics/groupthink. Accessed 26 Aug. 2021.

83. Pouzzner, Daniel. "The Architecture of Modern Political Power." *The New Feudalism*, 11 Nov. 2008, http://underpop.online.fr/o/omega-files/ architecture-of-modern-political-power.pdf.

84. Collins, Phillip Darrell, and Paul David Collins. *The Ascendancy of the Scientific Dictatorship*. Booksurge Publishing, 2006.

85. "Peer Review." *Cambridge Dictionary*.

86. Luskin, Casey. "Problems with Peer-Review: A Brief Summary." *Evolution News*, 10 Feb. 2012 https://evolutionnews.org/2012/02/ problems_with_p/

87. Ferguson, Cat, Adam Marcus, and Ivan Oransky. "Publishing: The Peer-Review Scam." *Nature*, 26 Nov. 2014, https://www.nature.com/ articles/515480a.

88. Chalmers, David J. *The Conscious Mind: In Search of a Fundamental Theory*. Oxford University Press, 1997.

89. Cook, Gareth. "Does Consciousness Pervade the Universe?" *Scientific American*, 14 Jan. 2020, https://www.scientificamerican.com/article/ does-consciousness-pervade-the-universe/.

90. Hamilton, David R. "Consciousness." *Dr. David R. Hamilton*, 11 Aug. 2015, http://drdavidhamilton.com/category/consciousness-2/.

91. Chalmers, David J. *The Conscious Mind: In Search of Fundamental Theory*. Oxford University Press, 1997.

92. Gefter, Amanda, and Quanta Magazine. "The Case against Reality." *The Atlantic*, 25 Apr. 2016, https://www.theatlantic.com/science/archive/2016/04/the-illusion-of-reality/479559/.

93. Ibid.

94. Sunim, Hwansan. "A Quantum Theory of Consciousness." *Huffington Post*, 19 July 2017, https://www.huffpost.com/entry/a-quantum-theory-of-consciousness_b_596fb782e4b04dcf308d29bb.

95. Matloff, Gregory. "Panpsychism as an Observational Science." *Cuny Academic Works*. City University of New York, 2020.

96. Perry, Philip. "The Universe May Be Conscious, Say Prominent Scientists." *Big Think*, 25 Jun. 2017, https://bigthink.com/philip-perry/the-universe-may-be-conscious-prominent-scientists-state.

97. Kastrup, Bernardo. "Consciousness Cannot Have Evolved." *Mind Matters*, 9 Feb. 2020.

98. Ibid.

99. Penrose, Roger. *Shadows of the Mind: A Search for the Missing Science of Consciousness*. Oxford University Press, 1996.

100. Ibid.

101. Massimini, Marcello, and Tononi, Guilio. *"Sizing Up Consciousness: Towards an Objective Measure of the Capacity for Experience."* Oxford University Press, 2018.

102. "Emergence." *Internet Encyclopedia of Philosophy*.

103. Griffin, David Ray. "Panexperientialist Physicalism and the Mind-Body Problem." *Journal of Consciousness Studies*, vol. 4, no. 3, 1997, pp. 248–68.

104. "Process Philosophy." *Internet Encyclopedia of Philosophy*.

105. Ibid.

106. Pribram, Karl H. *Brain and Perception: Holonomy and Structure in Figural Processing*. Psychology Press, 2013.

107. Siegel, Ethan. "How the Anthropic Principle Became the Most Abused Idea in Science." *Forbes*, 26 Jan. 2017, https://www.forbes.com/sites/startswithabang/2017/01/26/how-the-anthropic-principle-became-the-most-abused-idea-in-science/?sh=68d882677d69.

108. Gribbin, John, and Martin Rees. *Cosmic Coincidences*. Bantam Books, 1989.

109. "John Wheeler's Participatory Universe." *Futurism*, February 13, 2014.

110. "Using Quantum Physics to Prove the Existence of God." *Thought Company*, May 30, 2019.

111. Peter Kreeft is a professor of Philosophy at Boston College. He has written 95 books on a variety of subjects, including *Because God Is Real*. His criticism of statistical populations theory on his website (Argument from Design) is particularly insightful.

112. Shacklett, Robert L., and William C. Gough. "The Unification of Mind and Matter: A Proposed Scientific Template." *Foundation for Mind-Being Research*, 12 May, 2006.

113. Ross, Gilbert. "A Multi-Dimensional Theory of Mind." *Brewminate*, 22 Jan. 2018, https://brewminate.com/a-multi-dimensional-theory-of-mind/.

114. Ibid.

115. Pruett, David. "Toward a Post-Materialistic Science." *Huffington Post*, 1 Oct. 2014, https://www.huffpost.com/entry/toward-a-postmaterialistic-science_b_5842730.

116. Raman, Varadaraja. "Reduction and Holism: Two Sides of the Perception of Reality." *Metanexus*, 15 Jul. 2005.

117. Ibid.

118. Rosenberg, Alex. "Reductionism in Biology." *ScienceDirect*, 2007, https://www.sciencedirect.com/topics/social-sciences/reductionism .

119. "Public's View on Human Evolution," Pew *Research Center*, 30 Dec. 2013, https://www.pewforum.org/2013/12/30/publics-views-on-human-evolution/.

120. Crowther, Robert L. "Over 500 Scientists Proclaim Their Doubts about Darwin's Theory of Evolution." *Evolution News*, 20 Feb. 2006, https://evolutionnews.org/2006/02/over_500_scientists_proclaim_t/.

121. Spector, Dina. "The 6 Reasons Creationists Think Evolution Isn't a Sure Thing." *Business Insider*, 18 Sept. 2012, https://www.businessinsider.com/scientific-weaknesses-of-evolution-2012-9.

122. Light, Alexander. "9 Scientific Facts Prove the 'Theory of Evolution' Is False." *Humans Are Free*, 11 Dec. 2013, https://humansarefree.com/2013/12/9-scientific-facts-prove-the-theory-of-evolution-is-false.html.

123. Seiglie, Mario. "DNA: The Tiny Code That's Toppling Evolution." *Beyond Today*, 21 May 2005, https://www.ucg.org/the-good-news/dna-the-tiny-code-thats-toppling-evolution.

124. Ibid.

125. Denton, Michael. *Evolution: A Theory in Crisis*, Third Edition. Adler & Adler, 2002.

126. Roberts, Kyle. "But Where Are All the Transitional Fossils?" *Patheos*, 11 Aug. 2015. https://www.patheos.com/blogs/unsystematictheology/2015/08/but-where-are-all-the-transitional-fossils/.

127. "Physical Constant." *New World Encyclopedia*.

128. Feynman, Richard P. *QED: The Strange Theory of Light and Matter, Revised Edition*. Princeton University Press, 2014.

129. "The Fine-Tuning of the Universe for Life Just Got Finer." *Evolution News*, 15 Mar. 2013. https://evolutionnews.org/2013/03/the_fine-tuning_1/.

130. Bailey, David H. "Is the Universe Fine-Tuned for Life?" *Science Meets Religion*, 2 Jan. 2021, https://www.sciencemeetsreligion.org/physics/fine-tuned.php.

131. Deem, Rich. "Evidence for the Fine Tuning of the Universe." *Evidence for God*, 7 May 2011. https://www.godandscience.org/apologetics/designun.html. This summary lists 34 fine-tuning parameters that demonstrate the unique fine-tuning of the universe. Taken together, their existence proves a designer.

132. Ball, Philip. "Why the Many-Worlds Interpretation Has Many Problems." *Quanta Magazine*, 18 Oct. 2018, https://www.quantamagazine.org/why-the-many-worlds-interpretation-of-quantum-mechanics-has-many-problems-20181018/.

133. Ibid.

134. Tarade, Daniel. "Physics and the New Religion." *The Meaning of Life*, 17 Aug. 2018, https://www.lifetypestuff.com/blog/2018/7/8/physics-and-the-new-religion.

135. Nunes, Débora. "A Post-Materialist Science Already Exists." *International Press Agency*, 12 Nov. 2019, https://www.pressenza.com/2019/01/a-post-materialist-science-already-exists/.

136. Ibid.

137. Beauregard, Mario. "The New Science of Consciousness: Toward the Next Great Scientific Revolution." *Thrive Global*, 6 Sept. 2018, https://thriveglobal.com/stories/the-new-science-of-consciousness-toward-the-next-great-scientific-revolution/. Dr. Beauregard's website lists his numerous scientific articles and his books, *The Spiritual Brain* and *Brain Wars*.

138. "Manifesto for a Post Materialist Science." *OpenSciences.org,* https://opensciences.org/about/manifesto-for-a-post-materialist-science.

139. Baruss, Imants. "Beyond Scientific Materialism: Toward a Transcendent Theory of Consciousness." *Journal of Consciousness Studies,* vol. 17, nos. 7–8, 2010, pp. 213–31.

140. Zohar, Danah. "Spiritual Intelligence: A New Paradigm for Collaborative Action." *Systems Thinker,* https://thesystemsthinker.com/spiritual-intelligence-a-new-paradigm-for-collaborative-action/. Accessed 27 Aug. 2021.

141. Horgan, John. *The End of Science.* Basic Books, 2015.

142. Brockman, John. "Why I Think Science Is Ending: A Talk with John Horgan." *Edge,* 6 May 1997, https://www.edge.org/conversation/john_horgan-why-i-think-science-is-ending

143. Cowen, Tyler. *The Great Stagnation.* Dutton, 2011.

144. Globalization causes homogeneity, but breakthroughs happen through diversity. A number of sources, including the National Bureau of Economic Research, have noted this linkage. The task for humanity is to benefit from interconnection without stifling originality.

145. Horgan, John. "Facing the End of Science." *Scientific American,* 1 Dec. 2018, https://blogs.scientificamerican.com/cross-check/facing-the-end-of-science/. In this article, Horgan references Patrick Collison and Michael Nielsen who note the diminishing returns of modern science and offer tremendous insight into the causes of societal stagnation. They, like others, emphasize the importance of a large-scale government response in first acknowledging the problem and then providing solutions.

146. Collison, Patrick, and Michael Nielsen. "Science Is Getting Less Bang for Its Buck." *The Atlantic,* 16 Nov. 2018, https://www.theatlantic.com/science/archive/2018/11/diminishing-returns-science/575665/. Collison and Nielsen have provided useful historical analogies to the discussion,

and their arguments are both logical and compelling. Nielsen's book *Reinventing Discovery: The New Era of Networked Science* offers solutions on how to improve science.

147. Hossenfelder, Sabine. "The Present Phase of Stagnation in the Foundations of Physics Is Not Normal." *Nautilus*, 23 Nov. 2018, https://nautil.us/blog/the-present-phase-of-stagnation-in-the-foundations-of-physics-is-not-normal Hossenfelder's book *Lost in Math: How Beauty Leads Physics Astray* is an extremely courageous criticism of the rigidity of her discipline and its lack of progress.

148. Tainter, Joseph A. *The Collapse of Complex Societies*. Cambridge University Press, 1990.

149. Ibid.

150. Cooper-White, Macrina. "People Getting Dumber? Human Intelligence Has Declined since the Victorian Era, Research Suggests." *HuffPost*, 6 Dec. 2017, https://www.huffpost.com/entry/people-getting-dumber-human-intelligence-victoria-era_n_3293846.

151. "Why Have Our Brains Started to Shrink?" *Scientific American*, 1 Nov. 2014, https://www.scientificamerican.com/article/why-have-our-brains-started-to-shrink/.

152. Diamond, Jared. *Collapse: How Societies Choose to Fail or Succeed*. Penguin Books, 2011.

153. "New Age Psychology." *All About Worldview*. https://www.allaboutworldview.org/new-age-psychology.htm, Accessed 27 Aug. 2021.

154. Coppen, Alex. "A New Aquarian Age of Stupidity." *Devils' Lane*. 27 Dec. 2015, https://devilslane.com/a-new-aquarian-age-of-stupidity/.

155. Kuhn, Thomas S. *The Structure of Scientific Revolutions, 4th Edition*. University of Chicago Press, 2012.

156. "Erwin Schrödinger Quotes." *QuoteFancy*.

157. Egnor, Michael. "Is Information the Basis for the Universe?" *Evolution News*, 30 Aug. 2017, https://evolutionnews.org/2017/08/is-information-the-basis-for-the-universe/.

158. "Matrix." *Dictionary.com*.

159. "The Mind is the Matrix of All Master – Quantum Physics & Parapsychology." *Immaterial Power*, 13 Mar. 2019, https://immaterial-power.blogspot.com/2019/03/mind-matrix-quantum-physics-parapsychology.html.

160. "What Is a Singularity?" *Universe Today*, https://www.universetoday.com/84147/singularity/. Accessed 27 Aug. 2021.

161. Zyga, Lisa. "No Big Bang? Quantum Equation Predicts Universe Has No Beginning." *PhysOrg*, 9 Feb. 2015, https://phys.org/news/2015-02-big-quantum-equation-universe.html#:~:text=Quantum%20equation%20predicts%20universe%20has%20no%20beginning,-by%20Lisa%20Zyga&text=(Phys.org)%20%E2%80%94The,Einstein's%20theory%20of%20general%20relativity.&text=Only%20after%20this%20point%20began,did%20the%20universe%20officially%20begin..

162. Byrd, Deborah. "What If the Universe Had No Beginning?" *EarthSky*, 10 Feb. 2015, https://earthsky.org/space/what-if-the-universe-had-no-beginning/.

163. Fapesp, Agência. "Physicist Challenges the Idea That Time Had a Beginning." *Science Tech Daily*, 27 Nov. 2017, https://scitechdaily.com/physicist-challenges-the-idea-that-time-had-a-beginning/.

164. Grigg, Russell. "The Mind of God and the 'Big Bang.'" *Creation*, vol. 15, no. 4, September 1993. https://creation.com/the-mind-of-god-and-the-big-bang.

165. Hegel, G. W. F. *Phenomenology of Spirit*. Cambridge University Press, 2019.

166. "Spirit, Soul, and Body – How God Designed Us." *Faith and Health Connection*, 3 Mar. 2021, https://www.faithandhealthconnection.org/the_connection/spirit-soul-and-body/.

167. "What Is the Difference between the Soul and the Spirit?" *Compelling Truth*. https://www.compellingtruth.org/difference-soul-spirit.html. Accessed 27 Aug. 2021.

168. "Soul." *Encyclopedia.com*.

169. Lanza, Robert. *Biocentrism*, BenBella Books, 2010. This biology-based Consciousness and Thought philosophy is becoming a standard in challenging materialist orthodoxy.

170. Penrose, Roger. *Consciousness and the Universe: Quantum Physics, Evolution, Brain & Mind*. Cosmology Science Publishers, 2011.

171. "Is There Any Scientific Proof for the Soul's Existence?" *The Spiritual Scientist*, 15 Oct. 2011, https://www.thespiritualscientist.com/2011/10/proof-of-souls-existence/.

172. "Is There Any Scientific Proof for the Soul's Existence?" *The Spiritual Scientist*, 15 Oct. 2011, https://www.thespiritualscientist.com/2011/10/proof-of-souls-existence/.

173. Ibid.

174. Holden, Jan. "Veridical Perception in NDEs." *International Association for Near-Death Studies*, 25 Apr. 2015, https://iands.org/past-iands-conferences/2006-houston-tx/229-veridical-perception-in-ndes.html?highlight=WyJmYXNjaW5hdGluZyIsImZhc2NpbmF0ZWQiL-CJmYXNjaW5hdGlvbiIsImZhc2NpbmF0ZSIsImFzcGV-jdHMiLCJhc3BlY3QiLCJvZiIsIidvZiIsImFuIiwiYW5zIi wibmRlIiwibmRlcyIsIm5kZSdzIiwibmRl2vycyIsIm5kZXMnIiwiZm-FzY2luYXRpbmcgYXNwZWN0cyIsImZhc2NpbmF0aW5nIGFzcGV-jdHMgb2YiLCJhc3BlY3RzIG9mIiwiYXNwZWN0cyBvZiBhbiIsIm-

9mIGFuIiwib2YgYW4gbmRlIiwiYW4gbmRlIl0=. The International Association for Near-Death Studies has a wealth of information on the subject, including accounts, research, conferences, resources, references, and links to a number of experts and similar organizations.

175. Hornik, David P. "'I'-Sight: When the Blind-from-Birth Can Fully See during Near-Death Experiences." *PJ Media*, 8 May 2014, https://pjmedia.com/culture/p-david-hornik/2014/05/18/i-sight-when-the-blind-from-birth-can-fully-see-during-near-death-experiences-n152420.

176. Paccione, Charles Ethan. "Tunnel of Light: Making Sense of Near-Death Experiences." *Brain World*, 5 Nov. 2019, https://brainworldmagazine.com/tunnel-light-making-sense-near-death-experiences/.

177. "Out-of-Body Experiences." *Encyclopedia.com*.

178. Ibid.

179. "Soul Leaving the Body at the Moment of Death and Other Claims of Kirlian Photography." *Learning Mind*, https://www.learning-mind.com/scientist-photographs-the-soul-leaving-the-body-at-the-moment-of-death/, Accessed 27 Aug. 2021.

180. Vishnu, Anil. "A Scientific Look at the Concept of Soul: An Attempted Synthesis." *Proceedings of the 88th Indian Philosophical Congress*, October 2014.

181. Bar-Yam, Yaneer. "The Scientific Soul." *Medium.com*, https://medium.com/complex-systems-channel/the-scientific-soul-e31418ef3e5c, Accessed 27 Aug. 2021.

182. Jeans, James. *The Universe around Us*. Cambridge University Press, 1944.

183. This is a famous quote with much debate as to its originator. See Peckham, Hannah. "'You Do Not Have a Soul': C. S. Lewis Never Said It." *Mere Orthodoxy*, 5 Jul. 2012, https://mereorthodoxy.com/you-dont-have-a-soul-cs-lewis-never-said-it/.

184. Formica, Michael J. "The Soul in Body-Mind-Soul-Spirit." *Psychology Today*, 12 May 2008, https://www.psychologytoday.com/us/blog/enlightened-living/200805/the-soul-in-body-mind-soul-spirit.

185. Dürr, Hans-Peter. Quoted in Dr. Rolf Fröböse. "Scientists Find Hints for the Immortality of the Soul." *HuffPost*. 16 Aug. 2014, https://www.huffingtonpost.co.uk/rolf-froboese/scientists-find-hints-for-the-immortality-of-the-soul_b_5499969.html. Dürr had a distinguished academic career and advocated for consciousness surviving physical death. He was also a leader of the World Future Council.

186. "Simulation." *Cambridge Dictionary*.

187. "Simulation." *Wordnet*.

188. Bostrom, Niklas. "Are You Living in a Computer Simulation?" *Philosophical Quarterly*, vol. 53, no. 211, pp. 243–55, 2001.

189. Mitchell, John. "We Are Probably Not Sims." *Science and Christian Belief*, vol. 32, no. 1, April 2020.

190. Gleiser, Marcelo. "Why Reality Is Not a Video Game – And Why It Matters." *Marcelo Gleiser*, 9 Mar. 2017, https://marcelogleiser.com/blog/why-reality-is-not-a-video-game-and-why-it-matters.

191. Hays, Brooks. "We Are Not Living in a Simulation, Scientists Confirm." *United Press International*, 4 Oct. 2017, https://www.upi.com/Science_News/2017/10/04/Were-not-living-in-a-simulation-scientists-confirm/2701507120283/.

192. Masterson, Andrew. "We're Not Living in a Computer Simulation!" *Cosmos*, 1 Oct. 2017, https://cosmosmagazine.com/physics/physicists-find-we-re-not-living-in-a-computer-simulation/.

193. Beltramini, Enrico. "Simulation Theory: A Preliminary Review." *European Journal of Science and Theology*, vol. 14, no. 4, pp. 35–48, August 2018, http://www.ejst.tuiasi.ro/Files/71/4_Beltramini.pdf.

194. "Is the Universe a Simulation?" *Creation Ministries International*, 25 Feb. 2017, https://creation.com/is-the-universe-a-simulator.

195. Steinhart, Eric. "Theological Implications of the Simulation Argument." *Ars Disputandi*, vol. 10, 2010, pp. 23–37, https://www.tandfonline.com/doi/pdf/10.1080/15665399.2010.10820012.

196. Ibid.

197. Ibid.

198. Ibid.

199. Stratton, Tim. "How Does a Soul Provide Free Will?" *Free Thinking Ministries*, 1 Apr. 2016, https://freethinkingministries.com/qa-2-how-does-a-soul-provide-free-will/ .

200. Feit, Carl. Quoted in Sharon Begley, "Science Finds God." *Newsweek*, 1998, https://www.washingtonpost.com/wp-srv/newsweek/science_of_god/scienceofgod.htm. This is a fascinating article that discusses the positions of a number of thinkers who are attempting to fuse science and religion. What is remarkable is that science has shunned religion, but religion has incorporated science.

201. Brown, Lachlan. "Reality Is an Illusion: Everything Is Energy and Reality Isn't Real." *Hack Spirit*, 19 Jan. 2018.

202. Nelson, Robert H. "Existence of God: The Rational Arguments from Mathematics to Human Consciousness." *The Independent*, 30 May 2017, https://www.independent.co.uk/life-style/existence-god-rational-arguments-mathematics-human-consciousness-a7739841.html.

203. Tegmark, Max. *Our Mathematical Universe: My Quest for the Ultimate Nature of Reality*. Vintage, 2015.

204. Benzmüller, Christoph. "Independent Confirmation for Gödel's 'Proof' of Existence of God." *Freie Universität Berlin*, 17 Oct. 2013, https://www.fu-berlin.de/en/presse/informationen/fup/2013/fup_13_308/

index.html. Benzmüller of the Free University of Berlin and Bruno Paleo of the Technical University in Vienna ran computer programs confirming Gödel's Ontological Proof. Gödel's work was so brilliant that it is verified in limited computer processing time.

205. For this discussion, much is owed to the comprehensive article "Big Bang Theory" at *Encyclopedia.com*.

206. "Presentism." *Routledge Encyclopedia of Philosophy*, https://www.rep. routledge.com/articles/thematic/presentism/v-1. Accessed 27 Aug. 2021.

207. Proietti, Massimiliano, Alexander Pickston, Francesco Graffitti, Peter Barrow, Dmytro Kundys, Cyril Branciard, Martin Ringbauer, and Alessandro Fedrizzi. "Experimental Test of Local Observer Independence." *Science Advances*, vol. 5, no. 9, 20 Sept. 2019, https://doi.org/10.1126/ sciadv.aaw9832. This article is a collaborative work by a number of scientists and is extremely technical. Nevertheless, their findings demonstrate that different realities can exist concurrently.

208. "Growing Block Universe." *Oxford Studies in Metaphysics, Volume 2*. Oxford University Press, 2006.

209. Thomas, Rachel. "What Is a Block Universe?" *Plus Magazine*, 30 Sept. 2016, https://plus.maths.org/content/what-block-time.

210. Gribbin, John. *The Time Illusion*, Amazon Digital Services, 2016.

211. Stuckey, W. M., Michael Silberstein, and Michael Cifone. "Reconciling Spacetime and the Quantum: Relational Blockworld and Quantum Liar Paradox." *Foundations of Physics*, vol. 38, no. 4, pp. 348–83, 23 Jan. 2008, https://doi.org/10.1007/s10701-008-9206-4. This is an extremely technical article that examines many of the detailed arguments for the Block Universe. Quantum truths are interwoven into the authors' analysis and provide causal linkages for the Block Universe concept. An extensive reference list is included.

212. "Superdeterminism." *Dictionary.co*

213. "Create." *Dictionary.com*.

214. "Creative." *Vocabulary.com*.

215. Meyer, Stephen C. "Yes, Intelligent Design Is Detectable by Science." *Discovery Institute*, 26 Apr. 2018, https://www.discovery.org/a/17905/.

216. Esler, Ted. "Three Qualities of God's Creativity." *Mission Nexus*, 25 Jun. 2016, https://missionexus.org/creativity/.

217. "Scientist Says He Found Definitive Proof That God Exists," *Kalgidhar Society*, https://barusahib.org/general/scientist-says-god-exists/. Accessed 27 Aug. 2021.

218. Goff, Philip. *Consciousness and Fundamental Reality*. Oxford University Press, 2017.

219. Kastrup, Bernardo. *The Idea of the World*. Iff Books, 2019.

220. Jastrow, Robert. "Message from Professor Robert Jastrow." *LeaderU.com*, http://www.leaderu.com/truth/1truth18b.html. Accessed 27 Aug. 2021.

221. Jastrow, Robert. *God and the Astronomers*. Readers Library, 2000.

222. Chown, Marcus. "What If the Big Bang Was Not the Beginning?" *Science Focus*, 29 Apr. 2019, https://www.sciencefocus.com/space/what-if-the-big-bang-was-not-the-beginning/.

223. Robert Kuhn cites numerous experts, including Alan Guth and Paul Davies, to position Information as a force of the universe. His arrangement of their arguments combines different perspectives into a cohesive understanding that mirrors many of the findings discussed in this work.

224. Galeon, Dom. "CERN Research Finds 'The Universe Should Not Actually Exist.'" *Futurism*, 25 Oct. 2017, https://futurism.com/cern-research-finds-the-universe-should-not-actually-exist.

225. Allen, Adina. "God Created Us to Be Creative." *The Jewish News of Northern California*, 4 Oct. 2018, https://www.jweekly.com/2018/10/04/god-created-us-to-be-creative/. Although much of the article is beyond the scope of this work, its subject matter addresses in an interesting way how society limits human creativity through an elitism that is counterproductive to human advancement.

226. "Creativity." *New World Encyclopedia*. This article contains an excellent brief of the concept of creativity in all its various contexts.

227. "A Universe of Creativity." *Imago Arts*, https://imago-arts.org/a-universe-of-creativity/. Accessed Aug. 25, 2021.

228. "The Psychology of Believing in Free Will." *The Conversation*, 2 Jul. 2018, https://theconversation.com/the-psychology-of-believing-in-free-will-97193.

229. Thomson, Shelley, and John Brandenburg. "Possible States Theory and Human Destiny in the Cosmos." *Physics Procedia*, vol. 38, 2012, pp. 319–25, https://www.sciencedirect.com/science/article/pii/S1875389212025199. The theory concerns the propagation of change in the collections of possible states and relates to the concept of *superposition* and the *observer effect* frequently discussed in this work. In short, according to this theory, there is no collapse of the wave function that mandates a single outcome, but instead, a collection of different outcomes. The nonlinear directionality of time in the theory has been verified through *delayed choice quantum eraser* experiments.

230. Fuentes, Agustin. "Creative Collaboration Is What Humans Do Best." *The Cut*, 22 Mar. 2017, https://www.thecut.com/2017/03/how-imagination-makes-us-human.html.

231. "Direction." *Oxford Learner's Dictionaries*.

232. "Destiny." *Oxford Learner's Dictionaries*.

233. "Universal Intelligence." *Integrative Spirituality*. December 2009, https://www.wikidoc.org/index.php/Universal_Intelligence. The ideas discussed here contain elements of panpsychism and positions Information as a form of universal intelligence.

234. "Universal Intelligence." *The Co-Intelligence Institute*, http://www.co-intelligence.org/Universal_Intelligence.html. Accessed 27 Aug. 2021.

235. "Myth." *Oxford Reference*.

236. "Archetype." *Oxford Learner's Dictionaries*.

237. Campbell, Joseph. *The Power of Myth*, Anchor, 1991.

238. Campbell, Joseph. *The Mythic Image*, Princeton University Press, 1981.

239. Campbell, Joseph, quoted in Tom Snyder, "Myth Perceptions, Joseph Campbell's Power of Deceit." *Logos Resource Pages*, http://logosresourcepages.org/FalseTeachings/campbell.htm. Accessed 28 Aug. 2021.

240. Campbell, Joseph. *The Mythic Image*. Princeton University Press, 1981.

241. Much is written on the Innateness Hypothesis because of its centrality in the debate between the material and immaterial structures of reality. Recommended is the often-cited article by John Horgan in *Scientific American*, November 28, 2016. A number of works discussing both sides of the issue are referenced in the article.

242. "Dream." *Lexico*.

243. "Vision." *Lexico*.

244. "Dreams Dictionary: Meanings of Dreams." *Psychologist World*. https://www.psychologistworld.com/dreams/dictionary/. Accessed 17 Aug. 2021.

245. Trout, Susan. "Living Life Completely and Well." *Institute for the Advancement of Service*, https://www.showanotherway.org/susans-blog/living-life-completely-and-well. Accessed 27 Aug. 2021.

246. "Synchronicity." *Lexico.*

247. Grasse, Ray. "Synchronicity and the Mind of God." *The Theosophical Society*, https://www.theosophical.org/publications/quest-magazine/1441-synchronicity-and-the-mind-of-god?gclid=CjwKCAjwmqK-JBhAWEiwAMvGt6BJt_oHCBD95o37QCcwhPAcHLscb6CO2Q8G-9mH0ulqrTtKxajLwnkhoCr1IQAvD_BwE. Accessed 27 Aug. 2021.

248. "The Varieties of Synchronistic Experience with Richard Tarnas." *Synchronicity Symposium 2014 Videos*, https://synchronicity-symposium.vhx.tv/products/richard-tarnas-workshop. Accessed 27 Aug. 2021. A talk by the cultural historian Richard Tarnas illustrating an original point of Jung.

249. Perry, Robert. *Signs: A New Approach to Coincidence, Synchronicity, Guidance, Life Purpose, and God's Plan.* Semeion Press, 2009.

250. Ibid.

251. Vernon, Mark. "Carl Jung, Part 6: Synchronicity." *The Guardian*, 4 Jul. 2011, https://www.theguardian.com/commentisfree/2011/jul/04/carl-jung-synchronicity. This article discusses synchronicity and briefly explores the relationship Jung had with Pauli. They published a book together called *The Interpretation of Nature and the Psyche*. Pauli educated Jung on the realities of Quantum Mechanics, specifically *entanglement*, and as noted in our study, this provides a theoretical underpinning and mechanism for synchronicity.

252. Levy, Paul. "Catching the Bug of Synchronicity." *Awaken in the Dream*, https://www.awakeninthedream.com/articles/catching-the-bug-of-synchronicity. Accessed 28 Aug. 2021. Levy has written extensively regarding the parallels between Quantum Mechanics and the phenomenon of synchronicity.

253. *The Space Settlement Institute*, http://www.space-settlement-institute.org/, Accessed 27 Aug. 2021. This organization advocates for the

colonization of space but is sensitive to the standard criticisms of colonization such as the exploitation of indigenous populations. Their primary argument against these standard criticisms is that space is uninhabited.

254. *SETI Institute*, https://www.seti.org/?gclid=CjwKCAjwmqKJBhA-WEiwAMvGt6I2RU56eTKoKRhMPw3C2APYoRr6leMPP10k42Dd-NBSzqC_Yk2WH8jRoCOmoQAvD_BwE. SETI is headquartered in Mountain View, California. It works with a number of collaborators, including NASA and the National Science Foundation. Their scientists have written a number of extremely important articles regarding the cultural impact of extraterrestrial contact. Their website is at https://www.seti.org/.

255. Vakoch, Douglas A., and Matthew F. Dowd, Eds. *The Drake Equation: Estimating the Prevalence of Extraterrestrial Life through the Ages*. Cambridge University Press, 2015.

256. Maccone, Claudio. "The Statistical Drake Equation." *Acta Astronautica*, vol. 67, nos. 11–12, pp. 1366–83, Dec. 2010, https://doi.org/10.1016/j.actaastro.2010.05.003.

257. "Unidentified Flying Object." *Oxford Reference*.

258. Daugherty, Greg, and Missy Sullivan. "These 5 UFO Traits, Captured on Video by Navy Fighters, Defy Explanation." *History Stories*, 5 Jun. 2019, https://www.history.com/news/ufo-sightings-speed-appearance-movement. The government official is Luis Elizondo who headed a small study group initiated by the Defense Intelligence Agency to study the UFO phenomenon. His claims include that the United States government has recovered metal alloys and other materials from crashed unidentified flying objects.

259. *The Center for UFO Studies* has a number of classification systems for UFO sightings, including one from Jacques Vallée.

260. *LiveScience*, https://www.livescience.com/.

261. Fawcett, Larry, and Barry J. Greenwood. *Clear Intent: The Government Coverup of the UFO Experience*. Prentice Hall Direct, 1984. Also, Good, Timothy. *Above Top Secret: The Worldwide UFO Cover-Up*. Quill, 1989. These books are the gold standard for well-researched case studies of the UFO phenomenon.

262. J. Allen Hynck Center for UFO Studies. https://barusahib.org/general/scientist-says-god-exists/.

263. Vallée, Jacques F. "Five Arguments against the Extraterrestrial Origin of Unidentified Flying Objects." *Journal of Scientific Exploration*, vol. 4, no. 1, pp. 105–17, 1990, http://citeseerx.ist.psu.edu/viewdoc/summary?doi=10.1.1.557.770. Also, Randles, Jenny. "In Search of the Oz Factor," *Bufora*, July 1987, https://archive.org/stream/BUFORA_Bulletin_No_26_Jul_1987_Misses_page_343334/BUFORA_Bulletin_No_26_Jul_1987_Misses_page_343334_djvu.txt. Both Vallée and Randles are meticulous researchers and prolific authors.

264. Mack, John. *Abduction: Human Encounters with Aliens*. Scribner, 2007.

265. Ibid.

266. Good, Timothy. *Above Top Secret: The Worldwide UFO Cover-Up*. Quill, 1989.

267. Ibid.

268. Ruppelt, Edward J. *The Report on Unidentified Flying Objects*. CreateSpace Independent Publishing, 2011. Donald Keyhoe also wrote a number of significant books and articles and was considered the father of the UFO research community during its initial inquiry into the subject.

269. Lazar, Robert. Quoted in Morgan, David L. "Lazar Critique." *OtherHand*, https://www.otherhand.org/home-page/area-51-and-other-strange-places/bluefire-main/bluefire/the-bob-lazar-corner/a-physicists-critique/. Accessed 26 Aug. 1996. Robert Lazar is a controversial figure who alleges

to have been employed as a nuclear physicist at the secret Air Force installation known as Area 51 in Nevada. His claims include working on an extraterrestrial propulsion system from a recovered UFO.

270. From *Futurism*, a media company that aggregates news articles regarding technological developments and the future. Their website is at https://futurism.com.

271. Vallée, Jacques. *Passport to Magonia: On UFOs, Folklore, and Parallel Worlds*. Contemporary Books, 1993.

272. This is from a conversation with John Mack of the John Mack Institute in 1996. It is incredible that so many abduction experiencers report spiritual transformation as a central feature of the entire abduction phenomenon. In what should be a terrifying experience, witnesses often report a sense of environmental appreciation and spiritual awareness.

273. Kolbert, Elizabeth. *The Sixth Extinction: An Unnatural History*. Picador, 2015.

274. "The Fourth Industrial Revolution." *World Economic Forum*, 14 Jan. 2016, https://www.weforum.org/agenda/2016/01/the-fourth-industrial-revolution-what-it-means-and-how-to-respond/.

275. Brannen, Peter. "Earth Is Not in the Midst of a Sixth Mass Extinction." *The Atlantic*, 13 Jun. 2017, https://www.theatlantic.com/science/archive/2017/06/the-ends-of-the-world/529545/.

276. Stubbs, Phil. "The Best Environmental Books of All Time." *The Environment Show*, 26 Jan. 2019, https://www.environmentshow.com/best-environmental-books/. This is an excellent list of environmental classics and new works separated into practical categories, providing a balanced perspective on the issue of sustainability.

277. Kardashev, N. S. "Transmission of Information by Extraterrestrial Civilizations." *Soviet Astronomy*, vol. 8, no. 2, pp. 282–87, March–April, 1964.

278. The Spiritual Civilization Group, launched in January 2015, is an organization dedicated to advancing human culture through community and the promotion of spiritual values.

279. "Principle." *Cambridge Dictionary*.

280. "On Principle." *Lexico*.

281. Selfishness is closely related to narcissism, which, nearly all experts agree has proliferated with the advent of social media.

282. In addition to authoring many influential books such as *When Corporations Rule the World* and *Agenda for a New Economy*, David C. Korten is a founder of Yes Media and an often-cited expert on the environment and sustainability. The information used here is from *Climate Genocide*.

283. Information taken from United Nations Data, 2019.

284. "Emerging New Civilizations Initiative (ENCI)." The Club of Rome. https://www.clubofrome.org/impact-hubs/emerging-new-civilization/. Accessed 1 Feb. 2020.

285. International Studies has an extended history, beginning with the ancient historian Thucydides and proceeding to Machiavelli, Hobbes, Kant, Marx, and more recent thinkers such as Kennan, Gilpin, Grieco, and Mearsheimer. The discipline evolves with world events, although its basic formulations, particularly those linked to human nature, are largely determined.

286. *Acta Astronautica*, 2011, https://www.journals.elsevier.com/acta-astronautica.

287. Ibid.

288. Davies, Paul. "E.T. and God." *The Atlantic*, September 2003, https://www.theatlantic.com/magazine/archive/2003/09/et-and-god/376856/.

289. Bostrom, Niklas. "The Vulnerable World Hypothesis." *Global Policy*, vol. 10, no. 4, November 2019, https://www.globalpolicyjournal.com/articles/global-public-goods-and-bads/vulnerable-world-hypothesis